Shelter, Housing and Homes

SHELTER, HOUSING AND HOMES

A Social Right

Edited by Arnold Bennett

Montréal/New York
London

Copy right © 1997 BLACK ROSE BOOKS LTD.

No part of this book may be reproduced or transmitted in any form, by any means — electronic or mechanical, including photocopying and recording, or by any information storage or retrieval system — without written permission from the publisher, or, in the case of photocopying or other reprographic copying, a licence from the Canadian Reprography Collective, with the exception of brief passages quoted by a reviewer in a newspaper or magazine.

Black Rose Books No. Z236
Hardcover ISBN: 1-55164-043-0
Paperback ISBN: 1-55164-042-2
Library of Congress No. 95-79357

Canadian Cataloguing in Publication Data

Bennett, Arnold, 1951-
Shelter, housing and homes : a social right

ISBN 1-551640-43-0 (bound) -
ISBN 1-551640-42-2 (pbk.)

1. Housing--Quebec(Province). 2. Housing policy--Quebec (Province). 3. Quebec(Province). Régie du logement. 4. Regroupment des comités logement et associations de locataires du Québec. 5. People's Rights Over Urban Developoment. I. Title.

HD7288.85.C32Q8 1997   363.5'09714   C95-900779-2

Cover photo by Jason Halstead

Mailing Address		
C.P. 1258 Succ. Place du Parc Montréal, Québec H2W 2R3 Canada	250 Sonwil Drive Buffalo, New York 14225 USA	99 Wallis Road London, E9 5LN England

To order books in North America: (phone) 1-800-565-9523
(fax) 1-800-221-9985
In Europe: (phone) 081-986-485 (fax) 081-533-5821

A publication of the Institute of Policy Alternatives of Montréal (IPAM)
Printed in Canada

Table of Contents

Acknowledgements	vii
Preface to the English edition	ix

Part I: Québec

1 | A short (anecdotal and partial) history of the fight for housing in Montréal
    Arnold Bennett — 1

2 | For real rent control
    RCLALQ — 17

3 | For a Québec housing policy
    RCLALQ — 31

4 | The Régie du logement: Autopsy of a fraud
    RCLALQ — 52

5 | A critique of Montréal's Housing Code
    Arnold Bennett — 91

6 | Housing and poverty in Québec: An indictment
    FRAPRU/PROUD — 98

7 | The reform of the Civil Code: important changes for tenants
    Arnold Bennett — 124

Part II: Ontario and British Columbia

8 | Dispatches from the housing front: Ontario tenants take on the Harris government
    Editor's note
    Arnold Bennett
    Rent control is necessary in Ontario
    Dan McIntyre, FOCTA
    Tory alternatives to the Rent Control Act
    Howard Tessler, FMTA
    A brief with respect to possible new tenant legislation
    FOCTA
    Eight myths about rent control in Ontario
    Tenant Advocacy Group, FMTA, and CLEO — 141

9 | A comparative study of apartment rent control laws in Ontario and Québec
    Alexander X.S. Sabharwal — **159**

10 | Rental housing trends in the City of Vancouver
    Vanessa Geary and Leslie Stern — **193**

Appendix

Tenant information on the Internet — **227**

viii | Acknowledgements

first few years of the NDG clinic, as did my wife, Miriam Gelbard, and my mother, Gitelle Betnesky. A partial list of past participants includes Sam Tucci, JoAnn Duquette-Nickson, Eddie Springer, Joanne Cook, Jeanne Nicholas, Frank Remus, Frank Craig, Tivie Erais, Catherine Rideout, Marion Hewell, Arthur Levine, Carol Feldman, Steve D'Attoma, Ernie Dalgleish, Felicia Ross, David Over, Ruth Belfer, Tim Locke, Maeve Lopez, Deesh Mirchandani, Louise Durand, Marie-Rose Lonergan, Liza Douglas, Eileen Singer, Claude Lamontagne, Frank Povylius, Al Mazlavikis, Alan Feldman, Judith Adler, Deborah Mackenzie, Diane Downes and Philip Aronoff.

Acknowledgements

This book would not have been possible without Dimitri Roussopoulos of Black Rose Books, who vigorously promoted the concept from the start, Éditions Écosociété, which published the original collection of French documents and articles in 1994, and the Canada Council, which funded their translation into English.

Howard Tessler and Alexander Sabharwal of the Federation of Metro Tenants' Associations, Mike Walker of the Tenants Rights Action Coalition in Vancouver and Dan McIntyre of the Federation of Ottawa-Carleton Tenants Associations were absolutely indispensable in providing or directing me to the non-Québec material.

Michel Sauvé of the RCLALQ and Pierre Gaudreault of FRAPRU were kind enough to authorize use of their organizations' material, which constituted the core of the original French edition and a good chunk of the present book.

Darcelle Hall showed great patience in repeatedly extending the deadlines to allow new material to come in. Sandra Zarbatany spent countless hours retrieving and printing out the Internet references listed in the appendix.

Finally, I must thank the hundreds of staff and volunteers who since 1980, have helped keep the Montréal Housing Hotline and tenant clinics operating.

Current staff and board members include Ted Wright, Barba Cyr, Francine Poirier, Brian Curnock, Bob Jones, Sheila Scott, Staniewicz, Aloysius Ohiri, Rick Wood, Cheryl McLaughlin, Ver Gammon, Claudette Parkin, Margaret White, Claudia Hamilt Irene Codner, Sharon Dooner, Debra Rajotte, Judith Grant, Lo Thibert, Dwight Vaughan, Daniel Labonté, Paula Stewart, Reb O'Kill, Diane Piedmont, Rosemary Turpin and Grace Lucas.

Over the years, a number of lawyers have volunteered r hours of their time and contributed useful jurisprudence: Ch Takefman, Alan Zylbert, Martin Boyaner, Sally Butler and Friedman, who currently serve the clinics, as well as Domi Neuman, Kevin Cadloff, Wendy Jones, Stuart Russell, Dida Miriam Grassby, Rick Goldman, Herbert Brownstein and Laforest.

The late Lorne Cummings made an important contributio

Preface to the English edition

by Arnold Bennett

This book is not intended to be definitive or exhaustive. The original French edition was conceived as a first opportunity to collect the most important policy documents produced by Québec's two major federations of tenant organizations, the Regroupement de Comités logement et Associations de locataires du Québec (RCLALQ) and the Front d'action populaire en réaménagement urbain (FRAPRU), also known as People's Rights Over Urban Development (PROUD). The intention was to bring together these documents, previously published in limited quantities, in a single volume to make them available to researchers, activists and the general public.

The English edition makes the same information available to a wider audience, not only in Québec, but in provinces like Ontario where grassroots organizations are pitted against a government ideologically committed to undermining any interference with "market forces."

Since the Ontario government proposes to replace mandatory universal rent control with a tenant-initiated rent control system, supposedly based on Québec's, a new chapter (Chapter 9) by Toronto tenants' rights activist Sandy Sabharwal gives a comparative analysis of the existing Ontario and Québec systems and reviews their history.

This is preceded (in Chapter 8) by a review of the current debate in Ontario, based on documents supplied by the Federation of Metro Toronto Tenants' Associations and the Federation of Ottawa-Carleton Tenants Associations.

A chapter by Vanessa Geary and Leslie Stern of the Tenants Rights Action Coalition on rental housing issues in Vancouver has also been included, since the Harris government is trying to move toward a less controlled system similar to British Columbia's.

The RCLALQ and FRAPRU documents show the evolution of the main arguments behind the lobbying and community organizing efforts of the Québec tenant movement over the past decade: for a housing policy that serves the people who need it most; for mandatory universal rent control; for social housing; for a Régie du logement that works the way it should; and against cuts in social programs. Since these documents were published between 1990 and 1993, I have added footnotes to bring certain information up to date and explain what eventually happened. All four of these documents (Chapters 2, 3, 4 and 6) were published when the Bourassa Liberals were in power. Though both the RCLALQ and FRAPRU have been strongly critical of Parti Québécois shortcomings in housing policy, the documents show a residual assumption, left over from the 1970s when this was true, that the PQ would be more pro-tenant than the Liberals. In fact, the differences, if any, are now purely rhetorical. Both parties bow down to the same market gods whenever they can and do just enough to fend off the wrath of their tenant constituents.

When the reformed Civil Code came into force in Québec in January 1994, it brought some important technical changes in landlord-tenant relations. Two-and-a-half years of experience have shown how Québec jurisprudence has applied these changes in practice. Understanding the law and the jurisprudence is crucial for people who want to protect their rights adequately. The chapter on the Civil Code (Chapter 5) is an updated version of a series I originally published in the Montréal Gazette in December 1993.

This book also contains the text of a brief I presented to a Montréal City council commission on the proposed reform of the municipal Housing Code by the previous (Montréal Citizens Movement) administration. These changes were finally adopted by City council in August 1994, after the City incorporated many of the criticisms mentioned in this brief and by other tenant organizations. The problem is still one of enforcement.

This book begins with an "anecdotal and partial" history of the fight for housing in Montréal in this century, particularly since the 1960s — on the provincial and municipal political front, in the courts, and in the neighbourhoods. The facts and analysis are from my experience as an observer and direct participant since the late 1960s, whether as a student journalist with the McGill Daily covering the Milton-Parc struggle; as a radio phone-in guest and housing columnist with the Gazette, the Daily News and other newspapers; as a City Councillor for the Notre Dame de Grâce (NDG) district or a member of the Montréal Citizens Movement (MCM) central executive from 1974 to 1990; as one of those who became disillusioned with the MCM administration; as a tenant organizer and founder of the Association of Tenants Against Condo Conversions (ATACC); as a consultant to the Société d'habitation et de développement de

Montréal (SHDM) from 1991 to 1993; as an active member of the housing committee of the NDG community council, involved in the Benny Farm issue and other struggles; or as a director and founding member of two non-profit organizations that now manage nearly 500 social housing units, Habitations Sherbrooke Forest and Habitations Communautaires NDG.

Since 1975, when I helped establish the NDG Tenants' Association as a project of the NDG Community Council, tenants' rights have become my vocation, if not my obsession. In 1980 and 1981, a handful of us organized an information campaign on Bill 57, a one-shot deal that allowed tenants to claim substantial rent reductions due to the Québec government's abolition of apartment building surtaxes. What was originally intended to be one press conference and a leaflet distribution campaign turned into a marathon that reached its highest intensity in the last three months of 1981, coinciding with the start of my weekly column in the Gazette.

In previous years, we had organized tenant information clinics during the spring lease renewal period and considered a turnout of 20 people to be good. But now we were telling people how to get real money just by filling out a form (in those days the Régie didn't charge a deterrent fee). All of a sudden we were seeing mobs of 200 people at a time, packing them into the YMCA in groups of 50, filling Westmount's Victoria Hall to the rafters, passing out forms to an overflow lineup of 600 people one cold day as the December 21 filing deadline approached. We have never seen anything like this before or since.

Staff at the newly opened Régie office in Côte-des-Neiges weren't happy with us at all. We were sending them hordes of people with Xeroxed forms to be stamped and they had to stay open until midnight on the deadline date. Ultimately, out of 46,000 Bill 57 claims on the Island of Montréal, 32,000 were filed at the Côte des Neiges office.

After the Bill 57 deadline, we thought things would get back to normal. But it took a good three years for some of the cases to make their way through the courts, with the big corporate landlords resisting every step of the way. Jurisprudence had to be analyzed, bad decisions had to be appealed, and then there were all those other problems that people kept bringing in: rent increases, evictions, repossessions, renovations. We realized that the Saturday clinic was a permanent institution one day in January 1992: it was 20 below zero outside and the buses were on strike, but 50 people showed up at the NDG YMCA. Many of them needed information on how to fight their landlords' repossession notices.

Tenants and small property-owners showed up with problems to be solved and joined us as volunteers. Lawyers volunteered their services. We incorporated as Services d'animation Teninform and started using government programs to hire enough staff so that all clients could be accompanied to the Régie for their hearings. A telephone hotline was set up at (514) 488-0412 and now operates from 9 a.m. to 9 p.m., 5 days a week. Our people do more than answer questions and do referrals — on several occasions, we've had to talk police officers out of assisting illegal evictions, rounded up a lawyer to file a last-minute court challenge or mediated a repair emergency. Later we added a second hotline at (514) 990-0190. The clinic was already operating every Saturday at the NDG YMCA (4335 Hampton), 52 weeks a year. In early 1990, we added a weekly Sunday clinic at the downtown YMCA (1450 Stanley).

We found that people were coming to us from all over the metropolitan region, from places like Laval and Chateauguay and the West Island that had no local tenant organizations. In 1990, after tenants in the West Island suburb of Pierrefonds asked for our help after a major fire, we decided to set up a local organization staffed by local people, West Island Tenant Information, and established a backup Saturday clinic at the Pierrefonds CLSC (13800 Gouin West). A few years later, the Westmount Municipal Association asked two of our key staff, Ted Wright and Bob Jones, to start yet another clinic. It now runs every Wednesday at the Westmount YMCA (4585 Sherbrooke West). Francine Poirier and Bob Jones then founded a Tuesday night clinic at the Saint-Laurent YMCA (1745 Décarie).

So study these documents. Use them to fuel your community action and your knowledge of the issues. Inform your neighbours and start putting pressure on the politicians. And if you detect some movement, keep on pushing!

Part 1 | Québec

Chapter One

A short (anecdotal and partial) history of the fight for housing in Montréal

by Arnold Bennett, 1996

There was a time, at the beginning of the twentieth century, when Montréal trade unions launched a campaign against leases as the cause of tenant indebtedness and called on the government to decree one-month leases for working-class tenants.

There was a time, in the midst of the Great Depression of the 1930s, that the Montréal Property Owners' League demanded that the municipal administration guarantee the rents of unemployed tenants.

The 1930s were tough years. City Councils and religious orders were responsible for helping the poor. But the City of Montréal couldn't pay its debts and was put under trusteeship by the provincial government. There was no welfare, no unemployment insurance. In my grandmother's triplex on Drolet Street, the tenants took the shutters off the windows and burned them to keep warm.

Meanwhile, left-wing groups were mobilizing. Communists and social democrats competed for working-class support. In the garment industry, new unions were engaged in bitter struggles and the bosses' goons attacked union militants with lead pipes in their own front yards. A teenage girl stood in front of a truck full of scabs; instead of stopping, the truck ran over her legs.

These were the stories I heard from friends and family members who lived through those years. They were not untypical.

In 1937, Québec Premier Maurice Duplessis enacted the Padlock Law against "Communist propaganda" and invoked it against anyone who struck his fancy, even a Liberal Party candidate. Another teenager, then a militant with the Young Communist League, feared for her books. When a neighbour tipped her off that the police were about to raid, her father hid all her books under the coal in the back shed.

During the Depression, left-wing groups mobilized neighbours to resist evictions. On Saint-Urbain Street in the mid-1930s, an immigrant tenant, Nick Zenchuk, was gunned down by police as he tried

2 | A short history of the fight for housing

to prevent the bailiffs from entering. Zenchuk became a cause célèbre and a martyr, the Anthony Griffin or Marcellus François of his era.[1] The Left organized a funeral like the neighbourhood had never seen. An urban activist of a later period, MCM City Councillor Abe Limonchik, who was a child in those days, still remembers the Zenchuk funeral as a high point of popular struggle, an unforgettable experience of solidarity and a formative moment in his world view.

World War II ended the Depression and federal rent controls were instituted as part of a general package to ensure social peace. The war ended and thousands of veterans returned, only to find a housing shortage. While militant unions across North America fought industry-wide strikes to snag a share of postwar prosperity, the Left also operated on the housing front, organizing squatters' movements to put pressure on the government. The federal government built thousands of housing units for veterans in the late forties. But over the years, almost all these units, except for Benny Farm in Notre Dame de Grâce (NDG) which currently faces the threat of demolition, were sold off to the private sector. Some projects, like Côte St. Luc Gardens, resurfaced as cooperative housing in the seventies, but others were run into the ground by slumlords. The federal government's massive intervention created the only social housing that existed in Québec at that time. To understand why, we have to look back to the turn of the century.

The Catholic Church and right-thinking members of the Montréal elite, concerned about the effects of working-class migration to the City, looked at the horrible example of New York City and declared war on apartment buildings as sinkholes of immorality.[2] The Church required architects and contractors to develop a typically Montréal design: the row housing that we can still see today in Montréal's working-class neighbourhoods, with its outdoor stairways and individual entrances. It was essential, at all costs, to avoid the dark corridors of New York tenements, where promiscuity supposedly reigned. If it was a little slippery getting up to the third floor of a Plateau Mont-Royal triplex in the middle of winter, that was a small price to pay!

Forty years later, Mayor Jean Drapeau, during his first term in office (1954-1957), would oppose the Dozois Plan of Maurice Duplessis' provincial government, a plan that provided for "slum clearance" and construction of low-rental housing in downtown Montréal. Drapeau's arguments were identical to those invoked by the parish priests of 1910: as an authoritarian right-wing crusader for "morality," Drapeau insisted that "immorality" had to be prevented at all costs. Duplessis arranged for Drapeau's defeat in the very dirty municipal election of 1957. The incidence of ballot-stuffing and strong-arm tactics, now long-forgotten, made the 1995 referendum campaign look clean by comparison. Sarto Fournier briefly became mayor and the Jeanne Mance Housing Project was built.

After Drapeau swept back to power in 1960, Montréal refused its share of federal grants for construction of new low-rental housing units for nearly a decade, falling far behind Toronto. There was no political pressure on Drapeau to do otherwise. Until the 1970s, the only tenants who could vote in Montréal municipal elections were taxpaying heads of families. Most women and tenants were therefore excluded from the political process.

In the mid-1960s, the City finally decided to move in favour of "urban renewal" with the Little Burgundy project. From the architectural standpoint, the project was a success: designed on a human scale to encourage family and neighbourhood life, instead of the dehumanizing towers still being constructed in American cities. On another level, the exercise was paternalistic and even racist. The people of the neighbourhood, many of them black, were uprooted and expelled. Only former residents chosen by the civil servants were assigned new low-rental units once they were ready. By a strange coincidence, the new population was more racially "balanced."

Some of the talented urban planners who had made such a major contribution to the positive aspects of the Little Burgundy development, like American immigrant Andy Melamed, who had helped create a racially-mixed community in Philadelphia before fleeing the United States during the Vietnam War, were cut out of the loop by their bosses when they tried to help the local people organize against these injustices. Melamed resigned from the civil service, became a professor of urban planning at Concordia and later played a major role in the early years of the Drapeau regime's nemesis, the Montréal Citizens Movement.

In the meantime, Montréal was preparing for Expo 67, nostalgically remembered as the high point of the Drapeau era. An entire working-class neighbourhood, Victoriatown, was demolished for a parking lot to serve the Expo site. In the Centre-Sud district, east of Old Montréal, the City put up pretty pastel fences so that the tourists wouldn't have to look at urban blight. A new generation of activists promptly covered the fences with graffiti: "Visitez les slums!"

4 | A short history of the fight for housing

A booming economy and massive government spending, both now things of the past, weren't necessarily good for Montréal's poor in the sixties and early seventies. Victoriatown wasn't the only neighbourhood to disappear. The Décarie Expressway carved a trench through NDG and Snowdon in the early sixties, gutting two neighbourhoods and displacing thousands of people. Later the Ville-Marie Expressway did the same to St-Henri, Lower Westmount, Centre-Sud and Hochelaga-Maisonneuve. Place des Arts, Complexe Desjardins and the new CBC building, with its sprawling parking lot, were also built during this period, at the cost of thousands of homes. The people of these neighbourhoods paid the price for a policy of prestige projects and absolute priority to the private car. As in the case of the Expo fences, these events did not go completely unchallenged. Drapeau's right-hand man, Lucien Saulnier, called on the federal government to cut off funding to the Company of Young Canadians, a federal community organizing program. Its members, he declared, were "Communists." The federal program disappeared, but grassroots militancy increased.

In the 1970 municipal election, the opposition party, the Front d'action populaire (FRAP), created by the unions and east-end community groups, attacked Mayor Drapeau for his lack of interest in the housing crisis. But it was the October Crisis — the Cross-Laporte kidnappings — that caught the public's attention. "Lists of suspects" were prepared with the active collaboration of the Drapeau regime. Two FRAP candidates were arrested, among several hundred other innocent victims. Drapeau openly labelled FRAP as an affiliate of the terrorist FLQ, and his party swept every Council seat in the City.

Internal factionalism quickly destroyed FRAP and the activists returned to the neighbourhoods to do "travail à la base" — grassroots work — until the creation of the Montréal Citizens Movement (MCM) in 1974. In the meantime, an unchecked Drapeau prepared for the 1976 Olympics (and the fiasco of the billion-dollar Olympic debt) and increased the water tax, which hit the poor hardest. Welfare recipients demonstrated in front of City Hall and burned their tax bills.

Tenants' associations emerged in the neighbourhoods: Saint-Louis, Centre-Sud and Côte des Neiges. Within these organizations, militants debated the merits of "casework," or help to individual tenants, as opposed to collective struggles in which housing issues would serve as a tool for politicization. Other activists proposed a synthesis of these forms of struggle. But political ideas changed or evolved. Marxist sects disappeared and the problems of everyday life remained, as Murray Bookchin's disciples would put it. Praxis evolved accordingly.

Soon, new groups formed around the housing question — in Rosemont, Villeray, NDG, Verdun, Pierrefonds, Hochelaga-Maisonneuve, Québec City, Hull and elsewhere. They coalesced into the Front d'action populaire en réaménagement urbain (FRAPRU), also known as People's Rights Over Urban Development (PROUD), and the Regroupement des comités logement et associations de locataires du Québec (RCLALQ), to multiply the impact of their militant action and political lobbying.

In a dogged struggle that began in 1969, residents of the downtown Milton-Parc district mobilized against the demolition of their homes, occupied the developer's offices, got arrested, won acquittal by a jury of their peers, gained a partial victory, obtained government funding, bought up what was left of their neighbourhood, renovated it, formed cooperatives and non-profit corporations, overcame difficulties and internal disputes and emerged as a model for others. By using appropriate pressure tactics during the 1980 referendum on Québec sovereignty, they negotiated more affordable rent scales with the federal government. They also persuaded Québec to adopt a special law to preserve their community's heritage in trust and prevent resale to private owners. Over 600 social housing units were created, making this the biggest project of its kind in Canada.

In the 1974 municipal election, the newly-formed Montréal Citizens Movement (MCM) campaigned for the construction of social housing and against the hated water tax. The MCM surprised everyone, winning 18 of 52 Council seats. Drapeau saw the writing on the wall, and low-rental housing projects began to spring up in the urban landscape, though in insufficient number. The Drapeau-Lamarre administration also launched *Opération 20,000 logements*, not to build social housing but to attract respectable middle-class taxpayers to working-class neighbourhoods. Poorly conceived renovation programs triggered the "gentrification" of these districts. Either speculators found ways to get rid of tenants, or tenants could no longer afford the rents after renovation.

The MCM, at that time well attuned to grassroots demands, joined in a common front with community action groups in a number of struggles, but had to compete with the then-thriving, later-defunct Communist League for activist support. On upper Saint-Denis

Street, demonstrations were held in front of buildings where Clermont Motors wanted to evict its neighbours to expand a car dealership. Activists, including MCM Councillor John Gardiner, who years later, when in power, would blow his grassroots credibility by catering to developers, occupied the condemned buildings on downtown Saint-Norbert Street in a doomed attempt to prevent their demolition. During the same period, the MCM launched a public campaign for "collective negotiation of leases."

In 1971, the Québec Government enacted a law to "promote conciliation" between landlords and tenants and gave permanent status to the Rental Board which, in 1977, under the PQ, became the Régie du logement. The Rental Board had existed in Québec since Duplessis introduced it as a temporary measure in 1951. Its mandate had been renewed year by year ever since for pre-1951 buildings.

Tenant organizations began to campaign for mandatory universal rent control and registration of leases, while the big landlords looked for loopholes to undermine the existing protection. They found an excellent way around the law with conversion of rental housing to condominiums.

The conversions began with Presidential Towers in Cote St. Luc. The affluent tenants contested, but lost in court. But at least these tenants had the choice of buying their apartment or renting somewhere else. These options did not exist for the low-income tenants of the Elmhurst Development in the Liberal stronghold of NDG, nor for the Val-Martin tenants who retained the services of lawyer Bernard Landry, who made their cause his springboard to the Québec National Assembly and a PQ cabinet post. Both groups had similar horror stories to tell their elected representatives. At Elmhurst, the new landlord gave the tenants an ultimatum: buy your rundown apartment for $30,000 (no bargain in 1975) or I'll sell them to somebody else and the buyer will repossess and evict you.

This time the government couldn't ignore the bipartisan cries of alarm. Tenants accounted for 80 percent of Montréal's population in the 1970s. In December 1975, the first Bourassa government introduced a "temporary" moratorium on condo conversions until it could come up with regulations to "protect" the tenants against abuse.

The Parti Québécois replaced the Liberals in 1976. Civil servants studied one set of proposed regulations after another, but found no easy solution except wishful thinking. In other North American cities, under pressure from the real estate industry, these moratoria lasted one or two years at most until some kind of regulations were put in place. But in Québec, the total ban on condo conversions continued for almost thirteen years throughout the province, and even longer on the Island of Montréal.

In 1977, the Lévesque government enacted the *Act respecting the Régie du logement*. Housing activists, who had expected much better during the consultations leading up to the bill, were disappointed. There was no mandatory universal rent control, no registration of leases, no right to a rent strike. However, the new Régie du logement could order repairs, grant rent reductions and rule on the conditions of evacuation for renovation, in short, do all kinds of things that weren't in the power of the old Rental Board.

Landlord organizations applied to the courts to have the Régie declared unconstitutional, as they successfully did in Ontario in 1979 to block the creation of an Ontario Residential Tenancies Board with full powers. But in 1983, the Supreme Court of Canada, based on the powers given the pre-Confederation courts of Lower Canada, upheld all of the Québec Régie's powers.

In the early 1980s, annual rent increases were not limited to a mere one or two percent. The energy crisis, soaring municipal property valuations and record-high interest rates all converged to allow landlords to obtain rent increases of 12 to 20 percent at the Régie in 1982, before adding on the amortized cost of major repairs. In 1982, the Montréal Property Owners League publicly recommended that its members ask for a 30 percent rent increase to "catch up."

Landlords desperately looked for new loopholes and found a few: undivided co-ownership, limited partnerships with the right of occupancy and other more complicated variations on this theme.

In 1980, the owner of the middle-class Barrington Apartments in Outremont offered his tenants their apartments in undivided co-ownership for a price of about $50,000 each. His approach was similar to that of the condo-converting Elmhurst landlord five years earlier: if you don't buy, somebody else will and you'll be evicted for repossession. Some tenants bought and others left, but two stubborn and courageous widows, with apartments full of art and antiques, declared war. Before their fight was over, they had challenged the landlord at the Régie and in the courts, held press conferences, formed a coalition with tenants' and senior citizens' organizations, visited Premier René Lévesque's assistant at his office, lobbied the wife of opposition leader Claude Ryan after mass at the church they all attended, and demanded the dismissal of an incompetent Régie commissioner who had ruled to evict them in an error-filled judgment

8 | A short history of the fight for housing

(his contract wasn't renewed). Eventually, they won their case on appeal and remained in their homes. Their struggle was the exception that proved the rule: as well-connected members of the Québec establishment, with the resources and inclination to spend a lot of time in court, they could fight their landlord to a standstill.

More important was the fact that their lobbying efforts brought about an unusually rapid change in the law, partially closing the undivided co-ownership loophole. In June 1981, the Lévesque government amended the *Act respecting the Régie du logement* and banned repossessions by undivided coproprietors in buildings containing more than four dwellings. Smaller buildings were exempted so as not to penalize small property-owners, who often bought buildings as a family. For the tenants of the McGill Ghetto and Plateau Mont-Royal, where most buildings have four units or less, this proved to be a costly exception. Real estate companies jumped on the loophole like hungry sharks. Forced evacuation of tenants for major repairs went hand in hand with repossessions and, between 1981 and 1986, according to estimates done by tenant organizations, up to 20,000 tenants were expelled from their homes in these neighbourhoods.

It took longer to get this loophole closed than in the Barrington case. Undivided co-ownership was an unattractive option for investors in larger buildings. Even the notarial profession was against it because of the legal complications involved: notaries vastly preferred outright condo conversion, where each owner owned a unit instead of a share of the building. But for small properties, a much wider range of interests was at stake, including aspiring homeowners.

In November 1987, the second Bourassa government amended the law to prohibit repossession by undivided co-owners, except for legal and common-law spouses, regardless of the number of dwellings in the building. At the same time, the government made it more difficult to force tenants out for major repairs. The new law required three months' written notice, established the principle of tacit refusal (meaning that the tenant did not have to give a written refusal), obliged the landlord to take the initiative of filing an application at the Régie instead of the tenant (who previously had to get out if he didn't file an opposition within 10 days of the landlord's notice) and made it mandatory for the landlord to offer cash compensation in the notice.

Why was a Liberal government so generous to tenants? After all, both Daniel Johnson and Pierre Paradis, in their unsuccessful campaigns for the Liberal leadership, had called for the abolition of rent control. Robert Bourassa, typically, had dodged the issue. The answer was simple. The Liberals had committed themselves to lift the moratorium on condo conversion and wanted to sell this concept to tenants by offering what Housing Minister André Bourbeau repeatedly called *"une protection blindée"*: iron-clad protection, including a lifetime right of occupancy for existing tenants, a ban on non-urgent renovations in buildings for which a conversion proposal was announced, and heavy penalties (on paper) for harassment of tenants.

"Mon logement n'est pas à vendre" — my apartment isn't for sale — FRAPRU members responded, peppering some neighbourhoods with signs declaring this message. Tenants, especially the elderly, feared harassment and intimidation, the deterioration of their housing conditions and buyouts for a pittance, regardless of the protection that existed on paper, if the market ever became interesting.[3] The Montréal and Cote St. Luc City Councils adopted resolutions against the lifting of the moratorium. The MCM-dominated Montréal City Council held its own public hearings on the issue to put pressure on Québec. Even in Westmount, elderly tenants mobilized to elect May Cutler as mayor and defeat Mulroney crony Brian Gallery, who had refused to take a stand against the government's plans.

The MCM had bounced back from a crushing defeat in 1978 — a defeat caused by internal faction-fighting and a split opposition vote. Electing a strong opposition in 1982, largely due to its grassroots work with tenants in several key districts, they swept to power at City Hall in 1986.

But partisan politics produced strange bedfellows. Some of the militants of Saint-Norbert Street and Milton-Parc, like City executive committee member John Gardiner, were on the other side of the barricades when it was the turn of the Overdale tenants to face eviction: the MCM forgot its roots. Other councillors, like former tenant activist and hard-line ideologue André Lavallée, took a trip to the City Hall toilets when the Overdale issue came to a final vote.

Other activists and councillors, those who had not forgotten why they were in politics, began to leave the MCM, turning to the Democratic Coalition, Ecology Montréal or non-partisan work in their neighbourhoods. There were other issues that caused progressives to lose faith in the MCM, but Overdale was the seminal issue, the one that really stuck in people's craws.

What was the Overdale affair, after all? The destruction of a small downtown community in favour of a phantom condo development project, tearing a gaping hole in the urban fabric? The failure of the Doré administration, which tried to persuade the tenants to leave by offering them replacement housing "down the hill" at Lucien-L'Allier and Versailles, in a shoddily-built project known ironically as "Underdale"? The inability of the municipal administration to recognize that there were some individuals and some communities for whom principles came first? A conflict between "sell-out baby boomers" and newly militant members of Generation X? The rift between the old comrades of the Milton-Parc struggle: those like Dimitri Roussopoulos, Lucia Kowaluk and other "Bookchinists" who saw the Milton-Parc experience as a model for the future and those, like Gardiner, who saw it as an exception, something that could not be repeated because of cutbacks in federal housing programs? The City's shameful decision to hide behind its own housing code and condemn three dilapidated buildings instead of ordering the landlord to repair them? The spectacle of barricades and arrests when the tenants refused to leave the condemned buildings? The patent inferiority of the replacement housing at "Underdale," which the City had let the developer build, without adequate supervision, as part of the compensation package? The City, through its paramunicipal corporation, SHDM, negotiated a renovation and preservation agreement with the Anderson Coop, in the heart of Chinatown, instead of playing the game of another private developer, thus showing that it had learned something from the Overdale fiasco.

For some, Overdale was the last straw. For others, the end came when the MCM administration lifted the municipal moratorium on condo conversion. The MCM had opposed Québec's lifting of the moratorium, had worked with tenant organizations to get the Bourassa government to back down in 1987 and maintain the moratorium on the entire Island of Montréal. But during its second term, under the influence of John Gardiner, the MCM shrugged off the arguments of its former allies and adopted a by-law to "control" conversion. This was the public outcome of debates within the MCM between people whose priority was to protect tenants and people who wanted at any cost to encourage "access to home ownership," the return of the middle class to downtown Montréal and an expanded tax base. The latter group's ideas bore a strange resemblance to the priorities of the Drapeau-Lamarre administration.

If Overdale was the MCM's greatest sin, the creation of thousands of non-profit housing units, through a pumped-up acquisition and renovation program, was its crowning achievement. The Anderson Coop was only the tip of the iceberg. If there was one player that contributed to the "municipalization of urban land," a long-forgotten objective from the program of the old, radical MCM of 1974, it was the Société d'habitation et de développement de Montréal (SHDM).

A paramunicipal corporation created by the City of Montréal, the SHDM had a board made up of civil servants, people from community organizations and cooperatives, and a few business people, and was directed by Bob Cohen, yet another "veteran" of Milton-Parc. Between 1987 and 1994, the SHDM bought and renovated buildings in every Montréal neighbourhood, and then transferred management, with the eventual aim of transferring ownership, to housing cooperatives and community non-profit corporations.

Until budget cuts gutted the program in 1993, the three levels of government combined to subsidize 90 percent of the renovation cost (with 40 percent coming from the City of Montréal), thus minimizing the impact on rents. For example, $20,000 in repairs per apartment meant a rent increase of under $18 per month, instead of $180, if there were no subsidy.

In Rosemont, Saint-Michel, Cartierville, NDG, Côte des Neiges and elsewhere, SHDM accumulated a stock of 3,000 housing units and transferred management of most of them to neighbourhood groups.

These projects were not realized without conflicts or bureaucratic errors. There were problems with incompetent contractors and dissatisfied tenants. But the tenants participated, housing conditions improved, drug dealers disappeared from the buildings (to go to neighbouring streets where they weren't subject to close scrutiny), after-school programs, community kitchens and other projects developed, and multicultural and intercultural communities flourished.

The Barclay neighbourhood of Côte des Neiges isn't what it was ten years ago. Overcoming its previous reputation for crime, drugs and cockroaches, Barclay transformed into a construction site, with the recycling of 400 apartments by the SHDM and the Office municipal d'habitation, later becoming a revitalized neighbourhood of cooperatives and good-quality low-rental housing.

SHDM also participated in housing projects for special clienteles: rooming houses, AIDS hospices, and residences for ex-prostitutes and former psychiatric patients, among others.

However, some SHDM development projects aroused controversy, extensively reported in the media: hassles with the manager of the Blue Bonnets racetrack, acquired by SHDM for future large-scale mixed development; the slowness in filling the Centre de commerce mondial, in which SHDM was a joint venture partner; the controversy over archeological digs disrupted by the Faubourg-Québec project in Old Montréal, where SHDM had launched a 2,000 unit condo development.

Grassroots groups complained of the perceived conflict between the "housing" and "development" aspects of SHDM's mandate. At a time when public funds were scarce, when the Doré administration was cutting SHDM's "social" housing budget to 350 new units a year instead of 1,200, these interests criticized the priority given to "economic" projects, like the Centre de commerce mondial, or projects intended to attract the middle class.

The Faubourg-Québec project was designed to reconstitute an Old Montréal neighbourhood that had disappeared over a century ago, leaving nothing but a tract of vacant land by the waterfront. Though this project's design earned it international awards, community groups in the neighbouring Centre-Sud district were annoyed that Faubourg-Québec did not include social housing. They negotiated a tradeoff with the Doré administration to create more social housing in the adjacent district.

Housing budget cuts precluded any positive intervention by the Doré administration on the Benny Farm project in NDG. The federal government agency, Canada Mortgage and Housing Corporation (CMHC), proposed to consolidate the aging veterans on the site in two new elevator buildings, a move welcomed by a majority of the tenants. However, CMHC and the Mulroney government wanted to finance the new construction by selling off the rest of the site, including hundreds of housing units, to the private sector for demolition and redevelopment. Typically, after the Chrétien Liberals ousted the Tories, they proved to have the same agenda.

The Benny Farm controversy led to two rounds of public hearings, development of alternative plans, a bitter split between tenants favouring and opposed to CMHC's plans, and a loss of faith in the Doré administration's public consultation process by NDG community activists.

Everybody except a few true believers among the veterans (who would eventually lose their illusions) knew that CMHC's redevelopment scheme was bogus. There was no developer willing to pay $30 million for a $10 million piece of property in the middle of a real estate slump. This would have been a logical time for the SHDM to intervene. It could have made CMHC a serious offer to buy up and recycle the old apartment buildings over a five to ten year period, depending on the budget available. The renovated buildings could then be turned over to non-profit groups. But SHDM no longer had the funds for this type of large-scale venture, and the City authorities were more interested in pursuing the illusion of an expanded tax base.

If CMHC fails to find its private sector "white knight" and if governments eventually restore adequate funding for social housing, the community may yet save Benny Farm. With no intention to sell or demolish before 1997, the struggle continues.

Criticisms from the grassroots for not going far enough were no threat to the positive aspects of the MCM's housing policies. Rather, it was the attacks from the right, the interests nostalgic for the old regime, the enemies of social housing who complained of SHDM's "unfair" competition with private landlords, and the declared and closet racists who didn't want "foreigners" in their neighbourhoods and who waged campaigns against any form of social housing.

Prior to the 1994 municipal election, the question was seriously raised: If a party to the right of the MCM took power, would the SHDM continue to exist? Would its acquisition and renovation programs survive? Would the new administration try to privatize its housing stock?

In response to these concerns, SHDM began working on the concept of a City-wide land trust, permitted by the new Civil Code, with a board including representatives from cooperative federations and community groups, as well as the SHDM and financial institutions. This land trust would have five main objectives: ensuring collective, non-profit control of the social housing stock; maintaining rents at affordable levels; continuing the development of non-profit housing; ensuring the physical and economic integrity of housing projects; and contributing to neighbourhood revitalization. Management and ownership of the various buildings would be gradually transferred to local groups, but the land trust would maintain permanent control over the land. These structures were not in place by the 1994 election, but community organizations took the initiative to develop their own.

In the 1994 election, the MCM faced competition from two right-wing parties and one party on the left. Jérôme Choquette, leader of the Montréalers' Party, campaigned like a rampaging dinosaur who wanted to transform the City into *Jurassic Park* — a city designed for motorists, parking lot operators and militant landlords, who strongly endorsed him. Choquette wanted to sell off low-rental housing and SHDM units to their individual occupants, but didn't bother to ask whether they could afford the price. This position was completely contrary to the idea of collective acquisition of these buildings by cooperatives and non-profit organizations to protect the housing stock from speculators.

The eventual victor in the election, Pierre Bourque's Vision Montréal Party, was much more vague than Choquette. Some of Bourque's candidates attacked the SHDM for competing with the private sector, while others, mainly former MCM councillors, swore to preserve its social housing mandate. Other candidates seemed to take both positions at the same time. This wasn't surprising. Vision Montréal's slate was a mixed bag of retreads from Drapeau's Civic Party, opportunistic former members of the MCM caucus who saw which way the wind was blowing, one or two former left-wingers turned opportunist, and right-wing PQ nationalists who detested Doré for being "soft" on the language issue.

As it turned out, it didn't matter what the candidates thought. The real decisions were made by Bourque and a small circle of backroom boys who loathed the SHDM and all its works. The man handpicked by Bourque to run his administration's housing policy, a former caisse populaire manager named Robert Gagnon, took the axe to the SHDM in 1995 before losing his own job after conflict-of-interest allegations appeared in the media. By the middle of the year, its board of directors was gone and so was Bob Cohen. Most of the staff were redistributed to other City agencies and only a handful of civil servants remained to negotiate the transfer of management of non-profit housing to community groups. The SHDM was abolished and rolled into a new paramunicipal corporation, SDM, which would mainly be interested in development, not housing. The only good sign was Bourque's interest in the SHDM's land trust idea, which Cohen had pushed strongly before his departure.

In direct contrast to the tone of the election campaign, the Bourque administration retained the SHDM's megaprojects, which it decided were economically viable. However, it withdrew completely from acquisition and renovation of apartments for social housing. When the Québec government announced a new acquisition-renovation program for 500 units in 1995, the City of Montréal slashed the 350 units already budgeted by the previous administration.

Community groups are in a constant state of vigilance to ensure that the existing housing stock ends up with them, and not with private landlords. Their only reliable ally is Montréal's slumping real estate market, which makes the private sector more interested in selling than buying.

The public really had no idea what Bourque would do when he took power. Would he dismantle the district councils or simply change their role? Actually, he tried to do both. First he attempted to abolish all democratic consultation structures outright. But in a rare show of unity and common sense, PQ and Liberal members of the National Assembly refused to go along with his proposed City Charter amendments.

A humiliated Bourque went back to the drawing board and came up with a new scheme a year later. He created smaller neighbourhood councils, gave them some new cosmetic duties regarding local recreation programs, and stripped them of any power over zoning changes. A City-wide development commission was established to hear all zoning matters and promptly disgraced itself by ignoring the public's input on several controversial issues: zoning changes to allow more bars on certain commercial streets (successfully resisted in NDG but imposed on angry residents in the Plateau); a blocked attempt to allow a pool hall near a residential area of NDG; and the immensely controversial Précieux-Sang and St-Isidore convent projects, respectively involving construction on scarce NDG green space and demolition of an east-end heritage property.

No one entertains any illusions of massive investment in social housing in a context where all parties have bought into the ideology of budget cuts. Doré or Bourque, Bob Rae or Mike Harris, Bourassa or Bouchard, Mulroney or Chrétien — the bottom line is more or less the same. The difference is one of execution — how much gleeful damage will reactionaries or bungling ideologues do in addition to the harm caused by "necessity"? Constant vigilance and new coalitions will be needed to defend past gains against the new barbarians who only want to "slash and burn."

Reversing the trend will require governments and municipal administrations that will wake up, change their ways and know how to listen, and people at the grassroots, networked and organized, who know how to argue, lobby and negotiate, denounce and demonstrate when the need arises, but never give up.

16 | A short history of the fight for housing

NOTES

1. Anthony Griffin and Marcellus François were two young Black men slain by police in the late 1980s and early 90s under highly controversial circumstances.
2. The material on the early twentieth century and the postwar squatters' movement is from Marc H. Choko, *Crises de logement à Montréal: 1860 à 1939* (Montréal: Ed. Albert Saint-Martin, 1980).
3. In Montréal's Mile End district, a popular target for conversion of duplexes and triplexes into condos even during the housing slump, promoters were offering tenant holdouts as much as $15,000 in 1995 to give up their lifetime right of occupancy. On Ste-Famille Street, in the McGill Ghetto, the landlord used a loophole in the new Civil Code to combine smaller dwellings into larger units, a procedure under which could force at least some of the tenants to leave at the end of their leases. When the tenants banded together to fight him in court, thus delaying his plans, he offered buyouts of $2,000. Ultimately, most of the tenants settled for $6,500 each.

Chapter 2

For real rent control

by **Le Regroupement des Comités logement et Associations de locataires du Québec (RCLALQ), 1990**

Editor's note: This text was published in French and English as a manifesto for a rent control campaign by the RCLALQ in 1990. I have added a considerable number of footnotes to update the situation described to 1996.

For the Regroupement des Comités logement et Associations de locataires du Québec,[1] housing is a basic right that must be considered essential: all of the RCLALQ's actions are derived from these two premises.

The right to housing

This right is specifically recognized in:
• the *Universal Declaration of Human Rights* (Section 25, par. 1), as part of the right to an adequate standard of living;
• the *International Agreement on Economic, Social and Cultural Rights* (Section 1, par. 1), as part of the right to an adequate standard of living; Québec signed on April 21, 1976;
• the *International Agreement on the Elimination of all Forms of Racial Discrimination* (Section 5, par. 3, ii), as part of the right to equality in the enjoyment of economic, social and cultural rights, an agreement signed by Québec on May 10, 1978;
• the *International Agreement on the Elimination of all Forms of Discrimination against Women* (Section 14, par. 2, h), an agreement signed by Québec on October 20, 1981.

Housing is essential

Housing is not a commodity like any other. A person cannot survive the harsh Québec winter very long without a place to live.

Subzero weather kills homeless people, like the 41-year-old man who was found dead on a park bench in Viger Square, wrapped in a blanket, on Christmas Eve 1988.[2]

A. History of a campaign: from rent freeze to rent control

The Regroupement pour le gel des loyers (RGL), the coalition for a rent freeze, was created in January, 1978. Seven groups participated actively in a campaign against rent increases, demanding a freeze on rents with a slogan of "say no to rent increases." A growing number of groups came together to plan various actions, which extended far beyond the bounds of fighting rent increases in 1979. The RGL also focused on the issues of renovation and evictions.

In autumn 1980, the RGL became the Regroupement des Comités logement et Associations de locataires du Québec (RCLALQ). The new name was a better reflection of what the coalition had become in an increasingly wide range of interventions on evictions, urban renewal programs, discrimination, tenant blacklists and other issues. The main demands focused on rent control, increasing the number of social housing units and stopping cuts in essential services.

In 1981, the RCLALQ adopted a program for the coming struggle, a strategy that defined its objectives, orientations and demands. Since then, the RCLALQ has become a key player on all questions directly or indirectly related to housing. It lobbies federal, provincial and municipal governments and takes public stands on various issues. Over the years, these have included the unsuccessful attempt by landlords to challenge the constitutionality of Québec's rental board, the Régie du logement, the production of blacklists by landlord organizations, the Régie's imposition of a deterrent fee, the creation of rental agencies, and abusive rent increases.

The RCLALQ currently has thirteen member groups from Montréal, the Montérégie (South Shore), Québec City, Sherbrooke and Thetford Mines. Its goals are to win recognition for everyone's right to suitable housing, and to defend and promote the rights of economically or socially disadvantaged tenants. The RCLALQ operates on seven basic principles:
• ensuring that everyone has access to suitable affordable housing;
• ensuring the right of tenants to remain in their homes;
• ensuring the protection and preservation of the rental housing stock;
• favouring people's control of their living conditions;

- ensuring the right of association;
- ensuring access to collective property ownership;
- ensuring the State's responsibility to protect, safeguard and promote these principles.

At its December 1989 congress, the RCLALQ adopted a position for rent control and decided to make this its priority. This demand was included in the RCLALQ's housing policy, adopted at the same congress.

In this document, we explain why we have called on the Québec government to institute mandatory universal rent control for a minimum of five years.

B. An ever poorer population

In Québec, as elsewhere, collective wealth is unequally distributed among individuals. In 1980, it was estimated that the richest Canadians — accounting for 10% of the population — control nearly 60% of the wealth (income, stocks, bonds, real estate), while the poorest 40% share 0.8% of this wealth.[3]

1. Poverty on the rise

Poverty affects one out of three Québec households. This alarming situation becomes catastrophic when one realizes that poverty is growing in "la belle province." In 1986, 33.5% of the population was officially classified as poor, compared to 30.8% in 1973. These figures are frightening, especially since they do not reflect the real scope of poverty in Québec.

Statistics Canada only considers food, housing and clothing costs in setting the poverty line. Expenses inherent in health care, hygiene, education, transportation and insurance are not taken into account in this calculation. Yet these items are essential and represent real spending for anyone who wants to function in our society. The poverty line determined by Statistics Canada serves more to reduce and conceal the number of poor households than to present a true picture of poverty.

Poverty also has geographical implications. It is no surprise to note that poor families move from rural areas and small towns to major urban centres, hoping to reduce certain essential costs not considered by Statistics Canada.

2. Who is poor?

In Québec, poverty does not strike at random. Some classes of people are more likely to be poor than others. One-parent families headed by women, people living alone, people with handicaps and young couples (under 25 years of age) with children are very likely to be included in the poorest 33.5% of the Québec population.

This predisposition to poverty is confirmed in the basic data on poverty in Canada published by the Canadian Council on Social Development. The authors of this study found a high rate of poverty among people living alone.[4] What was new was that age had become a less valid indicator for measuring poverty in this group. Thus, 38% of singles and poor people were under age 35 in 1986. Another finding was that the economic situation of single individuals improved in all Canadian provinces except Québec.

3. Children

Another revealing point in this document is the rate of child poverty. In 1986, 30% of children lived in a poor household, compared to 16% in 1973. The high concentration of children in a sector has become a valid indicator for measuring poverty.

Child poverty has a direct impact on academic performance. Between 1973 and 1986, the school dropout rate doubled in poor environments. Without a high school diploma, the possibilities of finding a permanent, well-paid job are precarious.

This growth of poverty should incite our governments to take action and adopt measures to relieve the burden on poor people and alleviate the misery caused by this situation. At present, the majority of benefits paid by governments to Québec households are not designed to help the poor. Only social assistance (welfare) benefits, the guaranteed income supplement and spousal allowances are intended to relieve poverty. For example, if the guaranteed income supplement and spousal allowances did not exist in their current form, poor couples over age 65 would not have seen their financial position improve in the 1980s. However, people over age 65 living alone did not benefit as much from these government transfer payments.

Other existing programs, such as unemployment insurance and the Québec Pension Plan, guarantee an income to those who have contributed to these programs, without considering the level of their other income. Family allowances and old age security benefits are universal measures unrelated to economic needs. To eliminate poverty, government intervention in the definition of social programs should seek to redistribute wealth to reduce the gap between the rich and the poor.[5]

4. The minimum wage, subcontracting and job insecurity

The struggle against poverty cannot be won solely through government transfer payments. The State must also ensure that the working conditions offered on the job market do not perpetuate poverty. The refusal to increase the minimum wage on a regular basis impoverishes all Québec workers. In addition, companies are increasingly resorting to casual labour and subcontracting. Precarious employment creates insecurity and drives down wages. When combined with the stagnation of the minimum wage, this prevents many Québec workers from escaping poverty.

Nevertheless, it would be entirely to the State's advantage to control the conditions offered on the job market and adjust them upward. Governments that do not exert this influence are forced to provide financial assistance to a steadily growing number of people who do not have enough income to meet their minimum needs.

Current government interventions do not seek to relieve poverty or redress minimum labour standards. On the contrary, the State is cutting and tightening the criteria of eligibility to social programs and allowing private enterprise to dictate the working conditions prevailing on the job market. The unemployed have seen a reduction in their benefits (often their sole income) and in the number of weeks they are entitled to unemployment insurance. Welfare recipients, under penalty of having their benefits cut, are forced to accept dead-end jobs at compensation that is often less than the minimum wage.[6] Both of these measures keep wages down.

5. The GST

The introduction of the goods and services tax (GST) increased the financial burden on poor households. This tax applies to essential goods and services such as clothing, electrical and gas heating, furniture and electrical appliances. Even diapers are taxed. Despite a supposedly beneficial GST tax credit for poor households, they do not have the necessary cash on hand when making purchases. How can they meet their essential needs when working conditions are declining, social programs no longer fulfill their role of relieving poverty and the State is widening its tax base?

Governments must therefore ensure that there is a redistribution of the wealth produced by the economy. Otherwise, the inherent social costs of poverty, including physical and mental health problems, crime and illiteracy, will inevitably grow. To alleviate the harmful consequences of poverty, governments will have to increase the tax burden on working people. For many workers, however, this additional taxation will only accentuate their poverty. What the State absolutely must do is reduce the ever growing gap between the rich and the poor, since fighting poverty means improving our society's social and economic climate.

C. And what about housing?

Despite the "economic development" vaunted by the [former] Liberal government, Québec is still one of the poorest provinces in Canada. In 1986, there were 1,621,230 people living under the poverty line in Québec, or 25.4% of the population. For Canada as a whole, the figure was 5,182,780, or 19.1%. A very large proportion of Québec's low-income people are tenants.

1. Private enterprise controls the fate of millions of people
Private housing

There were slightly more than two and a half million households in Québec in 1987. Of these 45.8%, or 1,157,130, were renters. Slightly under one third of these tenant households, or 360,000, were classified as low-income.[7]

The number of property-owning households increased in the 1980s, partially due to the money invested by various governments to encourage access to home-ownership. Governments have always considered tenancy to be somewhat tainted. They have poured money into private ownership through tax shelters, subsidies to home buyers and other measures. These colossal sums of money go to people who do not necessarily have housing problems. To become a homeowner, you have to have money up front. All financial institutions demand at least a 10% down payment on the purchase price, even if the buyer benefits from a government program. This capital investment is one of the main impediments that prevent low and middle-income people from buying a home. The government and financial institutions do not want to change this practice. If anybody could become a property owner, this would kill the lucrative traffic in rental housing.

Social housing

Governments swear by private enterprise as a solution to the public's housing problems, even though it has proven incapable to do so. Cooperative ownership, which at best meets the needs of the lowest-income people, accounted for only 16,000 units in 1986, or 0.7% of the entire Québec housing stock. Low-rent housing increased by only 10,000 units between 1981 and 1986, reaching a total of 50,000 units. Governments have favoured a semi-private form of social housing: buildings managed by non-profit organizations. Between 1981 and 1986, the total number of these non-profit units rose from 15,000 to 47,000. By 1986, Non-profit housing only accounted for 4.8% of Québec housing units.[8] This does not provide real competition to private enterprise, which controls over 90% of rental units, concentrated in the hands of a small number of owners.

Ownership of rental housing in Québec

According to the Québec government's Green Paper on housing, 3.8% of landlords owned 53% of rental housing units in 1984.[9] Even though owner-occupants accounted for the vast majority of property-owners (85.1%), they only owned 32% of the rental units.

D. When the rent is paid, what's left for food?

Rising rents

To look at the rents charged nowadays, you'd think that you have to be rich to be a tenant. Unfortunately, this isn't true. More often than not, being a tenant means being poor. According to the 1986 census, 791,390 tenant households, or 74.5% of this type of household, earned under $30,000 a year. These income figures indicate that Québec tenants face a housing crisis.

Housing in Québec is expensive, with 45.5% of tenant households spending over 25% of their income on housing and 18.6% allocating over half their incomes. In contrast, only 20.3% of property-owning households spend over 25% of their income on housing.[10]

Since the current economic situation is deteriorating, it is important for governments to implement a series of measures that will lower this percentage. We do not want to be milked by an economic system that only widens the gap between the rich and the poor.

E. Housing: a lucrative business!

Tax loopholes

Landlords can practically do what they want with the housing they put on the rental market. They also enjoy a series of tax benefits. For example, a building's operating deficit can be applied against the owner's personal income or against the revenues of other properties. Mortgage interest and property taxes are also deductible.

Let's take the example of a non-resident owner of a triplex, who has a $144,000 mortgage and monthly rental income of $825. When he files his tax return, he can declare $9,900 in gross rental income and a net loss of $5,067, deductible from his other income. In 1990, for an individual with a gross salary of $35,000, this meant a $1,304 provincial tax rebate instead of the $46 to which he would have been entitled if he received no rental income. At the same time, this landlord's tenants would have to pay for any increases in renovation and maintenance costs, property taxes and insurance.

The landlord therefore could claim for the same expenses twice: through rent increases and on his income tax returns.

Now let's look at the big picture. In 1989, 313,579 Québec taxpayers declared nearly $7 billion in rental income from housing and commercial space. Only $169 million of this income was taxed, meaning that 97% went completely tax-free, even though the government needs money to balance its budget![11] It's time for the government to make this money serve the general public and stop allowing speculators free rein.

These figures are only the tip of the iceberg, since they only concern individuals. It is impossible to know what share of corporate income comes from rents, since the data is complex and big corporations have access to a multitude of tax loopholes.

The various Québec landlord associations have strongly attacked tenant organizations for demanding a maximum rent increase of 2% per year for the next five years. They claim that this would create a crisis in the real estate industry. The crisis already exists, and it's the landlords who are responsible for it, along with the various governments that have failed to act.

F. Rent control

The Québec government must treat housing as a basic right and an essential consumer good. The Québec minister responsible for housing must impose real mandatory universal rent control. This social measure has become necessary because the private market is incapable of supplying housing at prices that reflect the thousands of tenant households' ability to pay. The higher the rents that tenants have to pay, the less money they have for food and other necessities.

According to the Table de concertation sur la faim, the Montréal roundtable on hunger, one person in five suffered from hunger in

Montréal in 1989. This situation resulted from a lack of income and high housing costs. In 1989, the average price of a two-bedroom apartment on the Island of Montréal was $572 per month. At this rent, a welfare family of one adult and two children would have to spend 76% of its income on housing.[12] In this context, nobody should be surprised at the results of a study conducted in 1986 by the CLSC Centre-Sud, which showed that birth weights in that Montréal neighbourhood were far below the Québec average. In addition, according to the Saint-Vincent-de-Paul Society, the number of people requesting food vouchers increased by 200% in five years, rising from 6,600 to 20,000.[13]

According to the Société d'habitation du Québec (SHQ), 360,000 Québec tenant households were classified as low-income in 1987. Of this total, 266,120 were experiencing very serious housing problems in terms of financial accessibility, the quality of housing or a combination of the two. The number of households in difficulty can largely be explained by the fact that the average rent increased by 62% between 1981 and 1986.[14]

1. The Régie du logement does not control rent increases

Even though a certain form of rent control exists in Québec, there are many flaws in the rules governing the Régie du logement:

a) Every year, only 2% to 3% of rent increases are adjudicated by the Régie. For example, out of 1,092,000 rental units in Québec in 1986, the Régie only set the increases for 25,292, or 2.3%. The Régie explains this low participation rate by claiming that the majority of people reach "negotiated" settlements. These negotiations obviously didn't work in favour of tenants between 1981 and 1986, when the average rent rose 62%!

b) The increases granted by the Régie follow and confirm the trends of the speculative market. Thus, while the average rent increased by 62% between 1981 and 1986, the Régie allowed a 55% increase during the same period. (Even though our governments had declared war on inflation, they did nothing to stifle inflationary rent increases that mainly affect the lowest-income families.)

c) The Régie's rent fixation criteria are unfair because they consider expenses that never benefit the tenants. These particularly include:
• property taxes (tenants have to absorb annual tax increases that more often than not are the result of real estate speculation);[15]
• insurance (these are the premiums that an owner pays to insure a building; if a claim is filed, the tenant will not benefit);

- major repair costs (these expenses add to a building's value and are deductible from the landlord's gross income);
- indexation of net revenue (by indexing the landlord's profits, the Régie explicitly recognizes that the housing unit is also an investment and that it must be profitable, rather than essential).

We can therefore state that the Régie du logement rarely fixes rent increases, that it considers expenses that are of no use to the tenants and that it follows the laws of the marketplace rather than restricting and controlling the market.

2. The consequences of rent control

According to landlords, mandatory universal rent control would trigger a housing crisis. According to the RCLALQ, Québec tenants are already in the midst of a crisis because their rents are too high.

Landlord representatives claim that real rent control will have very harmful effects on housing for at least three reasons: deterioration, disinvestment and economic disaster:

a) Owners will no longer do renovations and repairs in rental units.
b) Real estate developers will no longer invest in housing construction, resulting in a shortage of rental units.
c) Disinvestment in the construction sector will trigger an economic disaster.

According to the RCLALQ, the basic problem of housing is access to affordable housing in good condition. Despite the absence of real rent control, landlords do not maintain the housing stock. In the City of Montréal alone, 60,000 housing units need major repairs. Every year, the City receives an average of 22,000 complaints under its Housing Code.[16]

When developers decide to invest in residential renovation, their main motivation is to speculate on the value of the renovated units. Rather than improving the quality of their tenants' lives, they displace them. The various residential renovation programs financed by the various levels of government favoured speculation and evictions during the 1980s. According to a survey by INRS-Urbanisation, over 90 percent of tenants "temporarily" evacuated to allow renovations never return to their dwellings. Until the Civil Code was amended in 1994, tenants could not contest the nature of the work and landlords did many renovations that were not necessary to make the dwellings liveable.[17]

As for the claim that rent control will cause a housing shortage because developers will stop building, thus triggering an economic disaster, this economic disaster is already a reality for thousands of Québec tenant households. The current [1990] situation in the construction industry was described by *La Presse* as follows:

> According to the Canada Mortgage and Housing Corporation (CMHC), which compiles these figures, the reduced construction activity is attributable to excess supply. The rental vacancy rate was 4.6% in October [1989], the highest in 10 years, and the supply of condominiums can satisfy demand for at least 16 months. Finally, uncertainty about interest rates has reduced the ardour of potential buyers...In Montréal, all real estate products were hit by the market decline of February 1990: only 58 rental units were built (-88%), 34 single-family units (-71%) and 84 condominiums (-34%).[18]

As for new housing starts, perceived as a lever for the Québec economy, it is important to note that:
• construction of rental housing accounts for only a small part of the real estate market (other areas are commercial, industrial, homes for owner-occupants);
• it has become increasingly difficult to build housing in most major urban centres in Québec because there is practically no land available. For example, Montréal estimated in 1989 that the bank of available land would be depleted within 10 years;
• real estate will always be a profitable investment vehicle for all kinds of speculators because it offers tremendous tax shelters and is not subject to stock market fluctuations.

G. Summing up: why mandatory universal rent control is necessary

Given the control of a large share of the rental market by a small proportion of individuals and companies;
Given the marginalization of social housing;
Given the impoverishment of Québec households and the increase in the number of tenant households spending over 25% of their income on housing;
Given the deteriorating housing conditions of many tenant households;
Given the tightened criteria for access to various social programs;
Given the difficulty of access to the labour market for a large segment of the population:

28 | For real rent control

The RCLALQ calls on the Québec government to institute mandatory universal rent control, supported by the deposit of all leases at the Régie du logement. This control will cover all rental dwellings except those located in housing cooperatives and leased to their members, those managed by municipal housing offices (low-rent housing) and those covered by a government program equivalent to low-rent housing. The cost of the rent will vary, without exception, by 2% per year for a minimum of five years.

The RCLALQ considers it important to institute real rent control in Québec. In the current context, this means restricting rent increases to 2% per year in order to limit the deterioration of housing conditions for thousands of Québec tenants. This is a measure of social redress that should be kept in force for at least five years. It is urgent to move away from the current rent fixation system which has proved its ineffectiveness by allowing too much room for real estate speculators to manoeuvre.

NOTES

1. The RCLALQ, a Québec federation of housing committees and tenants' associations, has its headquarters at 770 Rue Rachel Est, Montréal, H2J 2H5. Telephone: (514) 521-7114.
2. *La Presse*, January 4, 1989.
3. Jean Rochon, President, *Commission d'enquête sur les services de santé et les services sociaux*. (Les publications du Québec, 1988), p. 11. Rochon, who chaired a provincial commission of inquiry on health and social services in 1988, is now (1996) Québec's Minister of Health and Social Services; the Parti Québécois government's point man for cutbacks and hospital closings (editor's note).
4. Canadian Council on Social Development, *Basic Data on Poverty in Canada*.
5. Governments, of course, have been moving in the opposite direction since this document was published in 1990. There have been drastic welfare cuts, unemployment insurance has been slashed and shamelessly renamed "employment insurance," and the federal government is adopting a new pension system with clawbacks directed against some groups of seniors.(editor's note).
6. Under Québec workfare programs the government has to top up the income of workers (especially women heading one-parent families) whose employment income is less than they would receive on welfare. Similar top-up measures (the "APPORT" program) apply to low-wage workers, all at taxpayers' expense (editor's note).
7. Société d'habitation du Québec (SHQ), January 1989.

8. Under the Montréal Citizens' Movement (MCM), in power at Montréal City Hall from 1986 to 1994, more than 3,500 additional non-profit and cooperative units were added through acquisition and renovation funded by the three levels of government, with purchases concentrated in the neighbourhoods in greatest need of revitalization. The MCM originally intended to add 1,200 units a year, but was forced by budget constraints to cut this back to 350 units in 1994. However, when Mayor Pierre Bourque's Vision Montréal party defeated the MCM in 1994, the new administration abolished this program and abdicated responsibility to the Québec government and private non-profit groups (editor's note).
9. Gouvernement du Québec, *Se loger au Québec*. Also known as the *Livre vert*, or Green Paper, 1984.
10. The problem is even more acute on the Island of Montréal. A 1989 study by the City of Montréal found that over 60,000 households within City limits spent more than half their income on housing. This resulted in a short-lived commitment by the MCM administration to create 50,000 units of various types of "social housing" within 10 years, in the hope that economic development and job creation would solve the rest of the problem. A budget crisis and the defeat of the MCM put an end to any serious effort to meet this goal (editor's note).
11. Ministère du Revenu du Québec.
12. Canada Mortgage and Housing Corporation (CMHC), October 1989.
13. Guy Paiement, "La faim à Montréal," in *Relations*, March, 1990. After further cutbacks in social programs in the past six years, the situation has worsened and food banks, once considered a temporary measure, have become a fact of life (editor's note).
14. Statistics Canada. This was the period when Québec's rent control system allowed the highest average rent increases in history. For example, in 1982, a year of record-high interest rates, major municipal tax increases and an "energy crisis," the Régie du logement allowed increases of between 12% and 20%. Even though average rent increases levelled off in 1989-1996, with the Régie recommending around 2% and then 1% per year for units with no major repairs, other problems in the economy meant that low-income tenants never caught up (editor's note).
15. Real estate speculation fuelled tax increases in Montréal, with a resulting impact on rents, throughout the 1970s and 1980s. The Québec government's decision to switch to a three-year property assessment system in 1989, instead of annual assessments, alleviated the problem of sudden increases in most parts of the City two years out of three. The collapse of the inflated real estate market of 1987-88 has also played a role, except in certain high-speculation zones (editor's note).
16. *Habiter Montréal, Livre blanc*, 1989. White paper produced by the City of Montréal for a public consultation on housing policy.
17. Renovation was particularly used to displace tenants in the early 1980s. Legal controls were tightened to prevent this in 1987, and then again in 1994. Conditions to protect tenants and control post-renovation rent increases were also added to government renovation subsidy programs. Nevertheless, the inconvenience involved in renovations still means that many tenants leave and don't come back (editor's note).

18. *La Presse*, March 13, 1990, p. D7. On the Island of Montréal, rental vacancy rates were even higher, fluctuating around the 7% mark since the late 1980s.

Chapter 3

For a Québec housing policy

by Le Regroupement des Comités logement et Associations de locataires du Québec (RCLALQ), 1991

Editor's note: This text was published in French by the RCLALQ in 1991 as its basic position paper on housing. I have added several footnotes to update the context to 1996.

This document represents the point of view of the Regroupement des Comités logement et Associations de locataires du Québec (RCLALQ) on the entire housing question, based on the experience of people who have worked in this field for many years. The measures proposed, if implemented, would undoubtedly improve the situation of tenants in Québec.

The RCLALQ's thirteen member organizations, through many years of defending tenants' rights, have thought long and hard about this question.[1] The RCLALQ and its constituent groups represent over 500,000 tenant households.

The RCLALQ is an organization dedicated to the struggle for housing rights, with the daily task of promoting and defending the rights of underprivileged tenants. These last two words are more often than not synonymous, as this document will show. This situation leads us to promote six main social objectives:
• The right for everyone to have decent housing at a reasonable cost.
• The right of tenants to stay in their dwellings.
• The protection, preservation and, in many cases, restoration of the rental housing stock.
• The democratic assumption of control, by the people, of their own living conditions. The corollary is the right of association (which is still far from recognized, despite what some might be tempted to believe).
• Access to collective ownership of dwellings.
• The implementation of these principles by the responsible political authorities.

A Word of warning

A famous catch-phrase says: "Fifty percent of men are women." We are tempted to add: "...and even more among tenants."

All housing groups know from experience that a high percentage of tenants facing housing problems are women. All statistics and studies confirm this clearly.

Statistics Canada, after noting that one-parent families are the households with the most trouble finding housing, tried to explain the situation as follows:

Firstly, these households are generally headed by a woman, and women are less well-paid than men. Secondly, because they find it hard to reconcile the demands of employment with their children's education, many single mothers work part-time or are unemployed. Thirdly, it is known that single parents are subject to discrimination in the rental housing market, and consequently can find themselves obliged to pay more for their dwellings.[2]

Québec's Ministry of Manpower and Income Security acknowledges that: "In 1986, the poverty rate of families headed by a woman was 3.76 times more than that of families headed by a man, as compared to 2.39 times in 1973."[3]

We could add other quotes ad nauseam to show that, in Québec, poverty has a gender. Since we have used the masculine pronoun throughout this text, we wish to remind the reader that, unsurprisingly, housing problems affect women more than men, mirroring the place assigned to women in our supposedly democratic societies.

1. Housing in our society

A. A social right?

In official discourse, particularly on the political scene, housing is quite rightly recognized as a fundamental need. This is readily admitted because cold weather in this northern country lasts for more than half the year. Yet, no real action corresponds to the fine principles that are so broadly and generously proclaimed.

These are superficial and unfounded statements.Their lack of sincerity becomes obvious when compared to everyday reality. The right to housing is not recognized in either the federal or Québec Charter of Rights. In Montréal alone, there are thousands of homeless, and the situation is getting worse instead of better. All the relief services for persons living in poverty are overwhelmed by ever-growing numbers, and homelessness now affects some social groups that had been spared until now.

B. Under the law of the market

The tenant is mainly an urban phenomenon, as is the landlord. The emergence of masses of workers who had to be housed in cities, growing exponentially during the Industrial Revolution, provided a new source of profit for real estate promoters. From *Oliver Twist* to *The Tin Flute*, there is a large body of popular literature that describes the deplorable living conditions and the unhealthy and overcrowded dwellings of working class families, who were totally at the landlord's mercy. Property rights had replaced seigniorial rights in Québec, and were exercised just as arbitrarily. In Canada, the first steps to protect tenants were taken during the Second World War: rents were frozen and evictions were prohibited. The war effort required social peace, and this alone justified a belated intervention by the State in a field "normally" left to the law of the jungle, known by the gentler phrase, law of the market. In fact, once the war was over, the federal government lifted these controls.

However, the changes brought by the war altered society profoundly and permanently. The provincial government stepped in and established certain legal limits on the rental housing market. Even so, was the situation of tenants much improved? Was the almost feudal nature of property rights changed? This remains to be seen.

2. The state of housing in Québec

A. The rule of private property

In Québec, 55 percent of households (1,399,000) own their homes, while 1,135,000 rent.[4] The relatively recent trend toward a property-owning majority is due, in part, to several factors: higher earnings for unionized workers, government incentives for the purchase of new homes, suburban growth, the lure of the American model of single-family dwellings, and the increase in condominiums.

In the view of government, it seems that tenancy is a flaw to be eliminated. Hence, there has been a strong emphasis in recent years on access to home ownership in government housing programs. But it is well-known that loans are only made to the affluent, and only households that are already well-off have been able to take advantage of government measures to facilitate home ownership. The profitable business of rental housing continues therefore to flourish, although it does so more and more on the backs of the dispossessed. A large part of the meagre budget of the more disadvantaged in our society goes to pay for a roof over their heads, much to the benefit of the few: In fact, 3.8% of real estate owners own 53% of rental housing, according to the Québec government study *Se loger au Québec*.[5]

As for social housing, its availability is in proportion to government efforts. In 1986, non-profit housing accounted for only 4.8% of Québec's housing stock. Between 1986 and 1991, only 6,389 new low-rental housing units were added. The cooperative formula so often praised by the choristers of Québec nationalism has never been given a chance to prove itself in the housing field. In 1986, there were only 16,000 cooperative housing units, or 0.7% of all housing in Québec. As can be seen, there is not much competition for the near-monopoly in rental housing held by the private sector. Large property owners can no doubt sleep in peace, given the spellbinding oratory of our politicians who daily praise the alleged virtues of the free-market system as the universal cure for all of humanity's ills!

B. Landlord and tenant: an unequal legal status

While some limits have been established in housing legislation, property rights continue to rule unfettered in landlord-tenant relations. In fact, the section "rental housing" is found in the chapters on leasing, both in the Civil Code and other treatises on law. As stated earlier, the legal right to housing simply does not exist. Thus the landlord has the following privileges:
- The right to choose his tenants (an open door to all kinds of discrimination);
- The privilege to alter his property in any way he chooses, without the tenant's having any say in the matter (although the latter will pay the cost through rent increases);[6]
- The privilege of being exempt from all rent controls during the first five years' operation of a new building;
- The exclusive right to demand changes to the lease;
- The possibility of having a lease cancelled and the tenant evicted if the rent is still unpaid after three weeks, regardless of the cause of the delay;
- The right of access to the dwelling at any time.[7]

Furthermore, in practice, the few rights allowed the tenant have quite often been inoperative. For example, even though the landlord is required to indicate the rent paid by the former tenant on the lease of a new tenant, the landlord can omit it without penalty! In fact, to our knowledge, very few landlords abide by this so-called obligation. Furthermore, since a new tenant has virtually no legal rights until he obtains a lease, he may not find it in his interest to insist on having the information.

The same situation applies with regard to the tenant's right to stay in the dwelling. In most cases, the tenant does not return to his dwelling after vacating for major repairs, since in most cases he cannot afford the rent increase. Furthermore, the practice of repossessing the dwelling for occupancy by a close relative is very common.

A landlord can easily bring intimidation to bear. In most cases, the tenant is a disadvantaged person and thus more vulnerable to such undue pressures, which are hypocritically tolerated, indeed encouraged by the present system. Abuses had become so obvious that the Liberal government adopted a law in 1987 setting a fine (of $5,000 to $25,000) for harassing a tenant to get him to leave. Once more, good intentions do not stand up to scrutiny when confronted with the facts. Only judicial authorities are authorized to file penal charges of tenant harassment. It took two years after the law was adopted for the Solicitor General to appoint two investigators, who have been so overwhelmingly ineffective that, as of 1991, *no* case has resulted in a guilty verdict![8]

Even if a tenant decides to take his case to the Régie du logement (only if he is allowed to do so, of course), only the landlord may deduct the costs incurred at the hearing from his taxable income! This inequality must be ended.

C. Tenants' living conditions

According to the 1986 Census, 74.5% of tenant households (791,340 households) earned less than $30,000.[9] Tenant income averaged $22,147 (compared to the landlords' average of $38,730).[10]

Despite our governments' feeble attempts to promote economic development, Québec remains one of the provinces where the highest levels of poverty are tolerated. On a scale where a rank of first place identified the province with the lowest poverty rate, Québec ranked eighth according to the 1986 census.[11] On this same scale, since 1973, Québec had slipped from third to fourth place in the ranking of the five Canadian regions, nearly on a par with the Maritimes.[12] It is estimated that a third of Canada's poor live in Québec, although the province has only a quarter of the country's population.[13] In 1991, 700,000 people in Québec depended on social assistance.[14] In 1990, the poverty rate rose to 19% from 14% in 1980.[15]

Since, for obvious reasons, poverty and the status of tenants most often go hand in hand, the high cost of housing becomes a severe drain on the lowest incomes. Thus, according to the 1990 figures, 45% of tenant households spent more than 25% of their income to house themselves.[16] These statistics conceal the plight of the poorest people, since for 18.6% of Québec tenants (194,650 households), housing costs account for over 50% of their income![17] These figures could easily be higher, since severe cuts to welfare and unemployment insurance have further reduced the already meagre resources of low-income families while rental costs rose sharply in the same period.

One might at least expect that the other side of the picture would indicate a generally good quality of rental housing, given the high cost of rents. Yet according to Statistics Canada, 115,000 rental dwellings in Québec needed major repairs in 1990.[18] In addition, 21,300 tenant households occupied dwellings that were too small for them. Tenant households had to settle for an average of 4.1 rooms, while homeowners averaged 6.4 rooms.[19]

For many tenants, access to a dwelling and the right to stay in it continue to be a problem. Repossession, allegedly to house a close relative, and evacuation for major repairs, have traditionally been used by landlords to "get rid of" tenants they considered bothersome.

Under the present system, justice is random since the tenant's rights depend on the knowledge he is expected to have of housing laws and his ability to use the legal machinery of the Régie du logement.

Too often, a woman alone, a senior citizen,[20] a low-income worker, or a single parent on welfare will not dare appeal to the Régie when faced with an excessive rent increase or an illegal eviction. The insecurity inherent in their social status, the intimidating aspect of judicial procedures, the landlord's self-assurance, the tenant's ignorance of the law, health problems, difficulty speaking or the impossibility of getting time off from work or finding a babysitter on the day of the hearing, are all impediments that keep tenants — the majority as we have seen — from ensuring that their rights are respected.

There are other means of intimidation: personal files and blacklists. Before signing a lease, some landlords will ask the person looking for a dwelling to provide his social insurance number, health insurance number and driver's licence number, the name of his bank and his account number, the name and address of his employer, the name of the welfare agent, the name of the immigration officer, etc., all on the grounds of checking the person's solvency. Since insolvency is not recognized as a discriminatory reason for refusing to rent, the personal file becomes a legal shield to hide every form of discrimination.

Under this system, shockingly tolerated by the authorities, landlords can always find a way to refuse to rent to families, one-parent families headed by women, immigrants, members of ethnic minorities, disabled persons, etc. (In the case of welfare recipients, unemployment insurance recipients and low-wage earners, the issue is not hidden discrimination since insolvency is a legal reason for refusing to rent; the right to housing does not exist in Canada, as we have seen.) If a lease is signed, the landlord can always threaten that the personal data on the tenant who protests too much will be added to one of the blacklists of undesirable tenants, which are maintained by certain landlord associations in violation of individual rights. The tenant could then be denied access to all rental housing controlled by the owners who have access to these databases.[21]

3. For the right to housing

A. Access to housing

When a person has to spend more than 25% of his net income on housing costs, his entire quality of life suffers. Basic necessities such as food, education, health care and recreation can no longer be covered. There is no reason why, in a country such as ours, decent housing at a reasonable cost should be the privilege of the well-to-do. That is why it is important that housing rights prevail over property rights, and that the rental housing business respect a clearly-defined social right.

The right to housing must be recognized as a fundamental right, which is entrenched in the federal and provincial human rights charters and the constitution.

First come, first served, an old principle of natural justice, should also apply to tenants in search of a dwelling. In practice, a landlord must be required to rent to the first person who applies. This is the only simple rule that can prevent discrimination, whether subtly hidden or flagrantly displayed.

Recognition of the right to housing also implies a ban on various agencies that specialize in discriminatory practices or harassment, whether they are called "credit bureaus," "rental agencies," or "collection agencies." Whatever term is used to disguise these less respectable activities, blacklisting and recording of personal information must be prohibited. The Régie du logement should have its jurisdiction broadened to include cases of discrimination in housing, and the Human Rights Commission must be given the necessary resources and powers to investigate, inspect and intervene in the field to ensure these rights are respected. When necessary, the Commission could intervene at the Régie. Obviously, these fine principles will only have meaning if there are significant penalties for offenders.

B. Rent control

We stated earlier that the legal system currently in force for rental housing leads to randomly arbitrary justice. This is certainly true in the case of annual rent increases. Since the tenant has the burden of refusing the increase, many senior citizens, women living alone and fearful people in general become easy prey to the landlord's pressures, and do not dare challenge the rent demanded.

In fact, barely three percent of dwellings have their rents fixed by the Régie. When a dwelling changes tenants, there are often major rent increases, and the modest legal requirement that the old rent be mentioned in the new lease is not even respected.

According to a report by Canada Mortgage and Housing Corporation (CMHC), the range of rents for similar types of dwellings was between $596 and $1,054, depending on whether they were rented or vacant.[22] A 1989 survey by social work students at the Université du Québec à Montréal found that in Montréal's St-Henri district, tenants of less than two years paid 46.6% more than tenants who had occupied the same dwelling for over five years.

The result of laissez-faire policy is that rents are rising faster than the Consumer Price Index. Between 1981 and 1986, rents increased by 62%, while our governments, though officially at war with inflation, did not deem it necessary to intervene. These inflationary rent increases particularly affected lower-income families.

The present system has clearly proven ineffective. It is high time for a real rent control policy, based on two inseparable elements:
• ahe mandatory deposit of all leases with the Régie du logement;
• a single rate of increase, set annually, for all rental housing, whether recently constructed or not.

The costs of major repairs should be offset by tax exemptions rather than passed on to the tenants, as is now the case. The tenants' burden is already heavy enough. If putting an end to excessive speculation scares off certain real estate investors, the income stability resulting from universal controls will reassure serious investors who care more for long-term profitability than for quick excess profits. In short, except for a few greedy profiteers who want to retain their very profitable privileges, everyone would gain from implementation of these measures.[23] That is why the Regroupement has made this question a priority.

C. The lease

A lease, or any other amending clause that affects it, should be subject to cancellation within a given deadline, as is already the case for other types of contracts. Thus, leases signed under pressure or in the light of false information would not irrevocably bind the tenant.

In the event of the tenant's death, or a disabling accident or illness, it should be possible to cancel the lease with no penalty for the tenant or his estate, for obvious humanitarian reasons.

The standard residential lease forms issued by the Régie du logement should be mandatory and available free of charge at the Régie's offices.[24]

A tenant who is moving to a housing cooperative or non-profit housing should be able to cancel the lease on three months' notice, just as the law already permits for low-rental housing and nursing homes.

D. Financial assistance to the tenant

The difference between the amount of the rent and 25 percent of the net household income should be made up by a government rent allowance paid to low-income tenants. This would be an extension of the rent supplement now provided in low-rental housing and in certain dwellings managed by cooperatives and non-profit organizations, except that the allowance would be paid directly to the tenant.

This measure cannot be considered without a universal rent control policy, including mandatory depositing of leases at the Régie du logement. Otherwise, there is a risk that the allowance would be diverted to landlords through uncontrolled rent increases. The rent supplement formula would continue to be applied to non-profit housing units.

E. Repossession

Under the present system, the Régie will only hear repossession cases when the tenant does not agree to the landlord's demand. The tenant can then challenge the landlord's allegations. This is yet another example of random justice which results in the abuses we have already mentioned. If the tenant's right to stay in his dwelling is to mean anything, repossessions should simply be prohibited.

F. Renovation subsidy programs

Renovation programs to improve the rental housing stock have become an unavoidable necessity in Québec, given the political negligence which has led to the dilapidation of a large part of available rental housing. Unfortunately, these programs have served mainly to help landlords make a profit, without any concern for the rights of tenants. Unless the right to stay in one's dwelling is upheld in law, as stated earlier, renovation subsidies will only serve the landlord's interests, while the tenant ultimately pays yet again.

However, provided that there are strict policies to protect the tenant's right to remain in the dwelling, it is desirable that renovation subsidy and technical support programs be available to landlords, and that municipalities have the power to improve on these programs. On the other hand, tenants must be informed of their rights and be given an opportunity to make their views known. In any event, the Régie du logement should have the final say, whether on landlord-tenant relations, or on the proposed renovation work, the amount of compensation, etc. The Régie should also set the post-renovation rents automatically each year.

Owner-occupants should also have access to renovation assistance programs. In fact, many households with modest means, a significant number of them senior citizens, cannot afford the cost of maintenance of their homes as they watch them become more and more run down. Income-adjusted financial assistance programs should be available to them.[25]

G. Habitability standards

There are too many dwellings with major defects for governments to continue their current toleration of neglect. Renovation subsidy programs are expensive and will never make up for vigilance in keeping buildings in good condition. An ounce of prevention is worth a pound of cure.

Habitability and sanitation standards, including wheelchair access, must be legislated on a province-wide basis. Unlike existing codes, it should also cover soundproofing. This housing and sanitation code could be administered by municipalities which could improve on the standards.[26]

In the most serious cases, where the occupants' health and security is endangered by abusive or negligent landlords, an emergency fund should be established to allow municipalities to act quickly in critical situations. The costs would be recovered on the defaulting landlord's tax bill. Escalating daily penalties would apply against landlords who deliberately endanger their tenants' health and safety. Legal liability for housing code violations should be transferred automatically when the building changes hands.

H. Major repairs

Frequently, rental dwellings are converted almost overnight into luxury apartments that the tenants can no longer afford. To prevent this, tenants must be able to challenge the nature and expediency of any repairs that would change the dwelling. Therefore, any major improvements or repairs, other than those made necessary by an emergency, should require authorization by the Régie du logement, which would have the power to set the conditions. The Civil Code should specifically provide that the tenant who has vacated temporarily is the only person who may occupy the dwelling after the work is done, unless he gives the Régie written notice to the contrary. Mandatory depositing of leases would make it much easier to apply this measure, guaranteeing the tenant's right to remain in a dwelling.

I. Temporary housing

A stock of available units should be maintained in each municipality to accommodate people displaced by major repairs or by disasters. A tenant displaced for major repairs should pay the same rent as he paid in his vacated dwelling. The number of temporary units available would depend on the number of dwellings likely to be renovated that year and allow evacuated tenants to stay in their neighbourhoods.

J. A ban on condo conversions

A sharp rise in property values has been noted in all neighbourhoods where there has been a trend to conversion of rental housing into condominiums. This is a direct consequence of real estate speculation and creates upward pressure on rents in its wake.

Normally, when a building's selling price is about six times the rental income, rents can be maintained within a reasonable range. But if the selling price rises to eight, ten or eleven times the rental income, the landlord will want to increase the return on his investment by raising his rents. To this end, he will sometimes use unorthodox means of pressure. In addition, conversions reduce the stock of available rental housing, making it harder for tenants to find an acceptable dwelling at an affordable price.

The Regroupement therefore considers that any conversion of a building into condominiums should be prohibited if there have been any rental housing units in that building in the past.

However, the Regroupement favours the conversion of rental housing to different types of collective ownership (cooperatives, non-profit corporations, etc.).

K. Rooming houses

Roomers have the poorest protection of all tenants. Almost none of them return to their dwellings after major renovations, either because they do not know the law or because the rents have become too high. Rooming houses are mainly located downtown, and tend to be replaced quickly by offices, businesses or luxury apartments.

It is therefore necessary to establish a real policy to protect roomers' rights to stay in their dwellings, by establishing controls and standardizing all municipal and provincial laws and regulations in this area.

The appropriate government agencies should take action to prevent demolition of rooming houses and their conversion to other uses. Renovation programs for rooming houses should be completely overhauled to fit into a general policy, designed to maintain and develop the stock of rooms for rent and respect the fundamental rights of rooming house tenants.

To prevent abuses, which often occur in renovations, the government must intervene directly by promoting the development of social housing in rooming houses.

L. Change of destination, subdivision, combination and demolition

Changing a dwelling's destination from residential to commercial use, and subdivision, combination or demolition of housing units are all exceptional measures which have the effect of breaking a lease. It should therefore be mandatory to obtain the Régie's authorization in any of these cases. It is also essential to ensure that tenants living near a converted building do not see their quality of life reduced.

Municipalities should have clear policies and real powers to force landlords to maintain their properties in habitable condition and continuously occupied by tenants. Must we continue to tolerate speculators letting properties go to ruin until their poor condition justifies a demolition order? Boarded-up, abandoned houses must be expropriated, renovated and transformed into social housing, or they must be demolished if they cannot be renovated. Vacant lots created by demolitions should automatically be used for social housing.

Zoning by-laws must be reviewed if they have the effect of reducing the rental housing stock. Too often, the proliferation of businesses or of certain types of establishments in residential areas (restaurants, bars or sex shops, for example) brings about an increase in vehicular and pedestrian traffic which literally transforms a neighbourhood and greatly affects the quality of life of its residents. Municipal by-laws should prevent such commercial invasions in mainly residential areas.

M. Fire insurance

Many tenants do not have any fire insurance coverage. Their incomes are too low to cover the insurance premiums, or insurance companies set prohibitively high rates for coverage in what they consider high-risk zones. Fire insurance must be recognized as an essential service, and all tenants should be able to obtain coverage at an affordable rate. On the same principle as auto insurance, a universal fire insurance plan should be available to all tenants.

N. Low-rental housing

As we saw earlier, the need for social housing is self-evident. To meet that need, low-rental housing programs must be intensified, either through new construction, public ownership of part of the existing housing stock, or by recycling public buildings.

Moreover, low-rental housing should be managed according to democratic rules, whereby elected tenants' representatives would have decision-making powers with respect to site selection, construction, maintenance and administration. This of course implies that directors elected by the tenants would hold a majority of the seats on the board.

Tenants' associations will have to receive all the resources they need to fulfil their role as the tenants' representatives. Adequate community services must also be provided.

O. Housing cooperatives

Although cooperatives have been treated as an afterthought in the Québec housing market, they could be just as useful in solving tenants' problems as they have been historically in other areas of society. Programs for non-profit, non-equity housing cooperatives that are controlled by their members must become part of the mainstream instead of being kept on the sidelines of government housing policy.

They should be dusted off and modified so that they become accessible to low-income groups, thereby becoming real generators of economic and social development. To that end, the growth of cooperative housing must become a priority.

Programs should be flexible enough to allow for new construction, purchases for renovation, direct purchases or recycling of buildings. Governments should negotiate special low-interest rates with financial institutions so that cooperatives can borrow at the lowest possible rate. Budgets for technical resource groups that help set up cooperatives must be increased.

The market cost index used in setting the initial rents for co-op housing is tantamount to subjecting the principles of cooperative action to unbounded real estate speculation. Instead, rental rates must be set according to tenants' ability to pay.

P. Tenants' associations and class actions

As we have constantly stated, housing is a social right. Groups that promote this right, particularly neighbourhood or building tenants' associations, must see their mandates recognized and their efforts given practical encouragement.

Tenants' associations within a building must be considered as legitimate representatives with respect to landlord-tenant relations, and receive the necessary funding for their activities. These associations should have the right to represent tenants, file complaints and initiate legal action at the Régie du logement (particularly when the collective interests of a group of tenants are threatened).

It seems absurd that there is no class action procedure at the Régie du logement for a group of tenants who have the same landlord and the same problem. This situation ought to be corrected.

Q. Referenda and democracy

Residents of most Québec cities and towns can initiate referenda to decide on local issues. It is altogether unacceptable that such a procedure is not available to residents of Montréal and Québec City, where voracious real estate promoters has done so much harm to heritage buildings, disrupting residents' lives in complete disregard for their opinions. One notorious example, in the late 1980s, was the Overdale project in downtown Montréal, where condominium developers forced out the tenants.[27] In Québec City, there were the development projects affecting the Grande-Place, the Old Port and Parliament Hill.

All citizens have a right to pass judgement on anything that may alter their environment, especially if it affects their living conditions. Holding a referendum on development issues is one of the principal ways of exercising this right, and it is unthinkable for any municipality to be deprived of it. Given that citizens should have a say on urban planning, information on any development in a neighbourhood must be made public and readily available for consultation at no cost.

Public facilities must be accessible to the greatest number, without discrimination. The network of free community services meeting the basic needs of communities (such as daycare centres, green spaces, schools, etc.) must therefore be expanded and improved.

R. The key role of the State: the provincial government

Most of the measures proposed in this document require government action. This is perfectly normal: Because housing is fundamentally a social issue, collective solutions will have to be provided. Three measures requiring immediate and priority action are:
- the mandatory depositing of leases with the Régie du logement;
- universal mandatory control of rent increases;
- a right of first refusal for tenants if their dwelling is put up for sale.

These three measures would significantly reduce cases of discrimination and harassment which still affect the most vulnerable tenants every day.

The principle of protection for tenants is already recognized implicitly in current legislation. Yet the present legal framework has proven ineffective in bringing these principles to fruition. The credibility of our judicial system requires that our legislators reconsider the legal framework, since the way things are going, the objectives are a long way from being met. Given the generally accepted view that the State plays an auxiliary role in social sectors such as health, education and culture, where private enterprise cannot provide adequate services to the public under the impetus of ordinary market forces, we must conclude — in the light of all that has been said — that vigorous government intervention on housing is essential.

The most logical and obvious way of affirming that housing rights have become a true social priority would be to establish a Ministry of Housing. This ministry would have a mandate to coordinate every effort to ensure that all Québec residents have a right to decent housing at reasonable cost.

Similarly, the provincial government has a duty to support collectively-managed social housing, by providing increased aid to housing cooperatives or other kinds of non-profit community organizations. A capital gains tax should be levied on all real estate transactions to create a compensation fund for social housing.

Administrative procedures to obtain financing for purchases of real estate should be made easier to give tenants an effective right of first refusal.

When a rental housing building is put up for sale, there should be a compulsory procedure whereby the tenants may exercise the right of first refusal on the property, for conversion into joint ownership according to one of the social housing formulas (cooperative housing or non-profit organization). Tenants would have three months to set up an association and make an offer to purchase. If the tenants make an offer, a further three months would be allowed to complete the negotiations.

Alternatively, if the tenants do not exercise their right of first refusal, the owner must offer the property to other housing cooperatives or non-profit organizations, technical resources groups in the housing field, a municipal housing office or some other non-profit purchasing corporation that would be willing to convert the property to social housing.

S. The legal framework

As already stated, we would like to see the Régie du logement not only maintain its present role as court of first instance on questions arising from residential leases, but also widen its jurisdiction to issues of discrimination in the choice of tenants, renovation of dwellings, enforcement of the eventual habitability code, etc.

Since housing is a right, we doubt that the Régie's conciliation process is relevant. Substituting negotiation for law is a negation of all gains through jurisprudence and makes housing problems part of interpersonal relations. In the present context, this can only be done at the tenant's expense. The Régie should abandon this erratic process and concentrate on its primary roles of providing information, adjudicating disputes, publishing statistics and registering leases.

Procedures at the Régie must be speeded up. Cases related to heating, harassment, discrimination, or any other matter affecting the health and safety of tenants must be heard within one week.

Moreover, given that procedures are very often mysterious and disconcerting to the uninitiated, we believe that the commissioners should make sure all parties know the rules of procedure, explaining them if necessary. More generally, the Régie should expand its information services to tenants. In other words, we want the Board to fulfil its mandate as an administrative tribunal, at which any ordinary person can present his own case without being handicapped by the absence of legal counsel.

Finally, the Régie's services must be free. The $41 deterrent fee must be abolished.

T. The municipal administration

When a renovation program is initiated in a municipality, whether it is a local initiative or is federally or provincially funded, politicians invoke the tenants' interests. But when people try to obtain information on the progress of a project and its impact on tenants, they quickly learn that their inquiries are not welcome at City Hall. As for trying to find out the status of a complaint reported to City inspectors, in some municipalities you'll get farther consulting an astrologer than the department concerned.

Nevertheless, since the municipal administration is closest to citizens, it is in the best position to manage certain programs. Municipalities should therefore have the following powers with regard to housing:
• to apply and administer renovation programs;
• to establish technical and information services where tenants can obtain information on the processing, approval and subsidization of renovation projects submitted by landlords and their own legal recourses;
• to enforce and administer the Housing Code;
• to have expropriation rights for the construction and development of social housing and for installation of public utilities;
• to build and manage low-rental housing;
• to issue construction, renovation and demolition permits;
• to enforce zoning by-laws;

- to set up and manage a compensation fund earmarked for social housing. This fund would be constituted from an anti-speculation tax, compensation and top-up measures, as well as the fines levied for violations of municipal housing by-laws.

Under the current tax system, both homeowners and tenants pay municipal taxes. Homeowners often loudly challenge property valuations which increase their tax load. On the other hand, landlords can pass on the entire tax burden to their tenants, and any speculative increase in property values results in substantial capital gains.

The system must therefore be changed so that municipal finances favour the social objectives of the right to housing. Thus, variable property tax rates should be applied, depending on the building's use. This would result in lower taxes on housing cooperatives and non-profit community housing corporations. Increases in property valuation should be the same for all rental housing, and should be uniformly based on the general rise in the cost of materials and skilled labour, not on turbulent rises in real estate prices triggered by speculation.

U. The federal government

The federal government must direct its actions towards promoting the right to housing. It must therefore maintain and develop its rental housing renovation programs and encourage collective ownership of rental housing by tenants, by supporting housing cooperatives and non-profit community housing corporations.

V. Public utilities

We believe that the decision to cut off an essential service such as gas or electricity should not be left to the discretion of corporate bill collectors. A dwelling without heat or power becomes unusable. Such service cuts should be prohibited as an attack on the right to housing. It is bad enough to live through difficult economic circumstances without having to face the threat of a cut in services essential to the user's health and survival.

In extreme cases, where there is demonstrable and unequivocal bad faith on the part of a user who does not pay his or her bills, the utility could be allowed to cut off service after a decision by the Régie du logement.

4. Conclusion

Mayors of major Canadian cities are now sounding the alarm about the dramatic plight of tenants across Canada. Meeting in Montréal in April 1991, sixteen big-city mayors acknowledged that at least 30% of tenants in their jurisdictions have to spend over 30% of their gross income on rent. In Montréal, 40% of tenants were in this category, leading Mayor Jean Doré to declare housing a national priority, unlike the huge amounts going toward military spending.

That normally conservative administrators should make such statements is yet another sign that the Reagan years, during which social programs were cut in order to give tax cuts to the rich and the big corporations, are now over. In fact, regressive policies have largely proved to be ineffective, particularly in the economy, where, according to the politicians, they should have produced full employment and reduced the deficit.[28]

Housing committees, tenants' associations and other groups defending social rights are no longer preaching to deaf ears. The publication of these demands by Québec tenants is timely because their adoption by government bodies seem conceivable, as long as the entire progressive movement carries on the efforts initiated by the defenders of tenants' rights.

Given that present government policies lead to a dead end, effective rent controls are seen as a necessity by a growing number of people on the public stage. From now on, such controls should be at the centre of demands for social justice and the reduction of inequalities.

NOTES

1. As of 1996, three of these groups have over 15 years of experience in their field. Four others have been working on tenants' rights for over 10 years (editor's note).
2. Pierre Filion and Trudi E. Bunting, *Accessibilité du logement au Canada*, (Ottawa: Statistics Canada), no. 98-130, 1990, p. 14 (translation).
3. Ministère de la Main-d'oeuvre et de la Sécurité du revenu, *La pauvreté au Québec, 1973-1986: les faits saillants*, brochure no. F114, p. 4 (translation).
4. According to Statistics Canada, *Enquête sur l'équipement ménager 1990*, publication no. 64-202.
5. Ministère de l'Habitation et de la Protection du consommateur, Éditeur officiel, 1984, p. 28. This profile of investor-landlords is based on 1981 data. To our knowledge, no other study has been produced since, which would allow

anyone to accurately estimate the increase in the concentration of ownership of rental housing over the past fifteen years [as of 1996].
6. Until the Civil Code amendments took effect in January 1994, the tenant did not have the right to contest the nature of major repairs proposed by the landlord. This allowed for many abuses (editor's note).
7. The landlord can inspect the dwelling on 24 hours' notice. However, no notice is required to show the dwelling to prospective tenants after the current tenant has given legal notice of non-renewal (editor's note).
8. With the help of their organizations, tenants have been considerably more successful in filing civil claims for damages at the Régie du logement. Damages have been awarded for harassment, failure to do renovations after a tenant has been forced to vacate for that purpose, abusive failure to do necessary repairs, malicious illegal entry, and "bad faith" repossession (failure to take occupancy after getting a tenant to leave for that purpose). The amounts awarded range from $500 or $1,000 "wrist slaps" to fairly interesting deterrents of close to $10,000 (editor's note).
9. Statistics Canada, publication no. 93-105, Table 14-9.
10. Ibid., Table 13-11.
11. Ministère de la Main-d'oeuvre et de la Sécurité du revenu, op. cit.
12. Report of the Québec Cabinet's Secrétariat aux affaires culturelles et sociales, cited by Jean-Pierre Bonhomme in *La Presse*, November 3, 1990, p. 14.
13. Data taken from the Association des Offices municipaux d'habitation, April 1991, referring to a recent study by the Institut québécois de recherche sur la culture.
14. Ibid.
15. Ibid.
16. Statistics Canada, publication no. 93-105, Table 12-2. "While 20.3% of homeowners spend over 25% of their income on housing costs, this expense is an investment which will increase household equity. Contrary to tenants, the situation of these homeowners improves as the years go by and their careers advance... and the gradual repayment of their mortgage reduces their ownership costs in relative terms. At the same time, the value of their real estate investment increases, often quite spectacularly, as their home increases in value." Pierre Filion and Trudi E. Bunting, *Accessibilité du logement au Canada*, Statistics Canada, 1990, pp. 13-14. (translation)
17. Statistics Canada, op. cit.
18. A condition also shared by 171,000 homeowners. This shows that individual home ownership is not the panacea to housing problems. See *Enquête sur l'équipement ménager* 1990, Statistics Canada, op. cit., Table 1.12.
19. Statistics Canada. op. cit. Table 10. Yet in 1985 "gross rent accounted for more than 20% of tenants' average income, while homeowner's principal property expenses accounted for 14% of the income of property-owning households." Ibid., p VII (translation).
20. Thirty percent of tenants are age 55 or over. The most vulnerable victims of abuse by landlords are elderly people living alone.
21. The Act respecting the protection of personal information in the private sector (Bill 68), which came into force in Québec in 1994, made this type of blacklist illegal. This law also imposes tighter restrictions on credit bureaus, which cannot provide information from their files without written

authorization from the person concerned. However, a landlord can still require a prospective tenant to authorize the disclosure of information in his file that is necessary to enter into a contract (editor's note).

22. Pierre Filion and Trudi E. Bunting, op cit., p. 39.
23. We should add that high rental costs can have a negative impact on regional development since "...it is well known that employers also feel the pinch of high housing costs. In cities with high housing prices, firms have difficulty recruiting workers unless they raise wages." Pierre Filion and Trudi E. Bunting, op. cit., p. 14 (translation).
24. In December 1995, following a campaign by tenant groups, the Québec government amended the law to make the Régie's lease form mandatory. Some landlord organizations had produced their own printed leases, with additional clauses, some not necessarily legal (editor's note).
25. Many moderate-income households lured into buying a new home by government programs designed to stimulate the construction industry may find themselves trapped in a nightmare during a recession, when incomes drop but interest rates and payments remain high. The Associations coopératives d'economie familiale (ACEF), a network of Québec consumer protection groups, has even thought it necessary to issue warnings to people who might be tempted to buy a family residence too soon.
26. Unlike Montréal and the bigger suburbs, many smaller municipalities, such as Ste-Geneviève and Montréal West on the Island of Montréal, have no inspectors to enforce decent housing standards. Tenants in these smaller towns can only rely on the courts to enforce their rights; their municipal administration will do nothing for them, even if the building is cockroach-infested or they have worms crawling out of the floor (editor's note).
27. Controversial developments in Montréal in 1996, which have aroused noisy public opposition, include the federal government's plan to demolish perfectly recyclable veterans' housing at Benny Farm, and the Précieux-Sang redevelopment next to the Villa Maria heritage site, which would destroy badly-needed green space (editor's note).
28. The obsession with deficit reduction and monetarism has continued, infecting supposed liberals and social democrats. For an excellent analysis of this phenomenon, see Linda McQuaig, *Shooting the Hippo: Death by Deficit and Other Canadian Myths* (Toronto: Penguin, 1995) (editor's note).

Chapter 4

The Régie du logement: Autopsy of a fraud[1]

by Le Regroupement des Comités logement et Associations de locataires du Québec (RCLALQ), 1992

Editor's note: The French version of this document was launched at a 1992 press conference as a "dossier noir," intended to expose the degeneration of the Régie du logement from its original mandate. I have added extensive footnotes where necessary to update the criticisms to 1996.

Introduction

The first permanent law[2] on rental housing in Québec was adopted in 1972. This legislation replaced the temporary 1951 law that had been adopted to compensate for the federal government's lifting of rent and price controls after World War II.

The 1972 law followed in the wake of the major social reforms that shaped Québec during the Quiet Revolution. After the reform of the school system and the establishment of universal medical insurance coverage, legislators sought to protect the right to housing for everyone, especially for less well-to-do people who were tenants because they could not afford to buy a home.

The *Act to promote conciliation between lessees and property owners*, at the time of its adoption and in the years that followed, was the target of vehement protests by all those opposed to social reforms. Even Liberal Justice Minister Jérôme Choquette, like Health Minister Claude Castonguay before him, was labelled a "socialist" by those who felt deprived of their absolute right to control their property!

Under pressure from landlords and influential people, major provisions were deleted from the law. In 1974, buildings constructed after 1973 were completely exempted from rent control for the first five years.

The Parti Québécois took power in 1976 with a program that

included a housing policy as one of its "good government" priorities. In December 1977, acting on this promise, Minister Guy Tardif published a White Paper on landlord-tenant relations. This policy document emphasized that "the government has a role to play so that each citizen can be housed suitably."

On December 18, 1978, a press release issued by the Minister's office informed the public that "the Honourable Guy Tardif today tabled Bill 107, *An Act instituting the Régie du logement and amending the Civil Code*, in the National Assembly." It also stated that "the Régie will not only have the mandate to settle disputes [...] but to ensure that *all* citizens, both property owners and tenants, are well informed concerning their rights and obligations."[3] The government "is laying odds that *this increased knowledge of the rules* will enable the vast majority of citizens *to reach agreement on their own, without resorting to the Régie.*"[4]

In another press release from the same source, also dated December 18, 1978 and entitled *The objectives of the law*, the government again stressed this aspect of the question: "Mechanisms that will ensure that each party respects the obligations arising from the lease will be adopted to favour conciliation."[5] To emphasize this intention even more, the press release added: "one of the essential conditions for the future law to achieve its objectives is that the parties be given adequate information."

One year later, Bill 107 was adopted after being subjected to no less than 270 amendments and numerous criticisms in parliamentary committee, with the most vehement attacks coming from landlord associations. It finally came into force on October 1, 1980 and continued to bear the brunt of the real estate lobby's ire in subsequent years.

The new Régie du logement instituted under the Act has extensive powers, making it the only court of first instance to hear rental housing cases under the Civil Code.[6]

Under its enabling legislation, the Régie was given the responsibility to inform landlords and tenants about their rights and obligations, foster conciliation between the parties, conduct studies and establish statistics on the housing situation, and periodically publish a compendium of decisions rendered by the commissioners.[7]

Under the Act, the Régie is made up of commissioners — the number set by the government — including a chairman and two vice-chairmen. The chairman is responsible for the Régie's management and general administration and directs the work of the commissioners who "must comply with his orders and directives."[8] In addition, the chairman is responsible for advising the government on all matters concerning the application of the Act and for providing the minister with whatever recommendations he deems expedient.[9] The commissioners are appointed by the government for a maximum of five years.

We can therefore see that the legislator wanted to make the Régie du logement the "secular arm" of the State for everything related to the tenants' right to housing. By its enabling legislation, and by the powers and mandates that devolved upon it, the organization was called upon to become a major player in the housing field. According to its creators' intentions, the Régie's primary role was to protect tenants' rights,[10] while ensuring that the performance of this mandate did not discourage private investment in rental housing. This was where the government drew the line.

To fulfil its mission, the Régie had to adopt clear regulations which, once they were known, would establish discipline in landlord-tenant relations. The organization's information and facilitation function was also seen as a cornerstone of the right to housing.

The Régie was also given the duty of keeping track of the changing housing situation through studies and statistics, adjusting its interventions accordingly and advising the Minister on the best way to achieve progress in this sector. The Régie therefore was not to confine itself to passive administration. According to the law, it was to participate actively in improving the condition of tenants.

What has become of these good intentions? Twenty years[11] after the adoption of Québec's first permanent law on rental housing, it is time to analyze how the Régie has become what it is today. Given the many expressions of tenant dissatisfaction, we feel it is more necessary than ever to examine the role of this quasi-judicial body, which has jurisdiction over all matters related to residential leasing in Québec. We therefore think that the best way to proceed is to return to the initial mandate adopted for the Régie du logement and see what has become of this body in "real life" since 1980.

Since the Régie's primary role is to protect tenants' rights, it is legitimate to examine the views of those primarily concerned and draw conclusions from the concrete experience of people active in housing committees and neighbourhood groups, who have to listen to and counsel tenants every day. This is why grassroots activists made up the majority of the editorial board for this document and why it was submitted to other tenant organizations throughout Québec for their comments. The Régie will therefore be evaluated in the light of its historical mandate, based on the expertise acquired in the field by men and women who are dedicated to promoting the right to housing, and who deal every day with tenants seeking justice.

Part I: Information

Cracks in the cornerstone

Informing landlords and tenants is one of the main means by which the Régie is supposed to fulfil its mandate. Indeed, this is the primary function the law assigns to it: "informing lessors and lessees about their rights and obligations."[12] In the legislator's view, this is how the Régie can best ensure out-of-court settlement of litigious questions and promote conciliation of disputes.

The Régie du logement's statistics show that far more landlords than tenants are plaintiffs. Between 1986 and 1991, the proportion of applications filed by tenants declined steadily from 16% to 12.3%. Even after subtracting applications to fix the rent (which, though filed by the landlord, result from the tenant's formal refusal of an increase), the Régie's annual reports show that *Québec tenants, who are 10 times more numerous than landlords, file four to five times fewer claims.*

Does this mean that the Régie du logement has fulfilled its mandate, that the information it provides results in private agreements, reducing the number of tenant court cases? There are several good reasons to doubt this.

A study conducted for the City of Montréal shows that nearly one out of six rental units, in that municipality alone, has major defects and that vermin are all too common in apartment buildings.[13] These are issues on which the tenant can normally take legal action to demand that the landlord supply a dwelling in good condition.

Tenants who are poorly informed about their rights and recourses may not be reflexively inclined to apply to the Régie to deal with these crucial problems. Yet under the terms of the Act, the Régie is supposed to keep tenants informed about the ways and means at its disposal to enforce the right to a habitable dwelling.

Let's take some concrete examples to examine the type of information transmitted by the Régie, whether it is information addressed to the general public or legal information intended for tenants who are in conflict with their landlord on a specific point of law.

Régie press releases
September 23, 1991: The Régie du logement wrote to the RCLALQ to announce that "given your privileged relationship with Québec's tenant population and the important role you play with tenants [...] we will be sending you all press releases issued by the Régie du logement."[14]

While press releases are far from the only route by which the Régie reaches the general public, it is nevertheless true that they are all issued by the Régie's top officials and that, taken as a whole over a long period, they give us a coherent picture of the general information policy imposed on the Régie by its management.

We therefore analyzed all press releases received during the six months following September 23, 1991, sent to the RCLALQ by the Régie's communications department. We wanted to see how the Régie informs tenants about their rights and the means available for tenants to enforce them.

September 25, 1991: After its September 23 announcement, the Régie issued a press release in language that seemed to conform to its mandate. With cold weather approaching, it reminded landlords renting a heated dwelling of their responsibility to ensure an adequate room temperature at all times. However, *there was no mention of the recourse for tenants deprived of adequate heating*. The press release merely mentioned that tenants shouldn't leave the windows open too long! It then referred both landlords and tenants to the Régie's pamphlet on heating.

November 13, 1991: A Régie press release announced the increase from $25 to $35 in the fee charged for filing cases. The Régie justified this increase on the principle that the user should share in the costs of opening a file. The press release ended with a paragraph emphasizing that the Régie, which primarily seeks to achieve harmonious landlord-tenant relations, offers free mediation services.

December 4, 1991: A Régie press release reminded the public of the legal deadlines for repossession notices in the case of undivided ownership. Again, readers were referred to a Régie pamphlet for more details, *without mentioning the tenant's recourses* in the case of a repossession that did not meet the legal requirements.

December 4, 1991: A second press release, on the same date, advised landlords that their deadline to send a repossession notice (for leases ending June 30) was December 31. The procedure was described in detail. While the press release mentioned that a tenant who does not answer within a month is presumed to have refused, it immediately added that if the tenant refuses, the landlord can file an application at the Régie du logement. The fact that the press release was sent out so far before the December 31 deadline clearly indicates its intended audience and the message it was conveying.

December 20, 1991: The Régie announced that its standard lease form, which it previously supplied free of charge, would now be sold for $1.75 at convenience stores. This Régie decision had serious implications for the information available to tenants on their rights, as we will discuss in more detail later.

January 17, 1992: The Régie issued a press release on its rent increase calculation method for 1992.[15]

January 18, 1992: Landlords and tenants were invited (always in that order) to information workshops on the rent adjustment calculation method. These workshops were given at the very beginning and throughout the legal period for sending increase notices, but at no other time.

Analysis of this sample, which includes all Régie press releases between September 23, 1991 and March 23, 1992, shows that the Régie directed its messages almost exclusively to landlords. Tenants were merely mentioned as a "stylistic precaution."

For example, information on how to request a repossession was sent out just at the time that this information could be useful to a landlord who wanted to get rid of certain tenants. However, after December 31, when tenants who had received such a notice would have the most need to be informed about their rights and recourses, the Régie's communications department suddenly became silent. (Yet according to the Civil Code, the right to remain in the dwelling takes precedence, and repossession is only allowed as an exception to this principle.)

The same goes for rent increases. All the information concerning the adjustment rates was delivered when landlords were considering what increases to impose on their tenants. But in April, once tenants had received these increase notices and would need to know the adjustment rates allowed under the regulations, they found it was too late to attend the workshops so generously provided by the Régie.

Everywhere in these press releases, the tenant was considered the passive object of events: *never in six months was there any reference* to the possibility that the tenant had legal recourse in case of abuses by landlords or problems in the dwelling.

Only twice was the possibility mentioned of filing an application at the Régie: once on November 13 to say that this would cost more and that mediation services were free. The only other instance in the sample where recourses were mentioned was the December 4 press release, which encouraged landlords who couldn't get their tenants to leave, after sending them a repossession notice, to use the Régie.

The mere fact of publishing two press releases in a row in December, in such exhaustive detail, on the question of repossession, represented a serious departure by the Régie from its stated objectives. Indeed, according to the Act, cases where repossession of a dwelling is authorized are considered to be exceptions to the tenants' fundamental right to remain in their dwellings. Yet in the information addressed to the media, the Régie only discussed the exceptions granted to landlords and kept silent on the tenant's basic rights when it was time to mention them.

As for two problems cited earlier in this document: the poor condition of certain dwellings and the presence of vermin — problems faced by many tenants, at least in Montréal, according to one study — the Régie published no press releases on these questions and the tenant's possible recourses during the six months covered by the sample.

A closed counter

In December 1987, the government strengthened the provisions of the *Act respecting the Régie du logement* in cases where a landlord exercised undue pressure to obtain a tenant's departure. Fines of up to $25,000 were stipulated for harassment, which was defined as a series of actions intended to restrict the tenant's right to peaceful enjoyment of his dwelling causing him to leave. The intention at that time was to create a special counter at the Régie to receive complaints and play an active role with victims of harassment to help them in their proceedings.

Nearly five years later, the Régie still had not established the special counter and *no* case had resulted in the sentencing of any landlord. Yet the Régie, in its communications with the RCLALQ, continued to claim that, in accordance with its mandate, it "informs tenants and landlords about their rights and obligations in the matter" and "assists plaintiffs in drafting their complaints."[16]

However, as we have seen, the Régie was substantially more explicit and wordy on how to get a tenant to leave. In the case of harassment, it was discreet to the point of silence.

Secret justice

Let's now look at the legal information to which a tenant plaintiff at the Régie could have access.

One might well imagine that the Régie, as an administrative tribunal with the duty of making justice accessible to ordinary people, would have found many ways to present its jurisprudence in a clear and practical manner. However, our analysis once again shows that, in fact, the Régie does not fulfil its mandate to inform and educate, or fulfils it poorly.[17]

Public but confidential files

Régie regulations have made the decisions rendered after its hearings inaccessible to ordinary people. Since May 1990, an amendment to the procedural regulations prohibits any person from consulting a file other than his own.[18]

A tenant receives a notice of repossession. He suspects that the landlord has abused the same procedure to force someone in another building to leave, while pleading good faith at the hearing. He goes to the Régie office, asks to see the decisions concerning a certain dwelling for a given year and is told: it's none of your business!

A fundamental principle of Québec law is that justice is public and that the decisions of all courts are accessible to everyone. How can such an aberration have emerged at the Régie? Since the Bar is fairly prompt in acting on cases like this, we asked several lawyers for their reaction to this denial of their free access to files.

We were told that the regulation did not apply to licensed lawyers, who could continue to obtain information hidden from the rest of the Régie's users![19]

Since in many cases, tenants do not have the means to retain the services of a lawyer and have to handle their own defence, this regulation constitutes a denial of justice. Yet administrative tribunals like the Régie were created so that citizens can represent themselves, without being handicapped by a lawyer's absence.

So what has become of the Régie's legal duty to inform landlords and tenants on their rights and obligations?[20]

Haphazard Publication of Jurisprudence

As in the case of any other court, it is essential to study the decisions already rendered in order to understand how judges will interpret the law. This is all the more true of a specialized court like the Régie du logement. Since it has sole responsibility for an entire area of law, its decisions carry weight.

Therefore, in addition to giving the Régie the imperative duty of informing tenants and landlords, the lawmakers, well aware of the very heavy responsibility entrusted to this body, spelled out the Régie's obligation to publish a compendium of decisions periodically.[21]

Over the past fifteen years,[22] collections of the Régie's jurisprudence have been published in several forms. At first, there were the decisions of the defunct Commission des loyers, or Rental Board, published under the acronym DCL. Until 1982, these were succeeded by the decisions of the Régie du logement, or DRL.

No copy of either compendium, DCL or DRL, is available at the Régie du logement. Their print run has been long exhausted and they have never been reprinted. These texts can only be studied in the libraries of law faculties or the Québec Bar, which are only open to law students and lawyers, respectively. (The lawyers themselves complain about the poor quality of these compendia, mainly for containing summarized decisions and a confusing index.)

The *Jurisprudence-Logement* compendia for jurists (JL) have been a clear improvement over previous collections, in everyone's opinion, mainly because the decisions are reproduced in full. Surprisingly, their rate of publication was suddenly reduced from ten per year to four in 1990. In a mailing to subscribers, the Régie justified this situation on the grounds that jurisprudence on housing questions had stabilized in recent years, so that the number of issues published could be easily reduced. This argument seems very dubious.

In at least one case, the Régie published an important Court of Québec decision concerning tenants' rights only after it was reported in two other general compendia of jurisprudence.[23] Reducing the number of published decisions would seem to indicate a certain way of orienting the Régie's interventions. We will return to this point later.

For the time being, we will focus on the most tangible aspect: the very content of the Régie's compendia is cause for caution. To guarantee a minimum of impartiality, the vast majority of Québec courts and quasi-judicial bodies assign publication and, most often, selection of jurisprudence to an independent organization, Société québécoise d'information juridique (SOQUIJ).

By unilaterally reducing the number and frequency of publication of decisions, the Régie, with sole control over publishing its own jurisprudence, puts itself in a compromising position.[24]

Finally, the Régie would undoubtedly find an additional advantage in entrusting a third party with the sorting and printing of its jurisprudence. In addition to gaining credibility, the compendia might appear on time! The consolidated *Jurisprudence-Logement* index for 1990 (yes, 1990!) was only published in 1992. As of September 1, 1992, no 1991 decision had yet been published. If this pathetic performance is compared with that of the main courts, which see their decisions published two or three months after being rendered, we can grasp the extent of the Régie's inadequacy in terms of the information it is supposed to provide.

The standard lease

As we saw earlier in the analysis of its press releases, the Régie decided, as of 1992, to market the standard lease that it had traditionally distributed free of charge. This basic document spells out the main obligations and rights of landlords and tenants in black and white. Its generalized use (though non-mandatory) constituted the main source of information for the majority of Québec tenants about their rights up to now.[25]

It can be foreseen that attaching a price to the lease will give landlords an incentive to produce their own lease forms which, in all probability, will be substantially more laconic about tenants' rights and landlords' obligations.

Remember that since a lease is a consensual contract, any scrap of paper can replace the standard lease form. It was so widely used in Québec only because it was free of charge.

A series of mentions must be added to the lease according to the Civil Code.[26] In general, these are the obligations of the parties as formulated in the standard lease published by the Régie. Yet according to the judgments rendered by the Régie's commissioners, failure to supply this written information does not constitute sufficient grounds to invalidate the lease.[27] Another compulsory mention in the lease,[28] also declared to be a matter of public interest by the lawmaker, is the indication on any new lease of the rent paid by the previous tenant. Though this section is almost never filled in by Québec landlords, this doesn't particularly bother the Régie. Under the Régie's jurisprudence, the mandatory mentions required by law have been made optional!

Telephone information

The interminable waits before connecting with an information officer have made the Régie's telephone information services notorious for their inefficiency, resulting in many complaints and pressure from the public and Québec's ombudsman.

The answers obtained over the phone are not always complete, and some information officers seem to be more competent than others. If access to justice, one of the Régie's primary mandates, were not to be in vain, it would have been essential to make telephone information a priority and ensure the service's efficiency a long time ago. While the Régie recently made some changes, this is no cause for celebration, especially when one looks at the Régie's overall track record on information. This is why the self-congratulation in which Housing Minister Claude Ryan engaged at the National Assembly committee session of April 14, 1992 appears presumptuous. While some very belated corrections have been made to the waiting time for users of the Régie's telephone services, it seems premature, to say the least, for Mr. Ryan to describe this as a "spectacular improvement." Elementary prudence would require that these so-called improvements be put to the test of time.[29] We believe that a final judgment on the question will also have to consider the quality of the information provided over the phone, not just the waiting time.

Nonexistent studies and statistics

As we have already seen, in addition to providing information on landlord-tenant law to encourage its application, the Régie is also supposed to generate new information on housing-related questions. The legislator explicitly gives it the obligation of "conducting studies and compiling statistics on the housing situation."[30]

How can the chairman who, according to Section 9 of the Act, has the duty of "examining the consequences of the application of this act and making to the minister such recommendations as he deems expedient" adequately fulfil her mandate without having a minimum of studies and serious data in hand?

However, as incredible as it may appear, the Régie, to our knowledge, has not produced, or at least has not made public any study of the Québec rental housing market, even though the first-hand information from the cases it hears would allow it to produce documents on various subjects. How much did real estate profits rise during the inflation of the 1980s? Why didn't the existing law have the effect of regulating rents as had been expected when it was adopted? What is the condition of Québec's rental housing stock? Does the Régie encourage preservation by the way it operates? Do Québec tenants pay a fair rent for their dwellings or are they being exploited? What is the percentage of concentration of ownership in the hands of big investors and how does this affect housing costs? This list of questions could go on for pages. The Régie should have at least started to break some ground in these fields of study. But despite its clear mandate, the Régie's contribution to housing studies has been a big zero.

When one of the rare specialists in housing law, Professor Claude Thomasset of the Université du Québec à Montréal, asked for a computer classification that would allow her to do her own jurisprudence research, the Régie refused her any assistance.[31] The Régie claimed that, for its own reasons, it does not have to classify files by type of application as Professor Thomasset requested. It is of little relevance that the Commission d'accès à l'information later ruled in the Régie's favour on this point. What is worth noting is that the Régie refused to make up for its own research failings, refusing to offer generous and disinterested cooperation to a person conducting serious work in this neglected field.

The Régie does publish annual reports containing a few tables on the number and type of cases filed during the year. From this succinct data, it is possible, by comparison, deduction or extrapolation, to arrive at some approximations about the state of landlord-tenant relations. However, since the tables and statistics are chosen to illustrate the comments of the authors of these brief reports, they vary greatly from year to year and thus are extremely difficult to use for anyone who wants to do comparisons over several years. Since this is the only Régie publication that contains any housing statistics, we would be entitled to expect some regularity. Indeed, the Régie's enabling legislation requires it to produce its annual report no later than June 30 of each year.[32] Unfortunately, the Régie has completely failed to fulfil its mandate in this area as well. For reasons that are still unexplained, the Régie only published its 1988-1989 report on March 31, 1991. Its 1989-1990 report appeared in August 1991 and its 1990-1991 report was released in August 1992.

Part II: Commissioners and applications

The commissioners, appointed by the government "in sufficient number" according to the Act, currently total 39 for the 29 offices still open in Québec. (Four offices were closed in 1990.)[33]

Commissioners "vested with the powers and immunity of public inquiry commissioners" hold hearings and rule on applications within the Régie's jurisdiction.[34] They are subject to the authority of the chairman and "must comply with his orders and directives."[35]

Special clerks, with the same powers as commissioners, can be appointed, but they can only rule on a limited class of cases: applications for fixing of the rent, recovery of unpaid rent (with or without cancellation of the lease), depositing of rent at the Régie or changes in the conditions of the lease (including fixing of the rent).

Since the commissioner alone hears the cases submitted to him and produces his own minutes of the hearings, he has sole responsibility for interpreting the law. Since 1985, commissioners have been governed by a Code of Ethics. They are supposed to "contribute to making justice more human and readily obtainable, in particular, through making themselves available and by showing consideration towards the persons who appear before them."[36]

The commissioners' decisions are supposed to be a concrete reflection of the public interest expressed by the legislators who wrote the law. How they do their job has a determining influence on the rights granted to tenants by the legislature. This is the question that we will now analyze.

A. Neutrality and impartiality

Since tens of thousands of cases are handled annually by the commissioners, it is difficult to produce a comprehensive picture of how parties are treated by the Régie du logement. The only thorough study on how justice is rendered at the Régie was directed by a professor in the legal sciences department of the Université du Québec à Montréal and published in 1987.[37] From a methodical analysis of 150 cases heard in the Montréal area, she concluded that "landlords have easier access to the Régie du logement than tenants"[38] and that "in the final analysis, landlords are in a more favourable position than tenants in relation to the Régie du logement."[39] As for the commissioners, the study concluded that "most of them seem to have developed an attitude more favourable to landlords."[40]

Has there been any progress towards fairness since the Thomasset study? Experience indicates the opposite.

On Wednesday, February 1, 1992, the *Journal de Montréal* reported that a decision of the Régie du logement had been overturned in Superior Court.[41] Two commissioners were removed from a case for having shown partiality in favour of a landlord. The first, Claire Courtemanche, had refused to allow the tenants to table a document proving that the landlord had undertaken to pay for certain work. Given this attitude, the tenants asked her to withdraw (*recuse*) from the case, which she refused to do with the subsequent support of her colleague, Michel Dubé, who heard and rejected the tenants' petition for *recusation*. The tenants then filed suit at the Superior Court, where Judge Pierre Viau concluded that the commissioners had completely ignored one of the fundamental principles of natural justice, the principle that guarantees every person the right to an impartial hearing of his case.

It obviously would be an exaggeration to conclude that all tenants who are frustrated with their experience at the Régie were victims of such abuse of power. However, without a shadow of a doubt, very few tenants who are confronted with an openly biased commissioner will petition for *recusation*. Even fewer will take such a case as far as Superior Court. The question, therefore, is how many tenants have suffered the same affronts without daring to react and have come out bitter and frustrated?

When one realizes how the Régie's administration has proved incapable of the least self-criticism, this question is even more acutely relevant. An interview given by Régie Chairman Louise Thibault to a publication defending the interests of property owners is a particularly sickening example of this attitude. She unhesitatingly asserted that the fact that few people use their right of appeal is a sign of the Régie's neutrality and impartiality.[42]

How could tenants, generally people of modest means, afford to pay the legal fees necessarily involved in appealing to a higher court?[43] Their lack of financial resources and fatalistic attitude at the incompetence of certain judges provide a much better explanation why few Régie decisions are appealed. Since Ms. Thibault cannot ignore this fact, she prefers to engage in sophistry to prevent any blame from being attached to the Régie's image. It is this obsession with "marketing" that we find disturbing, since it is hard to see how a person immersed in such self-satisfaction could preside over the type of transformation that is necessary at the Régie.

While Louise Thibault endeavours to silence all criticism that might tarnish the Régie's image, there are countless cases of tenants dissatisfied with the cavalier treatment to which they were subjected. A community worker from Comité logement Centre-Sud gives an eyewitness account of the attitude of one commissioner, Jean-Pierre Hurlet who, according to the law, is under Louise Thibault's supervision and authority. This is a good example of how some commissioners behave.

A Case Study

The landlord of the Lorne Avenue apartment building had begun major renovations in June, without obtaining a permit from the City of Montréal, without respecting the legal deadlines for giving notice of temporary evacuation and without compensating the tenants for their trouble.

One tenant came to see us. He had complained verbally several times since the start of the work, but with no results. Finally, he sent the landlord a warning letter on November 25.

He then filed an application at the Régie, asking it to order the landlord to stop the major renovations in the building. He also requested a rent reduction retroactive to the start of the work and damages for the loss of peaceful enjoyment to the constant noise that prevented him from sleeping, working and studying, as well as the reduction in service. The water had been cut off morning and evening throughout the month of October, and there had been regular interruptions in elevator service, use of the laundry room and electricity since the renovations started.

He received a notice of hearing for December 10.

In the meantime, we took the initiative, printing a leaflet and distributing it in the mailboxes to inform the tenants about their rights and invite them to visit us. Some tenants who came to our office had already sent a warning letter. Since most of them were Anglophones, we helped them write up an application to the Régie in French. We also encouraged them to complain to the City inspectors.

On the morning of December 10, the tenant whose hearing was scheduled showed up at the Régie with seven witnesses, all of them tenants in the same building. Only one of the witnesses tried to file his own application on that date, but was [wrongly] told by a Régie employee that this wasn't necessary because he was already a witness in the case of Tenant X.

Since Tenant X was eligible for free legal aid, he brought a lawyer, Mr. R. We learned later in the morning that Mr. R was involved in another case on behalf of Ms. G, the landlord's lawyer. R and G obviously knew each other very well, but this doesn't explain their behaviour. For nearly an hour, both of them put pressure on Tenant X to reach a settlement with the landlord. The agreement they proposed, while standing near the elevators, was a hopeless muddle. At one point, R approached me to ask who I was. I introduced myself and he admitted that he had a conflict of interest. I had already heard of him, and my doubts about his competence were confirmed by what I had witnessed. I therefore recommended that Tenant X dismiss him on the spot and insist that the hearing be held immediately, since it was getting late.

At 11:30, Commissioner Jean-Pierre Hurlet showed up and invited the lawyers into the hearing room. Tenant X, his impatient witnesses and I no longer understood what was going on. I took a few minutes to call Marlène at the Comité-logement to tell her what was going on. When I returned at 11:50, Tenant X and the landlord were already in the hearing room. Here are a few excerpts from the discussion that was going on:

The Commissioner: "You negotiated a long time before you came in here. Maybe you were on the verge of concluding an agreement?... You're asking me to issue an order to stop the work. It is already under way. What I should do instead is issue an order setting conditions for the performance of the work...The law allows landlords to do major repairs. After all, private property is a right. Just because you give the landlord the right to do work doesn't mean that you are authorizing him to abuse your rights."

Mr. R mentioned that the commissioner would "set fair and reasonable conditions."

Hurlet and R suggested that Tenant X "meet the landlord halfway." It was obvious that the commissioner had no intention of issuing an order. He referred to the "agreement" on several occasions. Tenant X finally lost patience and asked him: "What agreement?"

Ms. G: "To do the work from 9 to 5! (The work had begun at 7:00 and even at 6:30 am.)

Tenant X: "That's all? How long is this going to continue, with all the disruption it's causing? I have a container under my window!"

Ms. G: "We have to put the old carpets somewhere!"

Tenant X: "Not carpets, bathtubs!" (In a 16 storey building, the workers were throwing doors, sinks and other items off the balconies.)

Hurlet: "The container has to go somewhere... The work has to be done. You can't contest the nature of the work... There are recourses after the fact." (He cited the example of all the major buildings in the City that had gone through major renovations, such as the Alexis Nihon Plaza and Place Papineau, where "the Régie allowed a percentage rent reduction afterwards.") "How is it that you're the only tenant complaining in a 16-storey building?"

Tenant X indignantly pointed out that there were seven witnesses, all tenants in the building, waiting to testify and that they wanted to complain.

Mr. R was very insulted that his client was talking instead of him and announced that he was withdrawing from the case. Everybody got up and left. I asked the commissioner why he hadn't proceeded with the hearing at the scheduled time. "Because the parties were negotiating an agreement," he answered. Why didn't he set a postponement date? "There's no more room on the roll for urgent cases." Why didn't he proceed with the hearing instead of a discussion, given the urgency of the situation? "It's much too late... The case will be heard at the end of January or the beginning of February."

So Commissioner Hurlet:
- Conducted a discussion instead of a hearing despite the urgency of the application.
- Insisted on an "agreement between the parties," without hearing Tenant X's arguments and despite the fact that the landlord hadn't offered any fair and reasonable conditions.
- Didn't set a date for the postponement of the hearing, despite the urgency of the situation, on the pretext that there was no more room on the roll for urgent cases before mid-January or mid-February.

We concluded that Commissioner Hurlet had passed judgment before the hearing and that it was essential that he withdraw from the case so that it could be heard with the impartiality required by law.

This record of quasi-judicial blundering leads us to question the competence of the Régie's commissioners and how they are chosen.

B. An arbitrary nominating process

In 1987, a task force submitted a report to Liberal Justice Minister Herbert Marx on administrative tribunals in Québec.[44] It specified that the conditions for recruiting people to serve on administrative tribunals provided no guarantee of their independence or competence.

Three years later, with the committee's recommendations still on the shelf, Yves Ouellette, the report's co-author and a professor of administrative law at the Université de Montréal, raised the issue in *La Presse*: "Administrative tribunals are one of the last bastions of political patronage in Québec. [...] Governments appoint anybody to anything at will."[45]

In the specific case of the Régie du logement, the same article stated that, from 1980 to 1985, a public competition was held prior to the appointment of commissioners by the Cabinet. However, this practice was abandoned when the Liberals took power. At the end of their maximum five-year term, commissioners have to depend on ministerial goodwill for the renewal of their contract.

It is surely no insult to the truth to state that the Québec Liberal Party is closer to landlords than to tenants. In the absence of any specific criteria, when the cabinet appoints someone to the Régie du logement, there is a strong likelihood that this person is a friend of the party in power. Appointments in recent years include former ministerial aides[46] and a former counsel for the Sûreté du Québec.

The Ouellette Report rightly mentions "the moderate degree of public confidence in a decisional system in the hands of decision-makers who work under precarious conditions and are perceived as being at the government's mercy."[47]

At the Justice Summit held in Québec City in February 1992, Liberal Justice Minister Gil Rémillard made a commitment to reform administrative justice on the basis of the Ouellette Report, particularly by clarifying the status of the members of these tribunals to guarantee their competence.[48] For anyone who might entertain any hope of reform from a politician's words, we should note that the Ouellette Report took up the conclusions of a 1971 task force on administrative tribunals and a second report on the question dating from 1983.[49] Both of these reports had been gathering dust on the shelf, where the Ouellette Report would join them.

It is fairly ironic that the Régie du logement is currently [in 1992] the responsibility of Claude Ryan who, at one time, passed for a model of honesty and virtue. By not displaying the slightest inclination to change the way that commissioners are appointed, this minister lends his authority to political mores worthy of the "Duplessism" that he had once condemned.

The highly politicized method of selecting and appointing commissioners does not necessarily mean that they are all biased or incompetent, but leaves room for many doubts. These doubts are reinforced by the orientations adopted in certain recent decisions and the road taken by the Régie's administrative policies.

C. Guidelines that always run in the same direction

It is disturbing to see jurisprudential guidelines emerging at the Régie that tend to indicate motives of a non-judicial nature.

We can cite two examples in areas that are crucial to landlord profit margins: fixing the rent and the public order provisions of rental housing legislation.

1. Fixing the rent

Can a commissioner allow a rent increase bigger than the landlord had asked in his notice to the tenant? According to legal tradition, judgments that are *ultra petita*, meaning that they go beyond the initial application, are considered incompatible with law and justice. However, several Régie commissioners in the 1980s had granted substantial rent increases to landlords who had not requested that much. Two schools of opinion had developed at the Régie on this issue, with decisions going either way, depending on which tendency the individual commissioner supported.

Matters came to a head on March 20, 1990, when a review panel of commissioners,[50] who had refuted the arguments for *ultra petita* increases in their earlier rulings, suddenly reversed themselves, not for reasons of a legal nature, but to ensure consistency in the Régie's decisions. These two commissioners further asserted that they had been legally right in the previous cases, but that from now on they would defer to a position that was contrary to their convictions, so that future litigants would have a clearer idea of the state of law at the Régie.

> Despite the opinion and convictions that the undersigned may previously have expressed *and that they might be inclined to reiterate*, they believe it is their duty to be reasonable and come around [...] Justice is generally better served when those who render it voluntarily avoid rendering contradictory decisions.[51]

What was the sudden source of this imperative need for unanimity? And why, if unanimity was necessary, did the commissioners, by their own admission, rule in a manner contrary to their own convictions? Remember that, according to the law, the commissioners must comply with the orders and directives of the chairman[52] and that the renewal of their mandate, and therefore their perquisites of office, depend on a decision by the minister which in turn may be based on a recommendation by the chairman of the Régie. This is enough to still many consciences.

In 1991, another Régie review panel endorsed yet another very dubious practice by fixing the rent without the landlord presenting any vouchers. The commissioners affirmed that the law allowed the commissioner to use any means available to determine the rent, presumably including guesswork![53]

2. *Public order*

Freedom of contract is the general rule governing contracts in Québec. This means that whoever signs an agreement is bound to respect it in full. Certain public order provisions have tempered the rigours of this rule, however. Certain individuals, too naive or too trusting, could be tricked into signing documents contrary to their interests without realizing it.

The housing provisions of the Civil Code have been declared to be a matter of public order. This means that the clauses of a lease, even if it is duly signed, are invalid if they violate the Civil Code.

Surprisingly, the Régie's decisions very rarely endorse this point of law. Its decisions on these matters have frequently been overturned by the Court of Québec. Indeed, commissioners "often hesitate to nullify [...] a clause of the lease that is contrary to the public order provisions of the Civil Code" and therefore display "considerable reluctance to give full effect to the tenant protection desired by the legislature."[54]

There is a persistent rumour that applications filed by tenants under the public order provisions of the Civil Code, which would therefore run counter to the sacrosanct rule of freedom of contract, will henceforth be rejected systematically by the Régie. The pretext would be the same as in the *ultra petita* rulings: to preserve consistency and unanimity in the interests of the litigants.[55]

It could well be said that at the Régie, at least in the chairman's office where the guidelines and directives are decided, there is a strong tendency to treat the interest of the litigants as being identical to the interest of the landlords.

D. Access to representation

The negation of the tenant's right to the representative of his choice to assist him during a hearing is spelled out in the law itself. A natural person "may be represented by his consort, or by an advocate."[56] A corporation "may be represented by an officer, a director, an employee exclusively employed by it, or by an advocate."[57]

In her study, Claude Thomasset found that "over two thirds of tenants appear alone in front of the Régie" while "42% of landlords are represented by a professional (a lawyer or a professional property manager)."[58] Tenants only use a lawyer in 16.1% of cases.

In addition, there is more of a chance that a landlord who appears alone will have more experience with Régie hearings, especially if he owns several dwellings.

The facts speak for themselves. There is no need for a lengthy argument to show that one party has a clear advantage over the other in terms of representation.

The Québec government's 1979 White Paper on landlord-tenant relations, which served as a prelude to the *Act respecting the Régie du logement*, was written in a completely different spirit. It proposed that:

> At the hearing, a party may be represented, in the case of a natural person, by an attorney, by his legal

or common-law spouse, by a person who lives in the leased premises with the signer of the lease, by a co-tenant or by a person who holds a free and specific written mandate; and in the case of a corporation, by an attorney or by an employee or a duly mandated administrator.

This proposal, which sought to establish some balance between the parties, was subsequently modified. As a result of pressure by landlords' associations, the legislator glossed over an essential part of the right to representation, creating an inequitable situation.

We will not go into the whole debate on access to justice, which has been diminished by the high costs of professional legal services and the ridiculously low income level required to be eligible for legal aid. We will merely note that the right to representation by a lawyer is an illusion for many tenants.

These same tenants often tell organizations dedicated to the defence of tenants' rights that they would like a resource person from the group to assist and represent them at the Régie hearing. They rightly do not understand why their tenants' association cannot act as their representative, while other administrative tribunals such as the Commission des normes de travail, the Tribunal du travail, the Commission des affaires sociales and the Commission d'appel en matière de lésions professionnelles[59] allow individuals to be represented by a union official or by someone from an organization defending social rights.

What has the chairman of the Régie done on this issue? Doesn't she have the time to perform her function as advisor to the government on questions concerning housing?

Still on the issue of representation, there is yet another incoherent situation that penalizes tenants and that the Régie's chairman could usefully devote her time to correcting. When a lawyer accepts a legal aid mandate in a housing case, he will be paid $131 for a case where the tenant is the plaintiff. However, the fee will be $262 in cases where the tenant is the defendant. At these rates, the tenant is not likely to get a lawyer who is a specialist or even experienced. However, our main point is that *in the legal aid system, the lowest fees are paid for cases in which tenants demand their rights.*

E. Conciliation

If the Régie is to foster conciliation between landlords and tenants, it should primarily do this by performing its function of "informing lessors and lessees on their rights and obligations."[60] Only after establishing the Régie's jurisdiction as a court of first instance does the law discuss conciliation: "With the consent of the parties, the board may entrust a conciliator with meeting the parties and attempting to reach an agreement."[61] The authors of the law therefore saw mediation as a secondary recourse which should be treated as voluntary.

Not until four years after its creation did the Régie, in 1984, proceed to recruit the necessary personnel (legal technicians) to set up a conciliation service with the aim of reaching negotiated settlements in landlord-tenant disputes. The main reason invoked to justify the creation of this service was the need to reduce the burden on hearing rooms due to the buildup of cases. The Régie contacts the parties by mail and phone to offer conciliation after an application is filed.

In 1987, however, the Régie, on the pretext of conciliation, began moving towards a major reorganization of the way it deals with litigants. This change in direction was fairly important, with such serious consequences for tenants that it merits special examination.

Part III: Under the pretext of conciliation, a mandate betrayed

The Régie's 1990-1991 annual report informed its readers that henceforth "the Régie will focus on prevention and conciliation first."[62] In a press release published a little earlier, on July 9, 1992, the Régie had already been presented as "an organization providing assistance to landlords and tenants, [which] of course functions as a court, [but which] at first prefers to direct its action to preventing conflicts and, when necessary, settling them by negotiated agreement."

Several concrete forms of intervention can be distinguished in this sense:
• the *in-court* agreement when a commissioner invites the parties to agree before he settles the dispute;
• the conciliation session which brings the parties together *out of court*;
• so-called *preventive* mediation, when a Régie information officer tries to act as an intermediary between the landlord and the tenant so that they reach a negotiated settlement.

In the latter case, contact is established by mail and by phone. According to what we have understood from the Régie's current orientations, all these options can be considered before proceeding with adjudication as such, in the form of a court decision. "If conciliation does not produce the hoped-for result, the power to decide then acquires its full weight," the Régie's annual report stated.[63]

Obviously this process, deemed to be voluntary, requires the assent of both parties and can be interrupted by either one at any time.

Having seen the results of this Régie policy, tenants' associations remain opposed to this orientation, which has emerged more clearly since 1988. Let's look at one typical case of an agreement reached under the Régie's auspices, before further substantiating the arguments by tenant representatives against this practice.

A. A case among many others

In April 1988, Madame Turcotte (not her real name) refused a $30 a month rent increase. The landlord filed an application at the Régie and in October, at the hearing, the commissioner granted a postponement to the landlord who had not produced any vouchers in support of his application. The case was adjourned.[64]

Later, Madame Turcotte received a terse notice from the landlord that the heating system would be converted to electricity. Given the impossibility of obtaining compensation for inconvenience resulting from the work (particularly the purchase of a new electric stove), the tenant filed another application at the Régie, asking it to rule on fair and reasonable conditions for the proposed renovations.

She emerged from the Régie hearing with an agreement concluded with the landlord at the commissioner's insistence. Feeling that she had been shortchanged, she went to her local tenant organization, Comité logement de la Petite-Patrie.

Closer analysis showed that the client had been mugged at the Régie. The agreement she had signed gave the landlord a $20 increase. The conversion to electricity was mentioned, but there was no provision for any compensation for the tenant. Even worse, the written agreement did not mention that the rent increase had to cover the cost of major repairs, the very condition on which Madame Turcotte had accepted the increase. (Even if this had been the case, she had accepted a reduction in her rights by agreeing to pay for work in advance.)

Anne Thibault, the Comité logement's president, then wrote to the administration of the Régie, calling the imposed agreement an abuse of power and pointing out that the agreement concluded in front of the commissioner was neither fair nor impartial for the tenant. "A tenant using an administrative tribunal for the first time," she wrote, "cannot challenge the procedure followed by a commissioner, because he represents authority and the law."

Jean-Yves Landry, director of the Régie's central Montréal office, replied to Thibault in a letter dated December 15, 1988, promising to give her a more detailed answer upon his return from vacation in January. Eventually, Mr. Landry received Thibault at his office, telling her that he would refund the tenant the $20 fee she had paid to file her application, but that was all he could do. No more detailed answer was forthcoming.

The next year, Madame Turcotte had to assume the cost of major repairs in a $42 rent increase.[65] She never received compensation for the inconvenience suffered during the renovations. Determined not to be had this time, she appealed the increase and managed to roll it back to $33.50. Needless to say, she had no more faith in conciliation.

According to Claude Thomasset's study, *in-court* agreements at which observers were present are often unreliable. With the cautious wording required in an academic document, Ms. Thomasset asked

> whether the tenant derives any advantage from agreements and conciliation. He finds himself on the defensive, faced with a landlord who is represented by a lawyer and a commissioner who sometimes appears to be biased in favour of landlords. Agreements mainly seem to be reached because the tenant has brought more supporting documents than the landlord. *In these cases, is an agreement a stratagem by the lawyer or the commissioner in response to a tenant who has the means to defeat the landlord's application?*[66]

On the same page, she writes that "commissioners who have ratified agreements appear to be biased in favour of landlords."

Even though the Régie is inclined to conciliation in certain types of cases, it doesn't seem to hesitate to pass judgment when the problem affects the landlord's sensibilities. Are there many conciliation sessions in the case of non-payment of rent? No there aren't! Instead, the Régie proceeds with an urgent hearing.[67]

There are all too many negotiated agreements that are scandalously unfavourable to the tenants, and that they would never have signed if they had been adequately represented or properly informed of their rights. This is why tenants' associations are hostile to any form of Régie conciliation session leading to negotiated agreements.

For example, in one agreement written on the Régie's official stationery, a tenant consented to automatic cancellation of her lease if "the behaviour of the tenant or the occupants is the object of other complaints," without any other specification as to the nature or source of the complaints in question. In the same agreement, the tenant accepted liability for three months' rent if the landlord did not immediately find another tenant after cancelling her lease![68]

B. Out-of-court settlements

In the summer of 1989, several tenant organizations held a meeting to review the contents of out-of-court settlements, which were becoming increasingly common at the Régie, and compare them to what would have resulted from a strict application of the law through court decisions.

Their first finding was that conciliation opens the door to arbitrary action. In some rent increase cases, conciliators encouraged agreements without the landlord having to produce any supporting documents. In other instances, tenants agreed to rent increases for work not yet done in their apartments.

Secondly, the Régie's conciliators try to reach an agreement between the parties instead of ruling on the validity of the application. This deprives the tenant of the protection intended by law. In repossession cases, conciliators don't try to analyze the landlord's good faith as a commissioner would have to do at a hearing. Instead, they steer the discussion to the compensation the landlord might offer the tenant if he agreed to move out.

Thirdly, tenants have no recourse if an unfavourable agreement is extracted from them during conciliation. Written agreements are not always clearly drafted and leave a lot of room to the parties' good faith in subsequent application. This means they are very difficult to invoke if the landlord doesn't respect the terms. Whether the document is complete or not, signing it closes all doors. In the case of a bad decision, the parties at least have the possibility of review or appeal.

In some cases, the pressure exerted by certain Régie employees on tenants reluctant to get involved in conciliation has sown a lot of doubt about the "voluntary" nature of this process.

This is why tenants' associations condemn the conciliation and mediation system established by the Régie *in practice*. These arguments have been stated on many occasions, but in vain. Shrugging off all criticism, the Régie has gone even further into *preventive mediation*, via its information officers!

Now that the syndrome of conciliation at all costs prevails throughout the Régie, its practices are subject to criticism from a legal perspective.

C. The right to housing endangered

> Presenting negotiated settlements as a cure for judicialization is equivalent to excluding the justice of law. Man has found no better defence against the rule of force than imperfect laws interpreted by counsellors or arbiters who are as impartial as possible. The combination of these two factors ensures a minimum of justice that one is not at all sure of finding in an out-of-court settlement.[69]

In Québec, as we saw in the introduction, the right to housing has been established by creating an exception in the Civil Code, where freedom of contract is the general rule. The primary objective is to protect the tenant's right to housing, which is why property rights are mitigated. Usually, things are leased under contracts freely agreed between a lessor and a lessee.

The lawmakers sought to control and limit residential leasing practices as part of a tendency of social law which seeks to restore a balance in favour of the weaker or more disadvantaged party, in this instance the tenant. Obviously, in this spirit, the conciliation foreseen in the law can only be considered a secondary recourse. *Systematically resorting to negotiated agreements, as the Régie currently does, means a return to the total freedom of contract that the housing legislation was specifically designed to prevent, because of the abuses that follow in its wake.*

The law is not worded so obscurely that it can leave room to whimsical exegesis. *If the Régie's primary mandate were conciliation, the legislator would have spelled this out in the law.* In other words, arbitrary action is replacing the rule of law, thus betraying the mandate assigned to the Régie du logement.

Remember that this change in direction was prepared and executed in years when the Régie annual reports that mentioned it were not being published. While we can't be absolutely certain that the Régie intended to make these changes on the sly and present their eventual opponents with a *fait accompli*, this is what it looks like!

D. The zealots of conciliation

The authors of the Régie's 1990-1991 annual report, in their clear desire to make us understand the virtues of conciliation and the importance of the work accomplished at the Régie, did not contain themselves — scattering poetic metaphors through their text in a clear departure from the customary aridity of official documents. Thus, we read that the law "colours the [Régie's] role as a court with kindness" (p. 9). Participants in the Régie's information meetings are described as "happy and delighted to finally understand how to arrive at a reasonable increase with a minimum of good will, good faith and a little math" (p. 12). The landlord-tenant relationship is described as "intimate and special" (p. 11). The report explains that the Régie wants to "avoid the hardening of positions that filing an application almost inevitably causes" (p. 19) and boasts of "the clear satisfaction felt by all parties" (p. 20) after a brilliantly conducted mediation process. As a crowning achievement, "this year saw the introduction at the Régie of the Recognition of Excellence program" for deserving employees.

If this were nothing but stylistic overkill, we could laugh it off. Unfortunately, there is more to it. With unflappable pollyannaism, the Régie seems to believe that problems arise because landlords and tenants don't know how to communicate, that they don't talk to each other enough and that they therefore need psychological support! Yet it will be obvious to anyone familiar with the reality of tenants that they only go to court as a last resort, when all attempts at negotiation and discussion have reached an impasse.

To justify its policy, the Régie gives its clients the image of stubborn, undisciplined children whom it has to bring round to reason. Thus, the Régie's employees "encourage landlords and tenants to take responsibility for their relations" (p. 12). The information officer "henceforth will put more emphasis in his interviews on the behaviour to develop to avoid conflicts and maintain cordial relations" (p. 20). People seeking legal information are proposed "preventive attitudes and actions, possible solutions to explore, ways of negotiating an agreement." This will allow the Régie "to gradually empower its clients by teaching them techniques of communication, negotiation and conflict resolution" (p. 20).

"Not only must [the Régie] propose its new orientations but also sell them, persuaded that they are in the interest of the public in general, and landlords and tenants in particular," the 1987-1988 annual report concluded.[70]

A reading of the Régie's press releases and reports, with their strong emphasis on conciliation, clearly implies that any employee who wants a promotion will have to be very zealous in obtaining the negotiated agreements to which the Régie attaches so much importance. Out-of-court settlements are seen as the ideal solution and a court decision as a necessary evil in the last resort. The Régie seems to want to push people into mediation, to the detriment of the purely voluntary nature of conciliation as stipulated in Section 31 of the Act.

Given the many objections expressed by tenants' associations, we might expect the Régie to justify its position with facts and studies, proving that conciliation as the Régie understands it is a good thing for tenants.

Apart from the flowery rhetoric we have cited, the Régie's 1990-91 annual report contains a statistical table on conciliation, showing that 81 percent of disputes were settled during the process. Did these settlements conform to the rules of law or justice? How many Madame Turcottes were talked into an agreement that infringed on their rights by zealous Régie employees? Where are the independent studies that could give us an accurate picture? Where is the filing system for agreements signed by the parties (filed by type of case) so that we can analyze the documentary evidence?

Yet again, the Régie's obsession with marketing prevails. Its annual report bears closer resemblance to a promotional pamphlet for a New Age cult than to a serious analysis of how the organization really works. We can only remain perplexed at the number of unanswered questions and irritated by the Régie's triumphal paternalism.

E. Obstacles in the path of justice

Louise Thibault's career at the helm of the Régie could be likened to the gradual construction of a series of barriers, each pushing tenants farther away from effective judicial treatment of their housing problems.

Under the Régie's "preventive mediation" service, the Régie's information officer, stepping in as an intermediary, is supposed to contact the parties in an attempt to find common ground for agreement. Since the Régie's employee will try to settle the dispute by discouraging the plaintiff from filing an immediate application, the judicial process will be delayed even further if the negotiations fail. After a claim is filed, the Régie will attempt to get the dissatisfied tenant to accept conciliation, where it will try to obtain an agreement at any cost. As these additional delays and hassles become endemic, they will discourage tenants from looking to the Régie for help when they have problems.

As if all this were not enough, an amendment to the Code of Procedure for Régie hearings will drag cases out even longer. According to the draft version of Section 17 of these regulations, the Régie could summon the parties to a preparatory conference in front of a commissioner, before the hearing, to plan the procedures and the evidence to be presented at the hearing and examine any other question "that may simplify, facilitate and accelerate its progress, *particularly the possibilities for agreement*."[71] The very wording of this regulation implied that a tenant who holds out would again be urged to reach a negotiated agreement. Faced with unanimous protests from tenants' associations, the Régie backed down and deleted the reference to "possibilities for agreement" from the final draft. But is it enough to strike out a few words to change the intention? Representatives of all tenant organizations consulted in preparing this analysis were extremely skeptical about the sincerity of this last-minute change.

We should note that all these conciliation sessions, preparatory conferences and other discussions are not proper hearings (which must be public, according to the law) and *take place behind closed doors*. Given the abuses to which tenants are subjected at regular hearings (as described elsewhere in this document), the Régie's plans give good reason to fear legal irregularities and problems with respect for people's dignity. At a June 1, 1992 consultation meeting on the draft version of the new regulations, *every* tenant organization that responded to the Régie's invitation opposed its conciliation-at-all-costs approach, while *every* landlord organization in attendance supported the proposal. Both groups were well aware of where the interests of their constituents lay.

F. A guaranteed success!

At least the Régie did not pretend that this costly operation of setting up a conciliation system would save public funds. The cost of judicial processing of an application at the Régie was already lower than for any comparable government agency and it would be unlikely that conciliation could do better. Only Housing Minister Claude Ryan sought to invoke the argument that conciliation offered budgetary advantages.

However, in the new spirit of conciliation that now drives the Régie, there is an avowed desire to reduce the number of cases. Criticizing the first years of operation at the Régie, which "essentially geared its action to its role as an administrative tribunal," the 1990-91 annual report was implicitly reproachful of the fact "that landlord-tenant relations do not seem to have improved [and] that the number of cases has increased steadily."[72]

As we have noted, it is very likely that the many barriers of negotiation and discussion erected between the filing of an application and the hearing as such will discourage tenants from applying to the Régie or resisting abuse by the landlord. This reduction in the number of applications will be presented as a success, since the Régie will claim that this shows an improvement in landlord-tenant relations as a result of its program of "empowering its clientele."

However, this policy may have the opposite effect. Landlords, sure that the Régie will push for negotiated settlements, may make outrageous demands on their tenants to put themselves in a strong bargaining position for conciliation sessions, or they may cunningly offer minor concessions for the sake of form. If this situation arises, it is very likely that most tenants, running out of patience, will waive their rights and sign some kind of agreement along the way, dropping out before the hearing. This situation may also be presented as a great success, since the Régie will then boast of the great number of cases settled in conciliation!

Part IV: Standing between landlords and tenants

The April 1991 edition of the landlord monthly *Immobilier d'aujourd'hui*, featured a beaming Louise Thibault on the front page, with a biographical sketch and interview inside.[73]

It seems so long ago that landlord associations and landlord publications were demanding the repeal of the infamous Bill 107 and the outright abolition of the Régie du logement! Does this change of tone, and the reception granted the Régie's chairman in *Immobilier d'aujourd'hui*, bear eloquent witness to a change in philosophy among the upholders of economic liberalism? Have landlords, after failing to obtain the Régie's abolition, resigned themselves to its presence to the extent that they gladly publish the comments of its chairman? Have they adopted a strategy of "if you can't beat them, join them"? These are plausible explanations for the obvious sympathy evinced for Louise Thibault in the pages of *Immobilier d'aujourd'hui*.

However, the champions of free enterprise have lost none of their pugnacity nor their taste for hyperbole. In the same edition, the editorial resoundingly declares that "in the current state of affairs, being a landlord is much more akin to a religious calling and a vow of poverty." A different hypothesis therefore is likely: the Régie du logement has adopted orientations satisfactory to landlords, who now consider it in their interest for the Régie to continue along these lines. Before concluding, let's quickly review some recent meetings on housing-related issues and see what type of role the Régie has played.

A. Rental application forms

In 1991, after a series of complaints from tenant organizations, the Québec Human Rights Commission began to investigate the application forms that some landlords are requiring prospective tenants to fill in. On the pretext of checking the tenant's solvency, they are engaging in a major invasion of privacy, demanding social insurance, Medicare, passport and bank account numbers, the name of the applicant's employer or welfare agent, previous places of residence, and more.

Asked to take a stand on this issue, the Régie du logement promptly alerted the landlord associations and invited tenant groups to sit down with the landlord representatives. As soon as the landlords realized that the operation wasn't designed to clothe an attack on human rights in a mantle of respectability, they withdrew from the discussions. *The Régie's representatives then declared that if the landlords didn't participate in the talks, neither could they.*

The Régie never made the slightest comment on the flagrant abuses committed against tenants who were forced to provide the landlord with the details of their private lives before he would let them have an apartment.

It would be interesting to see how the authors of the Régie's 1991-1992 annual report (which should have appeared in July 1992, but which we probably won't see until 1993) recount these events in their euphuistic prose. The truth casts a shadow on the image the Régie seeks to present as the great conciliator, the teacher of dialogue and negotiation. Marketing specialists will have quite a job putting this black mark in a more attractive light.

B. Rent fixation criteria

Under the heading of "transparency," the 1990-91 annual report mentioned the Régie's deliberations on its rent fixation method. It referred to meetings with landlord and tenant associations which, as the report put it, "allowed for fruitful discussions."[74]

The RCLALQ participated in one of these meetings on February 13, 1992 at the Régie's headquarters. After pointing out the distortions in favour of the landlords produced by the Régie's method for calculating the goods and services tax, the tenant representatives asked the Régie to make the necessary adjustments immediately so that tenants would not be penalized.

The Régie's representatives then endeavoured to minimize the consequences of this distortion for the rent increases allowed and promised an in-depth reform by March at the latest. Of course, there was no question of correcting the errors that would work against tenants until then.

As of September 1, 1992, the promised corrections, supposedly imminent in March, were still unpublished, and the Régie hadn't even provided excuses for this unexplained delay.

Tenants certainly would not be inclined to describe such discussions as "fruitful."

C. A rent registry

In theory, landlords are supposed to indicate the rent paid by the former tenant on any new lease. In practice, this provision of the Civil Code is almost never respected. Yet excessive increases most often occur when there is a change of tenants.

To ensure that tenants can obtain the information to which they are entitled by law, the RCLALQ asked Minister Claude Ryan to set up a rent registry.

When tenant organizations lobbied the chairman of the Régie to solicit her support, she raised all kinds of objections to this proposal. The tenant representatives could feel the poorly concealed impatience of the Régie's top brass at seeing the groups propose solutions that didn't fit in with their plans.

What if landlords don't respect the law? According to the Régie, dissatisfied tenants need only exercise their recourses against the landlord as individuals. (Of course, this isn't the way to encourage the "good relations" that seem to preoccupy the Régie so much.)

This time the discussions were fruitful in one sense only: the people in the RCLALQ who still had faith in the possibility of cooperation with the Régie's current administration ceased to believe in this option.

Maybe a Régie conciliator could propose that the chairman, in her future relations with tenant representatives, adopt "preventive attitudes and actions, possible solutions to explore, ways of negotiating an agreement."

D. A policy of silence

The criticisms addressed to the Régie by all tenant organizations throughout Québec were echoed in the press to some extent. In *Le Devoir* of January 17, 1992, Caroline Montpetit wrote an article entitled "Tenants feel the Régie is on a dangerous course."[75] Similar headlines appeared in *Le Soleil* and *La Tribune*. The Régie never bothered to respond.

No doubt fearing that a public statement would put them on the defensive and hurt their corporate image, the Régie's top officials retreat into haughty silence when publicly challenged. The Régie behaves like it is unaccountable to anyone, and has developed a contemptuous attitude to the press and the general public.

It's ironic that for a long period Régie officials took the position that because both landlords and tenants criticized them, they held the middle ground. Now, landlord organizations no longer criticize and smiling Régie officials are profiled in *Immobilier d'aujourd'hui*. Otherwise, they keep silent.

Conclusion

In this document, we have analyzed how the Régie operates but we have said little about tenants. We should remember, in conclusion, that the vast majority are low-income people or have moderate means. Often they live alone or head one-parent families.

One of the major causes of poverty in Québec, especially for women, who make up the majority of the tenant population, was the out-of-control rise in housing costs of the 1980s. The high vacancy rate for rental housing, headlined in the business pages, is a consequence of the simple fact that fewer Québecers can afford to house themselves.

With the systematic somnolence at the Régie regarding the right to housing, another vital link in the social safety net is becoming undone. It is no exaggeration to blame the Régie's administration for its contribution to increasing the distress of the disadvantaged, worsening poverty and all the evils that come with it.

This sabotage of the Régie has been accomplished in the guise of scrupulous application of the law. This must be named for what it is: a social fraud. A change of direction requires a change at the helm. Louise Thibault and her team appear much too compromised by the current mess for there to be any hope of improvement while they are in charge.

Is there a government in Québec? Is there a doctor in the house? Is there a pilot on the plane? Claude Ryan's stubborn silence on everything concerning tenants' rights has stretched our patience to the limit. As the next election approaches, let's remind all politicians of all parties that tenant organizations will hold them accountable for what has been done and what has been neglected on the right to housing. We refer them to our document, *For a Québec housing policy* [chapter 3], which summarizes the main demands of Québec tenant organizations.

NOTES

1. This document was the collective effort of several housing groups throughout Québec. The main contributors were: Anne Thibault (Comité logement Petite-Patrie, Montréal); Denis Cusson (Bureau d'animation et d'information logement, Québec City); Mireille Lemelin (Association des locataires de Sherbrooke); Huguette Singler (Comité logement Saint-Louis, Montréal); Joëlle Raymond (Comité logement Centre-Sud); Hanh Bao Lam (Association des locataires de Longueuil); and Robert Trudel, a lawyer specializing in housing law. André Dudemaine, of the RCLALQ magazine *L'Artère*, served as secretary of the editorial committee and produced the final draft.
2. *Act to promote conciliation between lessees and property owners.*
3. *Livre blanc sur les relations entre locataires et bailleurs.* The government's emphasis.
4. Our emphasis.
5. Régie du logement, *Les objectifs de la loi.*
6. Sections 1, 4 and 5 of the *Act respecting the Régie du logement.*
7. Ibid., Section 5.
8. Ibid., Section 10.
9. Ibid., Section 9.
10. "The objective pursued by the legislator is to ensure that everyone has decent housing at a reasonable price," according to a press release issued by

the office of the Minister of Municipal Affairs on December 18, 1978, entitled *Jurisdiction de la Régie du logement*.
11. This document was written in 1992.
12. *Act respecting the Régie du logement*, Section 4.
13. We would have liked to cite a Régie du logement study but, despite the clear terms of reference provided in the Act, we have found none.
14. Letter from Jacques Chagnon, of the Régie's communications department, to Anne Thibault, president of the RCLALQ.
15. As housing groups have frequently stated, this method is based on erroneous calculations that favour the landlord at the tenant's expense. At a meeting with several tenant representatives in Montréal on February 13, 1992, senior Régie officials admitted this, but took refuge behind a hypothetical reform of the method, in preparation at that time, to refuse any change in this situation for 1992.
16. Taken from an August 3, 1992 document written by the Régie's legal activities branch (Vice-présidence aux activités judiciaires) and addressed to groups which had made comments on a series of draft amendments to the Régie's rules of procedure.
17. The following section refers to the situation as it existed in 1992. That same year, tenant groups in Hull and Québec City filed lawsuits against the Régie to force it to release thousands of decisions. One of the instigators of this strategy was a Hull activist named Bill Clennett, who later came to public attention in 1996 when Prime Minister Jean Chrétien used him as a punching bag.

Both court actions proved successful. Rather than file an appeal, the Régie reached a negotiated compromise with the tenant organizations. Instead of having to retrieve and copy thousands of old decisions, it agreed to computerize all rulings rendered under the new Civil Code, starting January 1, 1994 and make them accessible on a computer terminal in each of its offices.

In opposing the groups' demands, the Régie had argued that it was protecting tenants against the compilation of blacklists. However, the tenant organizations felt that this risk was outweighed by the benefits of unrestricted access to the information contained in these decisions.

On the whole, the new system has worked out fairly well, even though the various terminals aren't interconnected and each Régie office only has the decisions handed down in its own territory.

Before renting an apartment, a tenant can look up the address of the building or the name of the landlord to find out if there is a history of repair problems or abuses.

A tenant fighting a repossession can check whether the landlord has used this procedure as a pretext to evict other people in the past. Jurisprudence is retrieved by typing in a key word or phrase, such as "harassment," "rats" or "repossession," or a specific Civil Code section number. This strengthens subsequent cases on similar issues.

It is true that landlords can look up the names of prospective tenants to find out if they have been evicted for non-payment of rent or some other problem. But Québec's privacy legislation, Bill 68, which came into full force in July 1994, bans the compilation and use of blacklists (editor's note).

18. But only until the end of 1993, as explained in note 17 (editor's note).
19. This is a fine example of a corporatist attitude. The professional association representing lawyers is only concerned about rights when its own members are affected.
20. *Act respecting the Régie du logement*, Section 5.
21. Ibid., Section 5.
22. As of 1992 (editor's note).
23. Decision JL 89-51 rendered in the case of *J.-. Jarvis-Royston v. Gestion immobilière Warnet*, which was initially published in *Jurisprudence Express* and *Recueil de jurisprudence du Québec*. JL only published it a year later.
24. A 1992 Régie compendium proudly publishes a decision in its favour by the Commission d'accès à l'information. But one wonders if the Régie, so concerned about its corporate image, would have published a decision that did not favour it.
25. After a renewed campaign by tenant groups, the Québec National Assembly finally amended the *Act respecting the Régie du logement* in December 1995 to make its standard lease form mandatory (editor's note).
26. Section 1651.1 of the *Civil Code of Lower Canada*. This has been replaced by Section 1895 of the *Civil Code of Québec* (editor's note).
27. See Rousseau-Houle and de Billy, *Le bail du logement: analyse de la jurisprudence* (Montréal: Wilson et Lafleur, 1989), pp. 38 and 39.
28. Section 1652.2 of the Civil Code of Lower Canada. This has been replaced by Section 1896 of the Civil Code of Québec (editor's note).
29. Could it be that the poor reputation of the Régie's telephone services was the sole reason for the reduction in the number of calls? The Régie brags that it has shortened the waiting time but does not mention the number of calls received. All this was blissfully repeated by Claude Ryan at the Commission parlementaire de l'aménagement et des équipements on April 14, 1992. The Régie's 1990-1991 annual report, published subsequent to Ryan's statement, clearly indicates a slight reduction in the number of calls to the Régie from 1989 to 1990.
30. *Act respecting the Régie du logement*, Section 5.
31. See JL-90-58, *Claude Thomasset v. Régie du logement*. This was the situation until 1993. As explained in Note 17, it is now possible to look up Régie decisions rendered since January 1, 1994 by type of application or by any other key word (editor's note).
32. *Act respecting the Régie du logement*, Section 25.
33. In 1994, the Régie closed its downtown Montréal office, conveniently located above the Berri-de Montigny Métro station. At the end of 1995, in the dying days of the Parizeau government, the Régie announced its intention to consolidate all Montréal hearings at the Olympic Village in the east end. The Côte des Neiges (west end) Verdun (southwest) and Crémazie (north end) offices would only be kept open as information and application desks.

Community organizations in the west end organized a petition campaign (including thousands of leaflets distributed at the St. Patrick's Day parade), encouraged clients to inundate the minister's office with phone calls and obtained a meeting with government officials in April 1996 to reopen the discussion. They pointed out that the move was particularly inconvenient for senior citizens, would result in a four-hour round trip by public transit for residents of West Island suburbs, and would make it more difficult for tenants to bring witnesses to hearings.

In the name of deficit reduction, the government maintained its decision, and all hearings were moved to the Olympic Village as of July 2, 1996. In a subsequent meeting with tenant groups, Housing Minister Rémy Trudel promised to consider cheaper alternatives for restoring service on the western half of the Island (editor's note).

34. *Act respecting the Régie du logement*, Section 17.
35. *Act respecting the Régie du logement*, Section 10. At the time this document was published, the chairman was Louise Thibault, who had been in office since June 30, 1988 (editor's note).
36. *Code of Ethics for Commissioners of the Régie du logement*, Section 1.
37. Claude Thomasset, *La Régie du logement à découvert* (Montréal: Éditions Louise Courteau, 1987).
38. Ibid., p. 41.
39. Ibid., p. 3.
40. Ibid., p. 230.
41. *Journal de Montréal*, February 1, 1992, p. 7.
42. *L'immobilière d'aujourd'hui*, vol. 1, no 4, April 1991.
43. Only the lowest-income tenants qualify for legal aid. Even old age pensioners and low-wage earners are usually over the eligibility limit, and they can't afford to pay a lawyer for an appeal (editor's note).
44. Yves Ouellette et al., *Les tribunaux administratifs. L'heure est aux décisions!* (Les Publications du Québec, 1987).
45. See Alain Bisson's article in *La Presse*, September 24, 1990.
46. Including the Régie's then-chairman Louise Thibault, who previously held the very political position of Assistant Deputy Minister of Municipal Affairs.
47. Yves Ouellette, op. cit., p. 188.
48. *La Presse*, February 22, 1992, p. A16.
49. Yves Ouellette, op. cit., p. 148.
50. Certain types of Régie decisions, including decisions fixing the rent, can be "appealed" to a review panel of commissioners rather than to the Court of Québec. A review panel generally consists of two commissioners (editor's note).
51. Decision number 90-20 in the case of *Gina Robinson v. Gaston Tardif et al.*, by commissioners Jean-Claude Pothier and Gilles Langlois. The emphasis is ours.
52. Act respecting the Régie du logement, Section 10.
53. In the case of *Yves Blais et al. v. Marcel Paquet*, March 26, 1991, by commissioners Pierre Thérien and Johanne Gagnon-Trudel.
54. Claude Thomasset, "Le logement entre l'État et l'entreprise, genèse d'un droit en d'un droit devenir," in *Le droit dans tous ses états* (Montréal: Wilson and Lafleur, 1987), p. 253.
55. Since the initial publication of this critique in 1992, there is no indication that this rumour has become reality. The decisions of different commissioners are typically inconsistent.

The public order provision most frequently enforced by the Régie is the first paragraph of Section 1900 of the Civil Code of Québec, which states: "A clause which limits the liability of the lessor or exempts him for liability or which renders the lessee liable for damage caused without his fault is without effect." In plain English, any clause in the lease stating that the landlord is never responsible for repairs to the fridge or stove or air conditioner he has supplied is in violation of Section 1900 and therefore invalid (editor's note).

56. *Act respecting the Régie du logement*, Section 72.
57. Ibid.
58. Thomasset, op. cit., pp. 50-51.
59. These administrative tribunals respectively hear cases on minimum labour standards, union rights, welfare and occupational injuries (editor's note).
60. *Act respecting the Régie du logement*, Section 5.
61. Ibid., Section 31.
62. *Rapport annuel* 1990-1991, p. 9.
63. Ibid., p. 11.
64. This is not unusual. If a landlord doesn't bring the vouchers supporting his application, he needn't worry. He'll get a postponement, even though the tenant will have to show up in court a second time with all the inconvenience that this involves (taking more time off work, babysitting costs, transportation, etc.).
65. In other cases, tenants who accepted a larger-than-normal rent increase in exchange for repairs have convinced the Régie not to allow the landlord to claim the cost of this work a second time in the following year's rent increase (editor's note).
66. Thomasset, op. cit., p. 250. Our emphasis.
67. Resulting from the inflationary and uncontrolled increases in housing prices in the past 10 years (since 1982) and the economic crisis, non-payment of rent accounts for the majority of cases filed at the Régie. These claims are given priority and expeditious treatment: up to 120 cases per day heard by the same commissioner, or a record average of 1.5 minutes per case! As a legal novelty, when the Régie orders an eviction for non-payment of rent, the decision [often] stipulates that *the judgment is executory notwithstanding appeal!* The Régie thus ensures that landlords are very well served.

    Editor's note: The Régie does not always make its eviction judgments executory notwithstanding appeal, which would mean that the tenant could be evicted by a bailiff even while an appeal to the Court of Québec is pending.

    Commissioners have showed some discretion in this matter, especially when the amount of rent owed is small or when it is initially unclear whether the landlord's claim is justified. Sometimes they simply omit the "notwithstanding appeal" reference. However, in the mid-1990s, the incidence of "notwithstanding appeal" judgments seems to be increasing.
68. Incredible but true! This document (Régie case number 31-89-1215-022) is in the files of Comité-logement Petite-Patrie.
69. Jacques Dufresne, "Raminagrobis," in *La Presse*, February 22, 1992.
70. Régie du logement, *Rapport annuel 1987-1988*.
71. Our emphasis.
72. Régie du logement, *Rapport annuel 1990-1991*, p. 9.
73. Published by Le Groupe Proprio and "mailed free of charge to all members of the Le Groupe Proprio enr. and Crédit Proprio ltée."

74. Régie du logement, *Rapport annuel 1990-1991*, p. 21 (translation).
75. "Des locataires estiment que la Régie prend une "pente dangéreuse," *Le Devoir*.

Chapter 5

A critique of Montréal's housing code[1]

by Arnold Bennett, 1992

In April 1992, the City of Montréal held public hearings on a proposed reform of the municipal Housing Code, an essential tool for the enforcement of decent housing standards. The Montréal Citizens' Movement (MCM) and Mayor Jean Doré, elected in 1986 on a platform of protecting tenants and neighbourhoods, were still in office, but their grassroots image had been seriously tarnished by the Overdale fiasco.[2]

Tenant organizations, which had expected vigorous action against slumlords to enforce decent housing standards, found that bureaucratic inertia was still calling the shots. Even worse, in the Overdale conflict, the City had invoked unsafe housing conditions as an excuse to condemn two dilapidated buildings and expel the tenants, instead of forcing the landlord to do repairs.

As an MCM member of City council, I had made reform of the Housing Code my top priority. In 1988, along with Councillor Marcel Sévigny, Claude Dagneault of the Côte des Neiges tenant organization OEIL and Pierre Marquis of Comité de logement Saint-Louis, I formed a tripartite committee with City housing inspectors to rewrite the Housing Code. Conservative lawyers in the City's legal department gutted our report and only minor improvements were adopted by City council before the 1990 municipal election. The City's lawyers argued that the City should not "intrude" on areas of provincial jurisdiction, even where Québec's enforcement role was secondary or inadequate, as in the case of apartment elevators. As a result, only minor improvements were made to the by-law before the 1990 municipal election. The rest of the reform was sent back to the drawing board, with the understanding that the administration's declared housing priorities, and not legal pettifoggery, would be given priority.

When the administration finally got around to tabling its Green Paper in 1992, we were angered to discover that the tripartite committee's recommendations had been ignored. Tenant organizations therefore used the public hearings of City council's Housing and Planning Committee to make their point.

I submitted the following arguments at the April 1992 hearings. Most of the arguments raised in this document and in the other briefs presented by tenant groups were taken into account in the by-law that was finally adopted by City council in August 1994. Despite the defeat of the MCM in the November 1994 municipal election, the reformed Housing Code is still in place. However, the problem of enforcement remains.

The Côte des Neiges tenant organization, known as OEIL (Organisation de l'éducation et de l'information sure le logement), has responded to the Bourque administration's spotty enforcement record by conducting its own inspections of apartment buildings throughout the district and publishing the results.

****

In its Green Paper, the City of Montréal proposes a more "flexible" approach to enforcement of the Housing Code, based on "education and cooperation." This would have the following consequences:
• no increase in the number of inspectors to enforce the Code;
• no minimum fine for violations, although the maximum fine for a first offence is raised from $300 to $1,000;
• the elimination of certain standards from the existing by-law, especially those concerning cladding of outside walls and foundations and the presence of kitchen counters and cabinets;
• limiting of inspection reports to "the object of the request" except in cases of "danger" and "urgency." This would create an arbitrary and discretionary climate, reducing tenant protection.

An approach based on education and technical support only works if the landlord is working in good faith. It is ineffective with speculators, absentee landlords and slumlords.

A. The power to get things done

The City proposes to maintain its existing power of emergency intervention when landlords refuse to cooperate and the buildings pose a danger to their occupants. This means the power to have the work done at the landlord's expense and register a lien against the property to guarantee recovery of these costs, plus a 65 percent charge for administration. If necessary, the City has the power to seize the property for unpaid debts.

While this power looks very effective on paper, it has been very rarely used up to now: three cases (up to 1992) where the City has actually had the work done and twelve others where a firm expression of intent has been enough to get the landlord moving.

As an organization which operates a telephone hotline (handling 500 calls a week) and holds three weekly clinics, we often have occasion to ask Housing Code inspectors to intervene. In many of these cases, very strong intervention is justified, including the use of the City's emergency power. But despite the creation of a revolving fund and the higher priority given by the City's Secretary General to requests from the Housing and Urban Development Department (SHDU),[3] the City is still reluctant to apply this power. Even when it does, it limits its interventions to the most urgent repairs. There are two reasons for this behaviour: the limited financial resources budgeted for this purpose and an over-timid legal department, which fears that the City will be sued by the landlord if it does too much.

What is incomprehensible is that the City almost totally neglects to advertise its interventions for their deterrent effect, which would reduce the necessity for other actions. In fact, the only serious publicity effort has come from community organizations.

B. The power to pay bills

Even though it has the power to do repairs or have them done, the City does not have the power to pay electricity or gas bills that a landlord has neglected to cover. Furthermore, Hydro-Québec refuses to restore service or allow the City to restore it as long as the arrears aren't paid.

For several years, the SHDU claimed to have the right to pay such bills. But the City's legal department now contradicts it. Due to the pigheaded attitude of certain Hydro-Québec bureaucrats, tenants in two apartment blocks in Notre Dame de Grace (NDG) had to live for several weeks in the summer of 1990 with no electricity in the buildings' common areas, no alarm system and no hot water. (The landlords in question, who lived in Toronto, were in the middle of a divorce dispute and nobody was willing to pay the bills).

It is absolutely essential to amend the by-law so that the City has the emergency power to pay arrears and not just the power to perform work.

C. The need for new standards

The Green Paper disregards the earlier recommendations of a tripartite committee of civil servants, City councillors and tenant representatives to add some important new standards to the Housing Code.
1. Minimum security standards must be established for apartment building access doors, by requiring secure locks and obliging landlords to ensure that the lobby doors are kept locked.

    The cities of Westmount and Côte Saint Luc adopted by-laws for this purpose in 1988. If the City of Montréal really wants to prevent crime, it is absurd that it has not done the same.
2. The presence of garbage rooms and their sanitary maintenance must be required in apartment blocks. This would indirectly force landlords to provide basic maintenance services in the buildings.

    Such a requirement would also meet the concerns already expressed by City Council's environment committee, which is trying to find a solution to sanitation problems in some neighbourhoods. Tenants on these streets often put their garbage on the sidewalk between pickup days because there is nowhere to store it.
3. The Société d'habitation et de développement de Montréal (SHDM) must be given the explicit power to require the landlord of an elevator building to ensure that the elevator works safely.

    At present there is a regulatory vacuum: the Québec Ministry of Labour can padlock an unsafe elevator and the Régie du logement can order elevator service restored, but no government inspector has the clearly defined power to assist the Régie by requiring an elevator to be repaired.

D. Unacceptable elimination of standards

The Green Paper claims that insulation standards are difficult to enforce and that they can be eliminated without causing problems. The City argues that it is preferable to apply the existing standard, which obliges landlords to maintain a room temperature of at least 21° C (70° F).

But many tenants pay their own heating. Since the 1970s, many landlords have shifted the burden of paying for heating over to the tenants and have converted their buildings to electric baseboard heating, without improving the insulation. This means that some tenants have to pay excessively high electricity bills or freeze during the winter.

The City must deal with inadequate heating and insulation, especially for tenants who pay their own heating.

The Green Paper also claims that market forces will encourage landlords to install kitchen counters and cabinets, or other features involving comfort or aesthetics. But what can low-income tenants do when they are obliged to take whatever they can find? Market forces don't work for them. There are good reasons why a Housing Code is necessary.

E. Renovation and harassment

The Green Paper offers nothing to solve another problem: the need to give the City the power to suspend a renovation permit and even continue the work itself if the landlord does not respect the tenants' safety, health and comfort or uses renovations as a way to harass tenants into leaving.

Let's take the notorious example of Bérenger Lessard, landlord of a building at 6210 Northcrest Place in Montréal's Côte des Neiges district in 1990. In an April 15, 1992 judgment, the Régie du logement ordered him to pay $6,358.50 to the only tenant who had bothered to sue him.

> The tenant testified that she had occupied her dwelling since about 1982. Major renovations began without prior notice at the end of December 1989. At the beginning of January, she had no water or heat; the hallways had been gutted and were full of construction materials. Because of the condition of the premises, the tenant started looking for another apartment. She moved in the third week of January after being subjected to harassment, intimidation and many problems and inconveniences due to the lack of security in the building, including the removal of her washing machine at the beginning of January, the inability to receive mail, having to look for a dwelling in mid-winter and having to move.
>
> Among other things, the landlord had removed the balconies, demolished the common areas, converted

> the plumbing, broken up the asphalt and the lawn around the building and generally undertaken major demolition and construction work with no regard for the habitability of the dwellings and the health and safety of the occupants.

According to the City inspectors, who kept me informed of the situation in 1990, the landlord complied with their notices, but always found a way to continue his renovations by doing other things about which he had not been notified.

> Even if there initially was a problem with frozen pipes (the Régie noted), the landlord used this as a pretext for a whole series of minor jobs, the urgency of which was not demonstrated in any way — this in violation of the legal requirements of the City and the Civil Code, and in a display of contempt for the tenants' right to remain in the premises and to peaceful enjoyment of their dwellings.

It must be noted that, despite significant efforts by City inspectors and community organizations, 26 of 29 apartments were vacant by March 1, 1990. The vast majority of the tenants who left, without ever suing the landlord, were recent immigrants.

While this case is extreme, it is a typical example of the behaviour of a certain type of landlord. Many community groups could cite others.

F. The object of the complaint

The Green Paper claims that limiting inspections to the object of the complaint will allow the City to allocate more resources to perform systematic inspections.

It also claims that it isn't fair for one landlord to be hit with a whole series of requirements and charges, while the owner of the neighbouring building, which may be in worse condition, gets off scot-free.

The Green Paper's argument in this case is absurd and illogical. Its authors are forgetting about the importance of the deterrent effect, especially if the City takes the trouble to publicize its interventions. This policy leaves the door open to more manoeuvres of the type described in the Northcrest Place case. It makes the system less accessible and life more complicated for tenants who now will have to formulate their complaint in much more detail.

It also leaves inspectors in a state of uncertainty regarding their obligation to report a problem if it is not mentioned in the original complaint.

G. Fines

We endorse the comments of the Côte des Neiges housing organization, OEIL, which proposes a minimum fine of $300 for the first offence, a maximum fine of $2,000 for the third offence and fines of $300 per day for emergency situations when the landlord does not comply with the Housing Code inspector's notice.

In conclusion, we should remember that the Housing Code is an essential tool for protecting those tenants whose fear, ignorance or illness prevents them from using the Régie du logement. It also plays an essential role in reinforcing tenants' rights at the Régie.

NOTES

1. Brief presented to Montréal City Council's Housing and Planning Committee (Commission de l'aménagement et de l'habitation) on April 29, 1992., during public hearings on the former Doré administration's Green Paper on reform of the municipal Housing Code. These criticisms were similar to those raised by various Montréal tenant organizations, and most of them were taken into account in the final version of the by-law adopted by City Council in August 1994. Despite the Montréal Citizens' Movement's defeat in the November 1994 election, the reformed Code remains in place. However, the will to enforce it has been weakened.
2. See Chapter 1.
3. Service d'habitation et de développement urban (SHDU).

Chapter 6

Housing and poverty in Québec: An indictment

by People's Rights Over Urban Development (PROUD), 1993[1]

Editor's note: This manifesto was published in French in 1993. I have added a few footnotes to update the context. PROUD has a reputation for being very creative in its use of media gimmicks and direct action to hammer home its message: a winter encampment in Ottawa, a cardboard house used in demonstrations, a donation of old shoes to the Finance Minister, etc.

Part I: Housing: a societal issue

In June 1993, the United Nations Economic, Social and Cultural Commission published a report on poverty in Canada. It provided a damning portrait of the housing situation and expressed astonishment that "given the obvious existence of homelessness and inadequate housing conditions, spending on social housing does not exceed 1.3% of public expenditures."

What is true for Canada is even more so for Québec, which accounts for one third of the country's tenants with imperative housing needs. One out of three tenant households spends over 30% of its income on housing, and one out of six over 50%. Nearly 20,000 people can be considered homeless.

In the current period of exclusion — permanent exclusion from work, exclusion from basic social rights — the housing problem is becoming even more dramatically acute. Yet this problem is far from being considered a societal issue in Québec. It continues to be seen as merely an individual responsibility, a problem to be experienced privately within the home — at least for people who can still afford one.

It is to make the problem more visible, to reveal its collective nature and force debate on what is nothing less than a vital necessity, that PROUD is publishing this indictment of housing and poverty in Québec. Its publication is part of a constant struggle to oblige governments, starting with that of Québec, to produce 100,000 new social housing units by the year 2000.

A. Quality of housing still a problem!

Twenty years ago, the main housing problem was quality. The situation has certainly improved, but housing in pitiful condition still exists in Québec. A recent study by the Société d'habitation du Québec (SHQ) describes the prevalent conditions:

> According to a survey conducted by Statistics Canada in 1991, 9% of Québec dwellings, or 236,000 units, needed major repairs according to their occupants, while 12% of dwellings, or 317,000 units, required minor repairs. When only low-income households are considered, namely those incapable of finding other housing at the average market rent without paying over 30% of their income, we find that 62,000 occupied a deficient dwelling in 1988. Of these, 40% owned their own home.[2]

We don't have to look much further to find that one of the main problems is insulation, which has consequences for heating costs and the occupants' health. Soundproofing is also a serious problem. Yet rental housing restoration programs have invested the least in countering these problems since 1986. In fact, five times more money has been allocated to plastering and woodwork.[3]

B. The effects on health

The Health and Welfare Policy published in 1992 by the Québec government very clearly identifies the effects that poor-quality housing may have on health.

> Living in a deteriorated, poorly heated, poorly ventilated dwelling particularly affects the health of children and the elderly. Infectious diseases, flus, colds and otitis are more frequent. It is also noted that tension, sources of conflict and stress levels increase in families when they live in apartments that are too small or poorly soundproofed. The cost of housing also appears to have a crucial effect on family

organization. If food, clothing and recreation are constantly subject to radical cuts because of the price of housing, the quality of physical and mental health will be affected.[4]

To solve these problems, the Health and Welfare Policy proposed improvement of "access to moderately-priced housing, particularly for poor one-parent families" and "development of cooperative social housing formulas."[5] Is there any need to add that these programs have been shelved by the Liberal government?[6]

> Jeannette and Réal Béland, age 59, of Montréal were both pensioners in 1993. Mrs. Béland had to leave her job as a nurse's aide in 1983 due to arthritis. The company where Mr. Béland worked shut down in 1989. The couple had to live on $912 a month. They had been living in the same 4 1/2 for fourteen years. The rent isn't very expensive ($210 a month), but "it costs a fortune in winter to stay warm."
>
> "In fourteen years, the landlord came once to repair a hole in the floor next to the sink [...]. We're fed up holding the devil by the tail; we want to live like real people."

C. The official estimate: 341,000 households poorly housed in Québec

Governments estimate that 341,000 Québec households, including 280,000 tenant households, have imperative housing needs and are therefore eligible for social housing.[7]

They have the following criterion: "a household that has an affordability problem (with housing costs accounting for over 30% of its income) or a space or quality problem and that cannot afford to relocate at the average market rent in quality housing corresponding to the household's size without paying over 30% of its income for rent."[8]

But in the government's view, not all households that pay over 30% (and sometimes over 50%) of their income for housing or that live in slums necessarily have imperative housing needs. According to their perspective, many of these households could find housing at cheaper rents or of better quality in the city where they live, if they wished to. This method tends to underestimate the scope of housing problems. As the Canada Mortgage and Housing Corporation (CMHC) itself admits, these statistics "do not include households living on reservations, people placed in shelters, tenants of furnished rooms, boarders and the homeless."[9]

We should also note that governments use an income threshold and that any household earning over this amount is automatically excluded from the imperative needs category. In 1993, in Montréal, this threshold was $18,000 per year for a person living alone or a couple. For a one-parent family with one or two children, it was $22,000. In smaller cities like Drummondville, Shawinigan, Thetford Mines or Valleyfield, a person living alone or a couple could not receive over $14,500 per year to be considered as having imperative housing needs.

It is also difficult to believe governments when they claim that the number of tenant households with imperative housing needs has diminished slightly, when the census data shows, on the contrary, that the number of households paying over 30% of their income for rent increased by 25,000 between 1986 and 1991!

D. Becoming a property owner?

In 1971, 47.4% of the Québec population lived in property-owning households. In 1991, this proportion was 56%. Quebecers are no longer "a population of tenants," although this is still the case in the larger cities, including Montréal, Québec City, Longueuil, Sherbrooke and Hull.

That's not all: surveys conducted by the CMHC claim that it is still possible for a large percentage of tenants to become homeowners. In Montréal, slightly over one third of tenants could buy their first home. The necessary income is estimated at $38,930. In Québec City, this proportion would rise to 40%, with a necessary income of $32,680.[10]

These figures are certainly debatable. One may seriously ask whether, in seeking to take advantage of current mortgage rates and certain government measures, such as the use of their registered retirement savings plan (RRSP) or the possibility of making a 5% down payment, some households risk excessively indebting themselves to buy a home. They put themselves in the position of losing it the first time they experience a major financial setback, of which there are many in these tough economic times: plant closings, layoffs, reduction of working hours without financial compensation.

What these surveys primarily show is that for most tenants, becoming a homeowner is a completely impossible dream. While the average income of property-owning households was $52,269 in 1991, tenants only averaged $28,136. Even more revealing is the fact that half the tenant households earned under $24,382 per year.[11]

What the census data also shows is that for a minority of homeowners, buying a home has meant a disproportionate financial effort. In 1991, 82,590 property-owning households spent over half their income on housing. Over 80% of them had to pay a mortgage.[12] The federal and Québec governments consider that 61,000 property-owning households, or 4.2%, have imperative housing needs.[13]

E. Government and housing: Everything for the private sector!

In Canada and Québec, government housing interventions, since they first began in the 1940s, have given priority to assisting individuals and families that have the financial means either to buy residential property or to invest in rental housing. This has been done through direct subsidies and through an arsenal of tax exemptions. The best known of these, the capital gains exemption on the sale of a principal residence, cost the federal government nearly $4.7 billion in one year (1989), and another $500 million for the Québec government.[14]

In such a context, there has never been any question of mass producing social housing. This explains why there is much less social housing in Canada and Québec than in Great Britain, the Netherlands (where it represented 70% of the rental housing stock in the late 1980s) or in Sweden, where it accounted for 55%.[15] Social housing in Québec has only slowly emerged from the fringes, and even then only due to many grassroots pressures and initiatives. In 1991, it accounted for about 10% of the rental housing stock. One out of ten housing units therefore escaped the private market and real estate speculation.

Growth of Social Housing as a Proportion of the Rental Housing Stock[16]			
Year	Social housing	Rental housing	%
1971	4,000	843,000	0.5
1976	24,000	940,000	2.5
1981	60,000	1,015,000	5.9
1986	96,000	1,062,000	9.0
1991	114,000	1,169,000	9.7

F. The federal massacre of social housing

In the wake of the return to pure economic liberalism, the resurgence of "every man for himself" — exclusive reliance on the market and the general assault on social gains (in health, education, income, etc.) — the development of social housing has been put in neutral.

The first blow was struck by the federal government which, because of its spending power, had always played the leading role in funding social housing. Annual production of new social housing began to decline in the early 1980s under the Liberals, but the major cuts came with the Conservatives under Brian Mulroney.

The first of these cuts occurred in 1986, with the signing of the *Federal-Provincial Agreement on Social Housing*. Housing assistance was henceforth reserved for the poorest of the poor. Social housing subsidies, already inadequate, were also made available to private enterprise through rent supplements.

The second cut began in 1990, when the Conservatives, budget after budget, reduced transfer payments to the provinces for production of new social housing. This resulted in a dramatic drop in the number of units "committed"[17] each year.

The fatal blow came with the budget of April 26, 1993, which announced that Ottawa would no longer ensure the long-term funding of new social housing as of January 1, 1994. Since it had already abolished its housing cooperative assistance program in 1992, this clearly meant that the federal government would no longer fund a single unit of low-rental housing, cooperative housing, or urban native housing. The five-year freeze on CMHC's budget also forced it to turn to existing social housing to save money, creating the current risks of rent increases and deterioration in these units.

Number of Social Housing Units Annually "Committed" to Québec from 1985 to 1994[18]	
1985	6258
1986	4907
1987	4327
1988	3727
1989	3619
1990	3646
1991	3320
1992	2051
1993	1799
1994	0

It now remains to be seen what Jean Chrétien's Liberal government will do about this situation. Will it agree to reestablish certain budgets or will it endorse the Conservative cuts? Part of the answer will surely come from the amount of public pressure to which the government is subjected.[19]

G. The Québec government: a middle management role

Even though it has responsibility for housing, the Québec government has never really exercised it. Over twenty-five years after the creation of the SHQ, the Province still has no housing policy. Neither does it have its own social housing programs. Up to now, the Québec government has settled for getting money from Ottawa, adding its own financial contribution and managing these funds according to its priorities.

When it has taken initiatives in housing, this has been done almost exclusively to fund individual assistance programs, whether for recovery of the construction industry, access to home ownership, renovation or shelter allowances.

H. Privatization

...through rent supplements

Even in its use of federal programs and funds, the provincial Liberals[20] have chosen to favour the private market by making ample use of the rent supplement program. Out of 26,600 social housing units allocated by Ottawa from 1987 to 1993, 5,900, or over one in five, were sacrificed to the private sector.

This privatization of part of the social housing budget has favoured owners of rental units in a period of high vacancy rates. It has been the worst way to help people who are poorly housed, since it does not produce permanent housing, offers lower-quality units and does not remove any housing from the speculative market. The last straw is that studies have also shown that the rent supplement is more costly than real social housing in the long run.[21]

...through shelter allowances

Assistance to people who are poorly housed has also been privatized through development of the shelter allowance. Two programs currently exist: Logirente, which is aimed at seniors and for which the age of eligibility is gradually being reduced to age 55, and a shelter allowance for welfare families with minor children. In the latter case, the allowance is built into the welfare cheque. At the end of 1992, over 120,000 Québec households received a shelter allowance, compared to 36,000 in 1986, making this the leading form of aid to people who are poorly housed.

The shelter allowance is paid directly to tenants to help them pay their rent. However, aid is minimal and goes to the private market. In July 1993, the average amount granted to welfare families was $63 a month.[22] These families therefore continue to spend 40%, 45% and even 50% of their income on housing. The government could also take away the shelter allowance at any time. All this undoubtedly explains why the real estate lobby, usually little inclined to help people who are poorly housed, has always called for this measure.

Worst of all, even while the government congratulates itself for helping 74,500 welfare families with a shelter allowance, it has cut $100 a month from the welfare cheques of 111,500 people who share their dwellings. In 1993, $133 million was clawed from Québec's poorest residents through this measure.[23] What a fine way to help people who are poorly housed!

...and through residential renovation

As for PRIL (Programme de rénovation des immeubles résidentiels), the rental housing renovation program portrayed by the government as social housing, this claim is only true when PRIL grants are used for cooperative and non-profit units. In all other cases, PRIL only serves to increase property values. If real improvements are made to the dwelling, the same tenants benefit from them all too rarely.

Several studies have shown that restoration programs result in substantial rent increases and the forced departure of a large percentage of tenants. An evaluation of the existing program's application in Montréal shows that these problems still exist: "The rent increase when the lease is renewed proves to be an obstacle to reintegration. In closed subsidy files in 1990, 16% of tenants were unable to return to their dwellings because of this obstacle. To illustrate the problem, a survey of files recommended in 1989 showed an average $127 increase after the work."[24]

It does not seem that the federal government's pullout will induce the Québec government to abandon its trend to privatization in favour of a more resolute shift to social housing.[25] On the contrary, in their representations following the cuts, the Liberal government and Minister Claude Ryan asked Ottawa for financial compensation that would be used for private rent supplements, shelter allowances and residential renovation!

I. What about the cities?

The federal and provincial governments have the financial capacity to develop social housing. It is therefore unacceptable that they try to download their housing responsibilities onto city councils.

However, municipalities can play an important role in protecting the rental housing stock, for example by prohibiting demolition of buildings or their conversion into condos. They can also play a role in the development of social housing by using the tools currently or potentially at their disposal: zoning, use of land reserves, housing acquisition policy, and topping up renovation subsidies for non-profit housing or cooperatives.

However, very few cities are willing to do this. Most have no housing policy. Some municipalities no longer request new social housing or, even worse, refuse it, as in the case of the Québec City suburb of Sainte-Foy. Others, like Repentigny, don't even have a municipal housing office to look after their poorly housed residents.

J. Rent controls? What for?

Except during World War II and the immediate postwar period, when the federal government froze and then gradually unfroze rents under the Wartime Leasehold Regulations imposed in 1941, there has never been universal rent control in Québec. The Québec government, which should have this responsibility, prefers to allow free rein to the private market, limiting its role to attacking the most flagrant abuses. In 1992-1993, barely 8,032 applications for rent fixation were filed at the Régie du logement. At the same time, the Régie acted as a rent collection agency, opening 32,021 rent recovery files.[26]

The government has also indicated no serious will to wage a real battle against discrimination. A few landlords were recently condemned to pay fairly substantial damages after being found guilty of discrimination in renting a dwelling. However, such cases are still very rare, and the burden of the complaint falls on the prospective tenants, the vast majority of whom can't or don't want to get involved in procedures lasting months or years for a dwelling they have been unable to occupy.

K. Let's talk money!

While invoking the public debt to make cuts in social housing, Ottawa and Québec maintained and increased tax privileges. When the Conservatives came to power in 1985, the *Nielsen Report* reviewed all government spending and found that housing-related tax exemptions cost the State "considerable revenues" that "scarcely benefit Canadians in the greatest need of housing assistance" and that taxing these benefits to invest more money in social housing "would be a step forward on the socioeconomic front."[27]

Since 1985, governments have even allowed a lifetime tax exemption on capital gains of $100,000 or less. In 1989, this tax shelter deprived the federal government of $985 million.[28] In 1990, the same measure cost the Québec government $273 million.[29] Until 1993, this exemption could be used in the real estate field. This made a major contribution to speculation, rental housing flips, expulsion of tenants and inflation of housing costs.

This is only one example. Tax exemptions cost billions of dollars a year, are unproductive and mainly benefit the rich. It is largely due to these exemptions that governments face the deficits that they now claim they want to reduce at our expense.

Moreover, when the State dares to tell us that it has no more money for social housing, it should be reminded that this isn't the only type of housing that is subsidized. All dwellings, without exception, have been or will be, through taxation exemptions, subsidies to landlords and prospective landlords. In addition, the billions of government dollars spent on welfare, unemployment or old age security cheques that go directly to landlords to pay the rent!

Part II: PROUD's housing policy: For a real attack on the problem

This analysis shows that the private market is a failure, due to the contradiction between the needs of people who are poorly housed and the needs of the market. For poorly housed families and individuals, housing is a necessity, an essential consumer good. For the vast majority of landlords, it is an investment that must be made profitable at any cost, regardless of the victims. This is why PROUD proposes a comprehensive policy of access to housing, focusing on social housing instead of the sacrosanct marketplace.[30]

A. The principles
1. Housing is not a commodity like any other. It is primarily a basic right to which everyone must have full access, regardless of their income, gender, social status, race, physical or mental condition, etc.
2. Since private enterprise, based solely on the profit motive, is incapable of respecting this right and enabling everyone to have access to housing, the State must play a key role in housing.
3. Residents must have more control over their housing conditions and living environment.

B. 100,000 new social housing units by the year 2000
The development of social housing must be intensified in all its forms, including low-rental housing, cooperatives, non-profit organizations and native housing. At least 100,000 new social housing units should be produced in Québec by the year 2000, both through purchase and renovation and through new construction, under existing programs and by creation of other formulas, such as a Québec cooperative housing program and a rental housing acquisition program.

Why 100,000 units of social housing? Because it is necessary that by the turn of the century, large-scale action has been taken to reduce the scope of the housing problem and because social housing is the best vehicle to achieve this goal.

Social housing is the only way for poorly housed people to have access to affordable housing. It offers much better quality housing than the private market, dwellings which can also be adapted to specific needs and requests. Primarily under the cooperative formula, it can empower people and give them greater control over their living conditions. Finally, it contributes to the physical improvement of old neighbourhoods, maintenance of the resident population and a more general improvement in the quality of life.

C. Real social housing

While it believes in the development of social housing, PROUD is also fighting to ensure that it meets all of the public's needs even more adequately. This is why it makes the following demands:

Quality housing: Social housing should be of good quality and integrated into the surrounding community. It should have adequate services and facilities, including those for people with handicaps or reduced mobility. Finally, wherever necessary, it should include government-funded community support.

Low-rental: The rent should not exceed 25% of tenants' income. To prevent situations where households, which often have a short-term increase in their income, have to leave social housing, a rent ceiling should be set. The rent could also be based on the tenants' net income.

Wider access: Any individual or family in need should have access to social housing without any restrictions. Social housing should also encourage the greatest possible mix of low and moderate incomes, family situations, ethnic origins and cultures, etc.

Tenant control: PROUD favours the greatest possible control by tenants of their housing conditions, in all types of social housing.

Maintenance of existing tenants: All social housing produced in the existing housing stock should allow tenants already there to remain, with their acquired rights respected.

Permanent housing: The government should stop using rent supplements on the private market and should convert units for which these supplements have been allocated into real social housing.

D. Control of the private housing market

Even though it is impossible to change the nature of the private market, PROUD considers it essential to try to prevent the situation of poorly housed people from worsening even further. This is why it demands:

Mandatory universal rent control: All rents must be controlled annually by the Régie du logement. Access to the Régie must be completely free of charge.

Severe measures to fight discrimination: The government must take the responsibility to prosecute landlords who are guilty of discrimination in renting a dwelling.

Preservation of the low-rent housing stock and maintenance of tenants in their homes: The conversion of rental housing into condos must be prohibited throughout Québec. Rental housing renovation subsidies, which penalize the existing tenants instead of improving their lot, should be reserved exclusively for social housing.

Total abolition of the welfare cut for shared housing: The government must stop penalizing welfare recipients who are simply trying to make ends meet by sharing a dwelling.

E. Full responsibility for the Québec government

The Québec government should have full responsibility for housing. This requires that it adopt its own housing policy and social housing programs.

Municipalities must be involved in social housing by adopting a housing policy and tools for development of social housing and protection of the housing stock.

Furthermore, for as long as Québec remains within confederation, recognition of its responsibility for housing must be accompanied by a major financial contribution from Ottawa, in the form of direct financing or transfer of tax points. Québec's accession to independence would give it all the economic tools necessary to take over the housing question completely.

F. Review of budget and fiscal choices

A real social housing policy would require additional government spending, although it would allow major long-term savings in such fields on health and social services and would have a significant impact on the economy, particularly in terms of job creation.

To achieve this goal, governments must review their budget priorities. For example, the federal government continues to allocate at least 10 percent of its budget to military spending. This money would be more socially useful if it served to finance social housing. The same principle applies for certain Québec government expenditures, such as hydroelectric megaprojects or financing of the Montréal and Charlevoix casinos.

There must also be a thorough review of taxation, the means by which governments obtain revenues to finance their spending. Several tax exemptions should be abolished immediately, including the $100,000 capital gains exemption. Others should be seriously limited, such as the tax exemption on capital gains obtained from the sale of a principal residence or the rule that allows landlords to deduct certain expenses from their rental income. Corporation taxes should also be higher and loopholes should be closed.

A more equitable redistribution of wealth is necessary for a lasting in-depth attack on the housing problem. This requires a radical requestioning of the dictates of the market, which is synonymous with poverty for hundreds of thousands of individuals and families.

> *Johanne Beauregard*, age 33, mother of one child, lived in 1993 in "Aux beaux soleils," a Châteauguay housing project run by a non-profit organization. She paid a rent of $252, heating and electricity included, while a basement apartment on the private market used to cost her $500. "Before it was cold and damp. Now I'm finally warm and have enough to eat. I can stop worrying and get on with my life. I'm treasurer of the project, which is very worthwhile because it has gotten me out of my apartment and taught me accounting."
>
> *Ginette Fillion*, mother of four children, lived in the same project. Her large 6 1/2 costs her $303 everything included, compared to the $570 she previously had to pay for a small basement 5 1/2:
>
> The children were always sick. My basement smelled damp and I couldn't afford to heat it more. Now we have a good apartment. The children are happy and much less sick. They have a better self-image and a better image of their mother. I feel secure because now I can get along on my own while paying my rent and I can give my children a comfortable home.

G. Pay the rent... or eat?

Hundreds of thousands of tenant households ask the same question month after month: how to pay the rent? How to pay the rent when your income amounts to welfare, unemployment or old age security benefits or comes from insecure, underpaid or part-time jobs? How to pay the rent without cutting elsewhere — in food, clothing, transportation or the few types of recreation still affordable?

The 1991 Canadian census data[31] tells us that 517,825 tenant households in Québec[32] had to spend over one quarter of their gross income on housing, which includes electricity, heating and access to municipal services. Some of these households have good incomes and are not necessarily poorly housed. But for the vast majority, the opposite is true.

404,045 tenant households, more than one household in three, paid over 30% of their income for rent, the level that governments consider critical. Even worse, for 194,225 of these households, half their income went to housing. More than one out of six were in this dramatic situation.

H. Yes, but the rents haven't increased much…

From 1986 to 1991, the average rent in Québec increased by 13% to $480 per month. This increase was far less than the 62% average for the period from 1981 to 1986.

So how can we explain why the plight of tenant households has not improved? Simply because most of them have not benefited from the so-called economic recovery of the late 1980s. In fact, they never recovered from the setbacks of the early part of the decade.

Like all statistics, these figures are misleading. Since they are based on averages, they mask the reality experienced by many tenant households whose impoverishment was much more serious due to the permanent loss of employment, the application of Bill 37 on "income security" or unemployment insurance restrictions.

We must also remember that the 1991 census data could not account for the effects of the last recession, which created more than its share of permanent victims. No doubt the plight of tenants will be even more difficult next year.

I. What does it mean if you run out of money?

For low-income tenants, the first day of the month represents a puzzle that can only be solved through often painful sacrifices. In the fall of 1993, a press conference held by the Metropolitan Montréal Round Table on Hunger[33] identified the cost of housing as one of the factors contributing to the major increase in distribution of groceries at food banks and meals served by community organizations and charities. In November 1992, Harvest Montréal distributed over twenty tonnes of food every day, representing over 20,000 meals per day in the Montréal metropolitan region.

The president of Moisson Québec, describing the situation in the Québec City region, was just as explicit: "Families and individuals who live off unemployment benefits or welfare and who don't have enough income start by paying the rent and electricity, especially in winter. Then they think of feeding themselves and quite often they don't have any more money for personal hygiene products, which are expensive."[34]

For a growing number of households, even these sacrifices are no longer enough. Régie du logement statistics show that the phenomenon of non-payment of rent has grown. Applications filed by landlords for cancellation of lease and recovery of rent rose from an annual average of 14,500 between 1981 and 1984 to 36,500 between 1990 and 1993, a 250% increase! In 1992-1993, these applications accounted for 43% of all cases filed at the Régie.[35]

Another sign of difficulty paying the rent is the increase in the number of sudden abandonments, even though the problem is far from having the scope claimed by certain landlord associations. In 1992-1993, 8,908 cases of abandonment were filed at the Régie, an increase of 2,000 cases compared to 1989.[36]

J. When the electricity or gas bills arrive...

While rents have not increased much in the past few years, the situation is completely different for electricity bills which jumped 23% in just one year, 1990-1991. Under these circumstances, it is not surprising that the total amount of Hydro-Québec's bad debts soared by 81% between 1988 and 1991 before climbing slightly in 1992.[37]

Unpaid utility bills often result in service being cut off. In 1988, there were 26,000 service cuts,[38] increasing to 30,300 in 1992.[39] Hydro-Québec announced in 1993 that it would no longer disconnect anybody between December 1 and March 31, "except in cases of fraud or theft." It took the death of a man in the Mauricie, poisoned by propane heater fumes after his power had been cut, for the provincial crown corporation to agree to end this inhuman practice. In exchange, it announced plans to cut off service 90 days after billing instead of 120.

Gaz Métropolitain also increased its service interruptions for non-payment, which rose from 2,371 in 1990 to 3,613 in 1992.[40]

Jacqueline Cayen, age 32, mother of three children, lived on $1,442 per month (welfare and family allowance) in 1993. She had recently returned to school and expected to obtain a high school diploma in January 1995.

"My rent costs me $350 per month, plus $150 for electricity. It's cold near the windows in winter and I heat the shed. To put down $500 for the rent, I have to cut back on food and clothing. And there'd better not be any unexpected expenses."

Luc D., age 22, of Montréal's Pointe-Saint-Charles district, had lived in his apartment for four years in 1993 and hoped to work in theatre some day. He was making $580 on welfare, but because he hadn't managed to find a place in the school system to complete his education, they were threatening to cut him to $500 a month.

"My 3 1/2 costs me $340 a month, plus about $100 for heating and electricity. In a co-op at least I could manage and wouldn't be obliged to cut back on food."

Colette Charest, age 57, of Montréal, had to give up her waitressing job eleven years earlier for health reasons. Since then she had been on welfare. Every month, she received $662, with which she had to pay a $310 rent and an $87 electricity bill.

Because her former dwelling was very cold, to the extent that the water froze in the corner, and Hydro-Québec had underestimated her electricity costs, she also had to repay $331 by February 1994, or else she would be cut.

> *Johanne Lepage* lived in Châteauguay with her four children in 1993. She received $1,046 from welfare and $478 in family allowance. She paid 46% of her income for housing: $540 in rent and $160 for electricity.
>
> I don't go out and I'm very worried about the bills coming in. I'm lucky that Brother René helped us a lot with gifts of good. I sew my own clothes and I'm involved in a collective kitchen to make ends meet.

K. Who is poorly housed?

Behind the statistics, there are people, the majority of them women. Some of the data is revealing. The 1991 census showed that when a women is the principal financial support of the household, there are two chances out of three that she was a tenant. The proportions were reversed in the case of men! Even among tenant households, the ones most poorly housed are those whose principal financial support is a woman.

People living alone and one-parent families, increasingly numerous in our society, are the tenant households that spend the highest percentage of their income on housing. Close to half of people living alone sacrifice over 30% of their income.

Age also plays a major role: the categories most poorly housed are young people from 15 to 24, pre-retired people from 55 to 64 and seniors over age 65, even though the situation of this last group has improved significantly over the past two decades.

Finally, members of cultural communities, especially new immigrants, are among the categories of tenants most likely to be poorly housed. The Conseil des communautés culturelles et de l'immigration found that in 1986, nearly one quarter of households originating from third world countries had to spend over half their income on housing.[41]

L. Homelessness: The tip of the iceberg is growing

According to the last estimate available, from 1989, 15,000 to 20,000 people were "homeless" in Montréal, meaning that they had no fixed address and did not have the assurance of a stable, safe and sanitary dwelling for the next 60 days.[42]

Homelessness has many causes which help make it the tip of the iceberg of the housing crisis. According to the Réseau d'aide aux personnes seules et itinérantes, a support network for the homeless, there are several signs that this phenomenon is worsening.

More and more women are in a homeless situation, either on the street, in facilities for the homeless, in shelters for women in difficulty, or in the misery-drugs-prostitution network. Women make less use of resources, "getting along" in other ways. They account for 40to 45% of the homeless population.

An ever-growing number of young people are on the street. According to an estimate by the Régie régionale de la santé de Montréal-Centre, the regional health board for central Montréal, the percentage of youth among the homeless population rose from 15 to 20% in 1988 to over 30% today [1993]. Between 8 and 10% of homeless people are under eighteen years of age. Resources for youth are clearly inadequate. Those that exist are often nothing more than dormitories or mobile units that accommodate them for a few moments. Young people don't squat in abandoned buildings just because they have a taste for adventure; it's mainly out of necessity.

Refugees are a new but growing part of the homeless population. In 1992, over 500 of these people stayed in Réseau d'aide centres. Entire families were often separated in different centres for the night and met each other back on the sidewalk next morning.

Natives living in an urban environment also rank among the populations most affected by homelessness. There are at least 15,000 in Montréal, the majority of them women.

The health of homeless people obviously deteriorates quickly. The fact that they live on the street or in rooms in bad condition, eating little and badly, has catastrophic consequences for the lives of these men and women. Condemned to prostitution and often drug addicted, part of the homeless population is in a situation of epidemic development of diseases linked to these degrading living conditions. For example, tuberculosis is on the rise, causing great concern for hospitals. But the greatest catastrophe is the high rate of people living with AIDS. The HIV positive rate increased in the homeless population from 5 or 6% in 1987 to 15% in 1990 and 30% in 1993. The streets are becoming a place to die!

M. Busing continues

Although homelessness is not uniquely a Montréal phenomenon, this problem is concentrated in Québec's metropolis. The lack of resources in other Québec cities and towns, the systematic repression exercised by some municipal administrations against the homeless and their hardline refusal to develop social housing, mean that many homeless people end up in Montréal. Sometimes they are pushed to go there. The practice of putting homeless people on buses with a one-way ticket to Montréal still exists. Some off-island police forces also continue to dump them downtown.

Being homeless anywhere in the province but Montréal generally means having no resources. Some cities like Québec or Hull, where resources do exist, are now seeing their homeless population rise.

N. Women and homelessness: The many faces of misery

A growing number of women have no fixed address, but unlike men, less of them end up on the street. Because of the assaults to which they fall victim when they are on the street, many of them will prefer to take refuge with men who are part of their problem. They will tolerate the intolerable for a few weeks or a few months, living with their pimp, abuser (ex-husband, father, stepfather) or pusher, before going elsewhere, but never to a place of their own.

Poverty and violence constantly add to the number of homeless women, doomed to prostitute themselves or sell drugs. Society judges or condemns them, as we have seen several times in Montréal's Centre-Sud district, rather than dealing with the violence and poverty that have brought them to this situation.

Despite the development of some resources intended to serve them, several hundred women are refused by shelters every month and return to their "network." Shelters for battered women often cannot accommodate them, either because they have no children or because of their drug habit.

More and more women over the age of 40 end up homeless. An unexpected situation arises and their months of rent in arrears start to add up: they lose their apartment, and the stress often triggers illness and a hospital stay. When they get out of hospital, these women, for the first time in their lives, find themselves going to shelters. Some women are victims of their children who batter and rob them. Not daring to complain, they are totally deprived of resources.

While it used to be possible for some homeless women to escape their plight, deteriorating economic conditions now make this almost impossible. Society no longer allows women to recover.

Shelters now find themselves dealing with the same women who they had seen at age 30 or 40 a decade ago, more worn out, aged by misery and without hope. As for young women, while the government's adoption of welfare parity for recipients under 30 back in 1990 allowed some of them to get off the street, another welfare cut penalized over 3,000 young men and women in Québec who lived with their parents,[43] reducing their monthly cheques to $109 in some cases. This was a perfect invitation to go live on the street.[44]

O. Access to housing denied

Housing discrimination, though identified a decade ago by the Québec Human Rights Commission and by several studies as a major problem, remains largely misunderstood and unchallenged.

More than two out of three women are affected

A 1986 survey, conducted in three Montréal working-class neighbourhoods and published by the Comité logement Rosemont and PROUD, made the following observation: "40% of women have experienced situations of obvious discrimination and 47.8% have suffered from situations of harassment (in 15% of the cases, this involved sexual harassment). 68.4% of the women tenants interviewed have experienced one of these situations. This percentage is 86% in the case of women on welfare."[45]

Anne Roberge of Société d'habitation du Québec analyzed the problem in the following terms in a study of women's housing conditions: "The sources of discrimination and harassment are economic and ideological. Ideological factors are reflected in conflicts of values (marginal situation compared to the norm) and paternalism, and most often concern marital status, sexuality and economic status. The landlord-tenant relationship is compounded by the male-female relationship."[46]

"You're the wrong colour..."

The Québec Human Rights Commission has also conducted investigations of discrimination practiced against members of ethnic communities. One of these studies, dating from 1988, showed that one third of French-speaking Blacks and 15% of English-speaking Blacks were victims of flagrant discrimination, while landlords exhibited great suspicion towards black visitors, both Anglophone and Francophone.[47]

Other studies by the Commission have revealed that "in general, visible minorities pay higher rents for smaller apartments, end up living in small enclaves scattered across the city and have to put up with more discrimination for all types of housing."[48]

Economic discrimination

Another fast-growing form of discrimination is economic, based on income.

As the Québec Human Rights Commission observed: "In the logic of the rental market where housing is a business, proof of ability to pay or solvency is the condition of access to housing to all intents and purposes. [...] Yet because of their meagre economic resources, often combined with other disadvantages related to gender, family situation, ethnicity, age and ignorance of their rights, a growing number of individuals do not pass the "test" and therefore do not have access to housing."[49]

This last form of discrimination is applied in several ways: flat refusal to "rent to welfare recipients," rental forms or information forms, credit checks, requests for endorsers, etc.

The problem is that a substantial part of economic discrimination is "legal." As the Québec Human Rights Commission acknowledges, "the landlord is entitled to know whether the tenant is providing sufficient guarantees that he will pay his rent regularly."[50] What is clearly at stake here is the very nature of the private housing market, where housing is considered a commodity rather than a right. If you don't have enough money, that's just too bad!

> *Jocelyne Saint-Hilaire and her husband Luc*, of Pointe-Gatineau, were welfare recipients with four young children. In October 1993, the owner evicted them without even going to court, because the family, for the first time, was unable to pay the rent in full immediately. "She didn't fool around. The next day, she put a "for rent sign" on the door."
>
> Over the rest of the month, Jocelyne visited a dozen dwellings. Everywhere she went, she was given the same answer: "You have four children. They're too young. The yard won't stay clean," "The flat is new. The children will damage it," or "You're on welfare. The rent is too expensive. You won't be able to manage."
>
> "It was horrible," Jocelyne recalled. "The landlords didn't mince any words." After this nightmarish experience, the family finally managed to find a place, but at a high rent.

NOTES

1. Published as *Logement et pauvreté au Québec: Dossier noir* by Front d'action populaire en réaménagement urbain (FRAPRU), known in English as People's Rights Over Urban Development (PROUD) (editor's note).

    People's Rights Over Urban Development is a Québec coalition, founded in 1978 to fight for the right to housing. Because of their knowledge from daily experience that the private market does not work, PROUD and its forty member groups active in different Québec regions, have made social housing the focus of their concerns and efforts. For more information on PROUD/FRAPRU, subscribe to its newsletter, *Le FRAPRU frappe encore!* or become a member, by writing to FRAPRU, 1212 Rue Panet, Bureau 318, Montréal H2L 2Y7. Phone: (514) 522-1010. Fax: (514) 527-3403.

    PROUD/FRAPRU's member organizations included the following participating groups in 1993:
    - Alerte Centre-Sud, Montréal
    - Association des locataires de Thetford-Mines
    - Comité de logement de l'Accent, Sherbrooke
    - Comité de logement social de Châteauguay
    - Comité de citoyens et citoyennes du quartier Saint-Sauveur, Québec City
    - Comité Logemen'occupe, Hull
    - Comité Logement Bordeaux-Cartierville, Montréal
    - Comité Logement Rosemont, Montréal
    - Comité populaire Saint-Jean-Baptiste, Québec City
    - Fédération des locataires d'habitation à loyer modique du Québec
    - Info-Logement, Buckingham
    - Institution d'éducation populaire des Bois-Francs, Drummondville
    - NDG Community Council, Montréal
    - Popir Comité-logement Saint-Henri-Petite-Bourgogne, Montréal
    - Regroupement Information-logement Pointe Saint-Charles, Montréal
    - Réseau d'aide aux personnes seules et itinérantes de Montréal

    The following groups were associate members of PROUD/FRAPRU in 1993:
    - Association des locataires de l'Office municipal de l'habitation de Mont-Saint-Hilaire
    - Association latino-américaine de Côte-des-Neiges, Montréal
    - Bureau consultation jeunesse, Montréal
    - Carrefour d'aide aux réfugiés, Montréal
    - Centre des femmes de la Basse-Ville, Québec
    - Cité des bâtisseurs, Baie-Comeau
    - Comité Logement Centre-Sud, Montréal
    - Comité Logement Saint-Louis, Montréal
    - Comité pour le développement du logement social, Sorel
    - Fédération des coopératives d'habitation de la Montérégie
    - Fédération des organismes sans but lucratif en habitation de Montréal
    - Groupe d'aménagement du logement populaire, Joliette
    - Groupe alternative logement, Saint-Jean
    - Groupe de ressources techniques Beauce-Amiante
    - Groupe de ressources techniques de Laval
    - Habitations populaires de l'Est, Rimouski

- Inter-loge Centre-Sud, Montréal
- Justice et foi, Montréal
- Montréal City Mission
- Multi-Caf de Côte-des-Neiges, Montréal
- Opération populaire d'aménagement, Centre-Sud, Montréal
- Programme d'aide au logement, Verdun
- Project Genesis, Côte-des-Neiges, Montréal
- SOS-Logement, Beauharnois

2. *La rénovation résidentielle: un engagement commun pour la qualité de vie et la croissance économique*, information document for Les Entretiens sur l'habitat, April 1993, p. 5.
3. Ibid., p. 10.
4. *La Politique de la santé et du bien-être*, Ministère de la Santé et des Services sociaux, 2nd quarter 1992, p. 159.
5. Ibid., p. 160.
6. The track record of the subsequent Parti Québécois governments of Jacques Parizeau and Lucien Bouchard hasn't been much better. Deficit cutting has taken precedence over social programs (editor's note).
7. Canada Mortgage and Housing Corporation (CMHC), *Statistiques du logement au Canada 1992*, 1993, p. 66.
8. SHQ, *Les besoins impérieux*, 1993, p. 1.
9. CMHC, op. cit., p. 63.
10. *Habitabec*, May 21, 1993.
11. Statistics Canada, *Équipment ménager selon le revenu et d'autres caractéristiques, 1992*, February 1993, p. 51.
12. "Recensement 1991, Coûts d'habitation et autres caractéristiques des ménages au Canada," *Le pays*, May 1993, p. 79.
13. CMHC, op. cit.,, p. 66.
14. Government of Canada, *Compte des dépenses fiscales liées au revenu des particuliers*, December 1992, p. 15. Also see the letter to PROUD from Claude Ryan, Minister of Municipal Affairs responsible for housing, May 21, 1993, p. 2.
15. Richard Morin, Francine Dansereau and Daniel Nadeau, *L'Habitation sociale, Synthèse de la littérature*, INRS-Urbanisation, 1990, p. 7.
16. SHQ, op. cit., *Document d'information et de discussion pour la Table de concertation sur l'habitation*, March 1990, p. 6; for 1991, PROUD estimate based on census data.
17. This term refers to the budget estimates of the federal government, which are committed each year to pay the Québec government enough money to acquire a specified number of units intended for social housing.
18. This table, produced from data in the CMHC and SHQ annual reports, does not include units committed under the rent supplement program.
19. After nearly three years in office, the Chrétien Liberals have shown themselves to be Conservatives in sheep's clothing. Mulroney's social housing cuts have not been reversed, and even more social programs have been axed (editor's note).
20. This document was written when the Québec Liberals were still in power. Despite some reshuffling, improvement under the Parti Québécois has been minimal (editor's note).

21. Among other sources, see *La SHQ, propriétaires et locataires de logement*, SHQ, 1990, 29 pages plus appendices.
22. Ministère de la Main-d'oeuvre, de la Sécurité du revenu et de la Formation professionnelle, *Rapport statistique mensuel. Programmes de la Sécurité du revenu*, July 1993, p. 25.
23. Ibid. Rather than reversing the Liberal welfare cuts, the Parti Québécois has slashed even more from welfare cheques. Even participants in "workfare" programs were cut $30 a month in April 1996 as part of Lucien Bouchard's "we all have to share the burden" budget cuts. The penalty for sharing accommodation remains (editor's note).
24. *Bilan de la deuxième année d'intervention auprès des locataires*, prepared by Claude Jourdain for Atelier habitation Montréal, October 1990, p. 11. The evaluation covers the Programme d'amélioration résidentielle Canada-Québec (PARCQ), also known as the Residential Housing Improvement Program, which was replaced by PRIL after its abolition by the federal government in 1989.
25. At the time this document was written in 1993 (editor's note).
26. Régie du logement, *Rapport annuel 1992-1993*, 2nd quarter 1993, p. 19. The number of rent fixation applications fell to 4,575 in 1993-1994 and 3,726 in 1994-1995, according to the Régie's 1994-1995 annual report (editor's note).
27. *Rapport du Groupe d'étude sur les programmes de logement au Groupe de travail ministériel chargé de l'examen des programmes*, June 27, 1985, p. 141. The quotations are translated from the French version of the report.
28. Government of Canada, *Compte des dépenses fiscales liées au revenu des particuliers*, December 1992, p. 13.
29. Gouvernement du Québec, *Les Finances publiques du Québec: Vivre selon nos moyens*, 1st quarter 1993, p. 113.
30. The first version of the PROUD/FRAPRU housing policy was published in May 1984 until the title *Pour une politique globale d'accès au logement*. In February 1989, it was updated in a manifesto entitled *Une politique de logement social, ça presse*. The current version has been adapted to the positions adopted since then by PROUD/FRAPRU.
31. "Recensement 1991, Coûts d'habitation et autres caractéristiques des ménages au Canada," *Le pays*, May 1993, 253 pages; *Recensement 1991, Catalogue G9107. Ménages privés dans des logements hors-réserve et non agricoles occupés par un locataire selon le groupe d'âge et le site de soutien de ménage par loyer brut en % du revenu du ménage en 1990*. This data shows gross rent as a percentage of household income in 1990 for private households in off-reserve and non-farm dwellings occupied by a tenant, broken down by age group and household support site (editor's note).
32. A household may be an individual or a group of individuals occupying the same dwelling (couple, family with children, cotenants, etc.).
33. Table de concertation sur la faim du Montréal métropolitain.
34. Damien Gagnon, "Moisson Québec est dépassée par l'ampleur de la pauvreté," *Le Soleil*, November 25, 1993.
35. Annual reports of the Régie du logement.
36. Ibid.
37. Hydro-Québec, *Rapport annuel 1991*, p. 16 and Rapport annuel 1992, p. 12.

38. Fédération des ACEF du Québec, *Pour assurer l'accès et la continuité du service électrique à toutes les familles du Québec*, 1st quarter 1990, p.5.
39. Pierre Asselin, "Hydro accéléra bientôt ses débranchements, sauf l'hiver," *Le Soleil*, November 25, 1993.
40. Information supplied by Gaz Métropolitain's Public Relations Department.
41. Conseil des communautés culturelles et de l'immigration, *Le logement et les communautés culturelles*, avis à la Ministère, September 1971, p. 17.
42. Definition established by the Comité des sans-abri de la Ville de Montréal in 1987.
43. Ministère de la Main-d'oeuvre, de la Sécurité du revenu et de la Formation professionnelle, op. cit., p. 26.
44. This section is based on an interview with Micheline Cyr, Director of Auberge Madeleine, a Montréal women's shelter.
45. Comité logement Rosemont, PROUD, *Femmes et logement. Résumé du rapport de l'enquête: Discrimination, harcèlement et harcèlement sexuel*, 1986, p. 1.
46. Anne Roberge, *Données sur la situation des femmes et du logement au Québec*, SHQ, June 1988, p. 10.
47. Commission des droits de la personne du Québec, *Bilan de recherche sur la situation des minorités ethniques et visibles dans le logement*, Montréal, 1988.
48. Commission des droits de la personne du Québec, *Un toit pour Sarah. Guide d'animation sur la discrimination dans le logement,* 4th quarter, 1992, p. 8.
49. Renée Lescop, *Le projet-logement de la Commission des droits de la personne. Bilan, perspectives et propositions d'action pour 1990*, Commission des droits de la personne du Québec, November 3, 1989, p. 125.
50. Ibid.

Chapter 7

The reform of the Civil Code: Important changes for tenants

by Arnold Bennett, 1993

Editor's note: An earlier version of this chapter was published in the Montréal Gazette in three parts in December 1993. The last section on Bill 7 is based on an article I published in the Montréal Gazette of June 13, 1996.

Québec's code of civil law was first published in 1866 as the *Civil Code of Lower Canada*. After years of discussion, an overhauled code, the *Civil Code of Québec*, came into force on January 1, 1994.

While the general principle governing contracts in Québec law allows the parties considerable freedom of negotiation, residential leases are a major exception. Specifically, Section 1893 CcQ stipulates that "a clause in a lease respecting a dwelling which is inconsistent with the provisions of this section... is without effect."

****

When the new Civil Code took effect on January 1, 1994, many of the rules of the game in landlord-tenant relations suddenly changed. Dozens of important technicalities changed, while other sections of the law were rewritten in ways that require interpretation and that use different terminology, especially in the extremely literal English translation.

Ontarians and Americans not accustomed to the "franglais" of the Québec legal system will have to look up *succession* instead of "estate," *hypothec* instead of "mortgage," and *resiliation* instead of "cancellation."

Even the numbering of the Civil Code is completely different. The chapter entitled "Lease" now covers Sections 1851 to 2000, instead of starting at 1650 as it did under the old law. The numbers are important because they appear on all notices of hearings and often are used as a form of legal shorthand in the Régie and court decisions. It can be crucial to know whether your hearing concerns your request for a rent reduction or your landlord's attempt to evict you!

So what are the important changes? One major group of differences concerns ways in which a tenant can get out of a lease. Here are three typical examples:

A. Getting out of a lease

Case 1: You're a tenant in Montréal. You got a job in Toronto and you have to move within the next month, but you're stuck with a lease until July. Do you have to sublet, or can you "assign" the lease and leave without any further liability?

Case 2: You're a duplex owner. You send out a notice of rent increase in January for the July lease renewal but you don't state on the notice that the tenant has only one month to reply. Is your notice still as legal as it was in 1993? Or is it null and void because of your omission?

Case 3: You're 80 years old and you just broke your hip. You live on the top floor of a four-storey walk-up and you have no immediate prospects of getting into a government nursing home. Can you get out of your lease because of your disability?

Case 1: Sublet and assignment

Under the new law, no tenant in his right mind will want to sublet an apartment unless he plans to return after a trip or sabbatical or unless the new occupant is only willing to take the place at a discount.

If you want to move out and never come back, you're much better off "assigning" the lease. The old law made a distinction between a regular assignment or transfer, under which the tenant remained responsible for the lease, just as he would if he sublet, and transfer with "novation," under which the old tenant stopped being liable.

Under the old rules a landlord had to have valid cause to refuse a sublet or regular transfer, but did not have to give a reason for refusing a transfer with novation.

The new rules abolish this distinction. The landlord must have a "serious reason" to refuse any assignment or sublet. This refusal must be given in writing within 15 days of the tenant's notice, which must state the name and address of the proposed new occupant.

Obviously, since a tenant who assigns the lease would be completely off the hook, the landlord can require a credit check and refuse somebody who is insolvent or has bad references. But his reasons for refusal can't be frivolous. They have to be "serious."

Jurisprudence over the past two years has defined the concept of "seriousness" more clearly. In October 1994, one landlord refused a notice of assignment on the grounds that the person proposed had never rented before and had only been working at his first job for a few months. On the other hand, this person was steadily employed and was not in the habit of bouncing cheques. The Régie rejected the landlord's arguments and cancelled the original tenant's lease as of the date of the landlord's refusal.

A tenant who chooses to sublet rather than assign the lease should be aware of the following changes in the law:

- It is legal to sublet "part" of your dwelling. Since a dwelling is defined to include its "accessories" and "dependencies," this means you can sublet a room in your apartment, a parking space or a locker, for example.
- Under the new law, a subtenant and a landlord can sue each other directly for non-performance of obligations, such as failing to do repairs or not paying the rent. Under the old rules, the "principal tenant" had to be dragged in as the defendant if either the landlord or the subtenant wanted to file a claim.
- Under the new law, a tenant can be prevented from subletting to a series of different occupants, returning to the apartment just long enough in between to establish occupancy. The landlord has the right to cancel the lease if the dwelling is sublet for more than 12 months. Under the old law, this right to cancellation only applied if there was a sublet for more than 12 "consecutive" months. For example, a tenant could sublet for eleven months, move back in for a while and then sublet again. Now the sublet periods are cumulative.
- Under the new law, a subtenant can not be required to move out at the end of the lease before receiving 10 days' written notice from the landlord or the "sublessor" (the principal tenant). Under the old law, it was theoretically possible for a subtenant to be asked to leave at the end of the lease with virtually no notice.
- According to recent court decisions, a subtenant's insolvency or inability to pay the rent is not grounds for a landlord to refuse a sublet, because the original tenant remains fully liable.

Case 2: Illegal lease renewal notices

For years, tenant organizations have complained about the rule that allows a landlord to give a notice of increase anywhere from three to six months before the end of a one-year lease.

Many tenants did not realize that they only had one month to answer the landlord's notice, even if it were given in January for a July lease renewal. The Régie's rules on this issue are easy to misinterpret and give many people the false impression that they can wait until three months before the end of the lease to give notice that they don't want to renew the lease.

Under both the old law and the new law, the requirement that the tenant answer the landlord's notice within one month always takes precedence.

As a result, many tenants ended up stuck with lease renewals that they did not want, or with exorbitant rent increases that they had not refused in time.

The new law introduces an important change on this issue that turns the tables in favour of the tenants, to some extent.

Section 1943, paragraph 2 states that if the landlord gives a notice changing the conditions or the term of the lease, that notice must state the tenant's deadline to reply.[1] The written comments by former Justice Minister Gil Rémillard make it clear that this requirement was intended to apply to any "modification" of the lease, such as a rent increase. Because Section 1943 is one of the "public order" provisions of the law, a landlord's notice which does not state the tenant's deadline to reply could be invalid.

If the landlord does not follow up an invalid notice with one that is legal, he could lose his right to any rent increase or changes for that year. Two years of jurisprudence have confirmed this possibility, although the strictness of Régie commissioners varies.

If the tenant wants to leave, he could give notice at any time up to three months before the end of the lease. Failure to respond to an illegal notice could not be held against him.

However, a word of caution is in order. Some of the more recent jurisprudence considers it sufficient for the landlord's notice to request that the tenant reply within one month. The notice does not have to state unequivocally that failure to reply within this deadline will mean automatic renewal of the lease.

Verbal notice

All notices concerning the lease are supposed to be in writing. The new Civil Code allows a possible exemption from this requirement if the person who gave verbal notice can prove that this notice was given and that his failure to give written notice did not cause "prejudice" to the other party (Section 1898).

For example, a tenant who only *told* the landlord that he would be moving out might be able to argue that he gave valid notice of non-renewal, if he could prove it. But this situation cuts both ways and could cause a legal headache for the courts.

Case 3: Helping the handicapped

Under Article 1974 of the new Civil Code, a tenant can break the lease on three months notice if he can no longer occupy the dwelling because of a handicap. The tenant can also cancel the lease on three months' notice if he is permanently admitted to any residential long-term care facility or foster home.

The old law was much more restrictive and made no allowance for people who became handicapped and needed to be hospitalized or to move in with family members. They were stuck with responsibility for the rest of the lease period.

The new law does not define "handicap," so it will remain to be seen how far the courts are willing to stretch this new leniency. Could an illness or allergic condition be interpreted as a "handicap," for example? Could an asthmatic tenant invoke this clause to break the lease if she lives next to a polluted traffic artery like Décarie or Metropolitan Boulevard? How long-term does a disability have to be for the courts to consider it a handicap? Until the courts build up a body of case law, there will be no clear answers to these questions.

Under another important change, any tenant who gives three months notice to break a lease after he is accepted to public subsidized housing, no longer has to worry about being forced to move out before the three months is up.

Under the old law, somebody who gave notice after being accepted to a public housing project could be forced to leave early if the landlord found another tenant within the three months. If the project was a new one and not yet ready for occupancy, this could force the tenant to move twice.

B. Punitive damages for abused tenants

Section 1902 of the new Civil Code improves protection for tenants who are victims of harassment by their landlord. For example, if your landlord tries to evict you for organizing a petition to demand repairs, you could sue him under both Sections 1899 and 1902: discrimination for exercising a legal right, and general harassment.[2]

Under Section 1902, it is illegal for a landlord or "any other person" to harass a tenant "in such a manner as to limit his right to peaceable enjoyment of the premises or to induce him to leave the dwelling." In the case of such harassment, the tenant can ask the Régie du logement to condemn the landlord to pay punitive damages.

Over the past two years, new jurisprudence has emerged, interpreting a landlord's consistent refusal to do necessary repairs as a form of harassment. This is particularly provable when the landlord has not complied with a Régie repair order.

Section 1899 of the new Civil Code also provides for punitive damages if a landlord refuses to rent to a person for exercising his legal rights as a tenant, or imposes "more onerous conditions" on this person.

Discrimination against a prospective tenant for being pregnant or for having children is also banned by Section 1899, and is grounds for claiming punitive damages.

Finally, the Régie can award punitive damages to a tenant whose landlord has acted in "bad faith" in getting him to move out for one of the exceptional reasons allowed under the law. For example, a landlord who asks to "repossess" your half of the duplex to move in his mother and then rents to somebody else or puts the building up for sale is guilty of bad faith. So is a landlord who gets you to leave on the grounds that your apartment is being converted into an office and then doesn't follow through.

Under the old law, punitive damages were known as "exemplary" damages and generally were claimed under the Québec Charter of Rights. One tenant was awarded more than $9,000 in damages, including moving costs and the difference in rent, after the landlord repossessed in bad faith.

Damage awards of $5,000 were common for illegal eviction or not respecting the promised deadline to complete renovations so that a tenant could return. In one case, an untidy tenant, who certainly was not blameless, was awarded $1,100 because his landlady changed the lock on his apartment and removed certain belongings without his permission. These cases were won because various judges and Régie commissioners decided that it was time to apply the Charter of Rights to landlord-tenant relations. The principles established in these cases are now clearly stated in the Civil Code, for anyone to see.

One of the basic principles of Québec's landlord-tenant law since 1971 has always been the tenant's "right to maintain occupancy." The tough clauses on punitive damages are intended to support this right. So is the government's decision to make the "right to maintain occupancy" the title of an entire section of the Civil Code. According to tenant lawyer Robert Trudel, giving a right the status of a title strengthens the argument that the courts should be very restrictive in allowing exceptions to this right, such as repossession.

C. Repossession

And indeed, the new Civil Code does tighten the restrictions on repossession. An individual landlord can still repossess for himself, his parents or his children. However, if he wants to repossess for a grandparent, a grandchild, an in-law, an ex-spouse or any other relative, he must prove that he is that person's principal means of support.

Under the old law, this proof did not have to be made for grandparents, grandchildren and certain in-laws. The addition of ex-spouses to the list of permitted relatives appears on the surface to be a new right for landlords, but in fact several court decisions had already recognized this category under the old Civil Code. However, the fact that an ex-wife receives alimony does not necessarily mean that her ex-husband is her principal support.

Another loophole is slammed shut. To repossess, the lessor — the "landlord" whose name is on the lease — must also be the owner of the building, and not merely a property manager.

All the other restrictions in the old Civil Code are maintained. If a company owns the building, the owner of the company cannot repossess. Neither can a co-owner who has bought the property since November 1987, unless the only other co-owner of the property is his legal or de facto spouse.

The procedures for repossession also remain unchanged. For example, the landlord must give notice six months before the end of a one-year lease. If the tenant does not agree in writing within one month, the landlord has another month to apply to the Régie.

An unexpected bonus, due to the courts' new interpretation of the law over the past two years, has been the compensation awarded to tenants in "good faith" repossessions.

Under the old Civil Code, compensation was the exception rather than the rule. Tenants who had made permanent improvements to the dwelling, or seniors who would have trouble moving, might receive a monetary award in a contested repossession case. Most other tenants would get nothing, or at best, a token amount for moving expenses.

However, the new jurisprudence has reversed this presumption. Many commissioners and judges now consider that even though the court "may" impose "just and reasonable" conditions, according to Section 1967, this should be interpreted in terms of the tenant's "right to maintain occupancy," to which repossession is an exception.

In one typical decision, the Régie awarded $3,000 in compensation to a Greenfield Park senior who had lived in his home for 25 years. Only $1,000 of this amount was earmarked for moving expenses: the rest was compensation due to the tenant's age and the fact that he was being "uprooted." Other compensation awards, where such exceptional circumstances are not involved, have ranged between $800 and $1,500 under the new Code, compared to about $500 under the old rules.

D. Evacuation for major repairs

In 1987, the Québec government closed many of the renovation loopholes that had been a convenient way for landlords to get rid of low-income tenants. These reforms are maintained in the new Civil Code. The landlord must give three months' notice of any major repair requiring the tenant to evacuate for a week or more.

To be valid, the renovation notice must state the starting date, duration and nature of the work and offer compensation. If the tenant does not agree in writing within 10 days, he is considered to have refused and the landlord has another 10 days to apply to the Régie. For evacuations lasting less than a week or major repairs not requiring the tenant to vacate, the landlord must give 10 days' notice and the tenant then has 10 days *to apply to the Régie* if he opposes the conditions.

Under the old law, the tenant could not contest the "nature or expediency" of the work proposed by the landlord.

In a handful of court cases, tenants successfully blocked renovations which were intended to get them out by showing that the landlord was in "bad faith." But most Régie commissioners and judges refused to listen to this argument.

Even before the 1987 reform, renowned Canadian author Hugh MacLennan and his neighbours had blocked a forced evacuation from their apartments on Summerhill in downtown Montréal by arguing that the work could be done without forcing them to leave. The landlord then sold the building rather than proceed with his plans. But MacLennan's group only won this point after appealing an unfavourable Régie decision to the Québec Court.

The new Civil Code finally recognizes the principle won by MacLennan and closes the "nature or expediency" loophole. Section 1928 requires the landlord to show that the work and the conditions under which it will be done are reasonable and that it is necessary for the tenant to vacate.

This certainly would have helped one elderly Montréal tenant whose former landlord had already renovated in July 1993. The new landlord, obviously interested in emptying the building for other purposes, sent him a notice in the fall of 1993 demanding that he move out temporarily so that the same work could be done all over again.

However, the new Civil Code allows a landlord, without having to obtain the Régie's permission in advance, to demand that a tenant move out temporarily for urgent and necessary repairs, with compensation. A tenant could force this issue into court anyway by immediately filing an opposition demand at the Régie on the grounds that the work is not "urgent." However, this new section of the law creates ambiguity.

E. Getting the landlord to do repairs

Often, a tenant needs repairs that are the landlord's responsibility but the landlord doesn't want to spend any money. The tenant has sent him a registered letter giving him 10 days to do the work, but nothing has been done. What's the next move?

Under the new Civil Code, the tenant has a new recourse not previously available except in a handful of cases. The tenant can ask the Régie du logement for permission to do the work at the landlord's expense. This is in addition to the right to claim a rent reduction and have the Régie order the landlord to do certain work. It is also distinct from the tenant's right to do "urgent and necessary repairs" on very short notice after warning or attempting to warn the landlord.

The new procedure replaces the little-used recourse in the old Civil Code, which allowed tenants to ask the Régie's permission to withhold the cost of repairs from the rent. The reason the withholding procedure was so rarely used was that Régie commissioners would insist that tenants bring the repair person as a witness and not just show estimates.

According to lawyer Robert Trudel, the new rules are less of a burden on the tenants in terms of the proof required. However, for more expensive repair jobs, it would still be a good idea to bring the contractor as an expert witness. The big unanswered question is how fast will the Régie hear and render a decision on these cases. It isn't unusual to wait several months for a hearing, and government cutbacks have worsened this situation.

Working hours

Assuming that the landlord does want to do repairs, the tenant has to let him into the apartment a lot earlier in the day. The permitted hours of work in the new Civil Code run from 7 a.m. to 7 p.m. Under the old law, the starting time was 9 a.m.

When the landlord does any kind of work in the dwelling, including fumigations, he must restore the dwelling to "clean condition" at the end of the day. This goes farther than the old law, which only mentioned clean-up after "repairs" or "improvements."

F. Leaks and electrical fires

Another important change is the new principle requiring the landlord to guarantee the "good use" of the dwelling for the entire term of the lease. This provision, Section 1854, replaces the guarantee against "hidden defects" in the old Civil Code.

Previously, if a tenant suffered losses due to an electrical fire or a flood, for example, it was difficult to win damages in court, although the tenant was entitled to a rent reduction for the loss of rental value. Essentially, the tenant had to prove that he had not known of the hidden defect, while the landlord had been aware of it and had failed to take action. Not surprisingly, few could win these cases. According to Robert Trudel, the new rule will make it a lot easier for a tenant to claim compensation for damage.

G. Refusal to move in

What if an apartment is "unfit for habitation" and the new tenant refuses to move in? The new law gives the tenant the right to refuse to take possession of the premises under these conditions. This right was not clear under the old Civil Code, although some tenants had won court cases for this reason.

H. Dangerous neighbours

The new Civil Code allows a tenant to obtain cancellation of the lease by the Régie if the landlord's failure to perform his obligations causes serious prejudice to other occupants of the building. This means that a tenant no longer will have to prove that the drug dealers or criminals down the hall were bothering him personally. It would only be necessary to show that they were causing a serious problem for some of the neighbours. The old rules imposed a much tougher burden of proof on a tenant who wanted to break the lease.

Recent Régie decisions also make it clear that the presence of bad neighbours does not make a dwelling "unfit for habitation." In this type of situation, a tenant can't just move out and send a notice of abandonment within 10 days, the way he could if his apartment was fire-damaged, flooded or infested with cockroaches, for example. The tenant must file a demand for cancellation of the lease at the Régie, preferably before moving out. In some extreme cases, the Régie has heard the case several months after the tenants had to leave and has allowed them to cancel the lease retroactive to the filing date.

I. Deadlines for claims

The new Civil Code shortens the deadlines for claiming damages or recovery of unpaid rent. Under the old law, a landlord had five years to file a claim for unpaid rent at the Régie. The new rule is three years.

Under the old law, either the landlord or the tenant had 30 years to file a claim for damages. The new Civil Code reduces this deadline to three years.

Finally, after a final judgment is handed down by the court, the winner will have ten years to "execute" the judgment by seizing the other party's salary or property. The old rule was 30 years.

All of these new deadlines include all time already elapsed before January 1, 1994.

J. New buildings

The law still allows landlords to be exempt from rent control for five years after a new building is ready for occupancy. This exemption is now extended to formerly non-residential buildings which have been renovated for residential use.

Under the old law, landlords had to state this exemption on the back of the lease, but there was no clear penalty if they didn't. The new Civil Code closes this loophole. If the exemption is not stated on the lease, it cannot be used against the tenant. This means that rent control would apply.

K. Student housing

The new Civil Code's rules for student housing are tougher on students and easier on the universities. The right to maintain occupancy in student residences is limited to full-time students in residences operated by their own institution. For example, a Concordia student would have no right to maintain occupancy in a McGill residence.

Summer tenants of student residences lose their right to maintain occupancy at the end of their lease, and the university can have them evicted if they stay past their term.

Finally, universities are given the right to relocate students during the lease for "serious reasons." The new dwelling must be of the same type, in the same neighbourhood and at an equivalent rent.

L. Rules for co-tenants

However, because the new law gives every tenant on the lease a "personal right of occupancy," it is good news for many students in private housing. Under the new law, the landlord must send notices to every co-tenant if there is more than one tenant on the lease, and not just to one member of the group.

If one co-tenant agrees to a rent increase but another one refuses, the landlord will have to ask the Régie to set the rent and the Régie's decision will take precedence over any agreement with the other co-tenant. If one co-tenant gives notice that he is not renewing the lease, the other co-tenant now has the right to stay, as long as he is willing to pay the full rent or find another roommate.

M. Two big mistakes

Given the new Civil Code's stronger emphasis on the tenant's right of occupancy, two of the new clauses represent a glaring contradiction.

The new Code allows landlords to evict tenants in order to combine or enlarge apartments. This was not permitted under the old law and opens the door to abuse by speculators, particularly in neighbourhoods targeted for gentrification.

As in the case of subdivision of a dwelling or change of destination to commercial use, the tenant would be entitled to six months' notice before the end of the lease, three months' rent as compensation and moving expenses.

Secondly, under a completely different section of the Civil Code, the government allows a "syndicate" of condo owners to set a limit on the percentage of tenants in the complex and to ask for cancellation of any leases that the management signs beyond that limit. This section of the law is totally unrelated to anything in the chapter "On Leasing" and does not state what recourse the tenants would have in such a case.

They could apply to the Régie to oppose the eviction demand and could hold the condo manager liable for damages. The Régie has a discretionary power to rule on cases for which no specific rules are set down in the law.

Up to now, because of the high vacancy rate in the glutted condo market, the danger of mass evictions of condo tenants is more theoretical than immediate. There have been no cases involving this section in the past two years. Nevertheless, tenant organizations are lobbying the government to have this article struck from the law before it does any damage.

1996 update: Québec undermines the right of appeal[3]

In late June 1996, the Québec National Assembly quietly adopted fundamental changes to court appeal procedures that seriously undermine access to justice. The changes are contained in Bill 7, a 24-page collection of mostly innocuous amendments intended to eliminate "frivolous or excessive proceedings" in the courts.

While most of these amendments arouse no argument, and even deserve praise, a few paragraphs in the bill will fall like an atomic bomb on the type of people who most need the courts' protection — tenants and small landlords who can't afford a lawyer. Evictions, claims for damages over $3,000, contested evacuations for major repairs and many other types of cases would be affected.

Under the existing law, it's relatively simple to file an appeal at the Court of Québec if you disagree with a Régie du logement decision. Within one month of the decision, you write up a brief declaration stating your reasons, attach the appealed decision, pay $31 to have it stamped at the court and serve it on the other party by bailiff. Eventually you are called to a hearing, where the entire case is reargued in front of a judge.

Bill 7 changes this dramatically. Within 30 days of the Régie decision, you must obtain "leave to appeal" from another Court of Québec judge, and then file your appeal, all within the same deadline. No extensions will be allowed. To obtain "leave to appeal," you must attach other "documents of the contestation," which the proposed law does not specify, and without which you could lose your case on a technicality.

What does this mean in plain English? For starters, we're talking about two court appearances instead of one. Tenants and small landlords who have trouble scraping together a few hundred dollars for one appeal hearing can expect that the cost will be nearly double. This will discourage many people from exercising their rights, or will require them to go to court without a lawyer.

What about low-income people who qualify for free legal aid? Right now, it takes at least three weeks to get a legal aid appointment, if not longer. Some private lawyers who accept legal aid mandates draft appeals free of charge at community clinics, or do this relatively simple paperwork "on spec," while waiting for the bureaucracy to approve the legal aid mandate. But almost no lawyer will take a chance on appearing in court (and waiting a few hours until the judge has time to hear the case) unless he or she is guaranteed that legal aid will pay the bill. In any event, many landlord-tenant cases (just about everything except evictions) will no longer be eligible for legal aid once another bill, also rammed through the National Assembly in June, becomes law.

The judge who decides on leave to appeal would also define the issues that could be heard by the trial judge. Appeal hearings would no longer be "de novo" — that is, they would no longer review the entire case. According to one lawyer who has analyzed the bill, Dominique Neuman, judges could easily be tempted to limit the appeal hearing to points of law, thus making it impossible to correct factual errors in the Régie decision. But factual errors are the reason that many people appeal in the first place.

Another dangerous amendment in Bill 7 makes all Régie decisions executable "notwithstanding appeal." This means that a decision can be applied even while an appeal is pending. The only exceptions would be in cases of eviction, and the tenant would have to file a special motion to convince another judge to suspend the decision's execution until the appeal could be heard. Under the existing rules, Régie commissioners can decide whether or not to impose execution notwithstanding appeal. Under Bill 7, they will have no choice. This is bound to create all kinds of injustices.

The amendment is also poorly drafted. It makes an exception for evictions, but none for temporary evacuation for major repairs, which can be just as traumatic for elderly tenants.

It would make much more sense to limit extension of the "notwithstanding appeal" rule to Régie decisions ordering necessary repairs, which are frequently dragged out on appeal by recalcitrant landlords. This new possibility of enforcing repairs more quickly is the only positive aspect of Bill 7.

The problem with Bill 7 is that it has been written by lawyers and bureaucrats for lawyers and bureaucrats, with no consideration to how it will affect ordinary people. The public now faces an uphill battle to persuade the government to reconsider.

NOTES

1. 1943, CcQ: "In every notice of modification with a view to an increase of the rent an indication shall be made of the new proposed rent in dollars or the increase expressed in dollars or as a percentage of the rent in force. The increase may be expressed as a percentage of the rent to be determined by the court, where an application for the fixing or review of the rent has been filed."

    "Where the lessor proposes to modify the term of the lease, the proposed term shall also be indicated in the notice, and the time granted to the lessee to refuse the proposed modification."

2. 1899, CcQ: "A lessor may not refuse to enter into a lease with a person or to maintain the person in his or her rights, or impose more onerous conditions on the person for the sole reason that the person is pregnant or has one or several children, unless the refusal is warranted by the size of the dwelling; nor can he so act for the sole reason that the person has exercised his or her rights under this chapter or the Act respecting the Régie du logement."

    "Punitive damages may be awarded in cases where this provision is violated."

    1902, CcQ: "Neither the lessor nor any other person may harass a lessee in such a manner as to limit his right to peaceable enjoyment of the premises or to induce him to leave the dwelling."

    "A lessee who suffers harassment may demand that the lessor or any other person who has harassed him be condemned to pay punitive damages."

3. This is an updated version of an article, "New court rules could mean trouble for tenants," by Arnold Bennett, published in the *Montreal Gazette*, June 13, 1996.

Part 2 | Ontario and British Columbia

Chapter 8

Dispatches from the housing front: Ontario tenants take on the Harris government, 1996

Editor's note: This chapter contains four key documents produced by tenant organizations in Ontario as part of the current struggle against the Harris government's plans to gut that province's rent control system. The first two documents are opinion pieces by Dan McIntyre and Howard Tessler, active in the Ottawa and Toronto tenant federations. They are followed by an Ottawa tenants' April 1996 brief to the Ontario government on possible new tenant legislation, and by a "myths and facts" pamphlet that Ontario tenant groups have used as a mobilization tool.

Since abolition of rent control was not a stated objective of the "common sense revolution" that brought the Conservatives to power in 1995, the tenant lobby has been effective in attacking the government's lack of mandate on this issue. The debate has evolved from a head-on collision on outright elimination of tenants' rights to a fight on two main issues.

One is "vacancy decontrol," which, on paper, would not affect existing tenants but would certainly give their landlords an incentive to get rid of them by every means possible. Each time a new tenant moves into an apartment, the landlord could raise the rent. New tenants in Québec have the right to challenge rents if they are increased too much compared to the previous occupant. Although this right is used infrequently, it is a deterrent to getting rid of existing tenants in the hope of rent gouging. The existing Ontario protection in this area has long been considerably better than Québec's. For example, Ontario has a rent registry, something that Québec tenant groups have long demanded and have never obtained.

The other key Ontario issue is very familiar to Montréal tenants: conversion of rental units into condominiums. Harris wants to eliminate most of the existing provincial controls on such conversions, including the requirement of municipal authorization. If tenants could not afford to buy their units, they would lose their homes. This contrasts with the situation in Québec where, at least on paper, tenants have a lifetime right of occupancy if their rental unit is converted.

Rent control is necessary in Ontario

by Dan McIntyre, Executive Director, Federation of Ottawa Carleton Tenants Association, May 1996. This article was published in the *Ottawa Citizen*.

Tenants want and deserve fairness. Tenants do not want and do not deserve uncertainty. That is why a fair and effective rent control system is necessary.

Each of the three political parties in Ontario have brought in permanent rent regulations. Each system has been flawed in law and in administration. Flaws can be corrected.

Opponents of rent control have complained that rents have been held back unfairly and that rent control has ended the supply of new rental housing. These complaints are wrong and misleading.

Rent regulation has prevented exploitation of tenants who can be squeezed when choice is limited or when tenants have sought to exercise other lawful rights. But when it comes to raising prices, landlords have done very well. That is why there is much stronger argument for tightening rent controls, not loosening them.

Landlords are on a ten year winning streak as the annual rent guideline has exceeded inflation. Further, the system has permitted increases well above the guideline, which have then been compounded by the guideline.

In fact, the Ministry of Housing estimates that perhaps a third of rental units are renting below what rent control allows. This fact has already deterred some tenants from exercising maintenance rights. You can complain but the landlord can jack up your rent in retaliation.

The annual guideline is a floor, not a ceiling. Twenty years ago a typical unit might rent for $250 (those were the days). Applying the Consumer Price Index for those 20 years, the rent would be $777. The minimum rent guideline would give you a rent of $703. Considering that it is the same product, only 20 years older, and that average operating costs are about half of current rents, that is a lot of gain for the landlord. Even with all the buying and selling that went on, particularly in the late eighties, Citibank Canada quotes the average yield for a Toronto apartment at over 10%.

The issue of new supply has been the convenient whipping boy of landlords for years. New units are exempt from rent control. The fact is that the rent required to make new units viable far exceeds the market and tenants' ability and willingness to pay. That fact would be the same in a regulated or unregulated market. Developers would lose money regardless. Another way to look at it is to consider that 1976 unit renting for $250 and compare how much it would cost to develop right now. Can you imagine building another Bayshore today?

The other lame argument is that the system is too complex, especially for small landlords. It is only complex if you cannot live with the guideline increase above the level of inflation. To increase rent, a landlord need only fill out one form and give it to the tenant 90 days before the increase takes effect. Yes, even that form could be simplified as could the process of applications, but it is hardly a reason to leave tenants vulnerable to the whims of landlords.

An extra word about small landlords: Some of the best landlords are in this category — but also some of the worst. There are no standards set for being a landlord. Many people who make money in this business could not succeed in any other business because they would have to know their business, meet standards, and have a higher respect for their customers. Small buildings enjoy some advantages because they do not pay the double rate of property tax as do buildings with seven or more units, and they do not have elevators.

So given that landlords are making money, have received substantial increases, and that rent regulation does not impede supply, what should tenants expect? The Harris government should favour rent freezes and rent reductions with the same zeal as they favour tax freezes and cuts. That will not happen by telling landlords that they can charge anything they can get.

• A proper system should recognize that tenants have suffered disproportionately through recent tough economic times. Job losses, wage freezes and cutbacks, and draconian cuts to social assistance make it tougher to pay rent — not easier.

• A proper system should recognize that substantial amounts of money are in current rents for the specific purpose of repairs and long-term maintenance. Every year since 1987, the annual guideline has included a bonus for these costs. There has been absolutely no check that these monies have been used for this purpose.

• A proper system should allow tenants to seek rent reductions when maintenance is inadequate or services are reduced as the current system does. The effective use of these provisions has lead to better

levels of maintenance and substantial peace between landlords and tenants.
- A proper system should provide certainty so that incoming tenants are charged evenly with existing tenants. No surprises.
- A proper system encourages free participation without fear of retaliation.
- A proper system is not slowed down by the bureaucracy so that people lose faith in the law because of the system.
- A proper system requires skilled advocates to ensure fairness for all.
- A proper system can be achieved if fairness is the goal rather than right-wing free-market ideology at all costs.

Tory alternatives to the Rent Control Act

by Howard Tessler, Federation of Metro Tenants' Associations, 1996

The Harris government has said time and again that "everything is on the table" and has been very vague about what specific changes will be made.

However, they have said that they are looking carefully at other forms of legislated tenant protection especially that of rent review as administered in B.C. and Québec.

It should be noted that since 1975, Ontario has had actual rent control and not rent review. Despite the weak and porous nature of specific pieces of legislation, they still imposed limits on the annual rent increases landlords could ask. Studies done prior to the introduction of rent control in 1975 pointed to rent increases from 14.2% to 18.2%. A sample of North York buildings had average increases of 17.1%. Once rent control was instituted, the guideline increases were never greater than 8% (1975-1977).

The B.C. model

British Columbia's tenant protection began with the passing of the *Landlord Tenant Act* in the early 1970s under the NDP government of Dave Barret. While there was a rent increase guideline to compensate for inflation, the system revolved around the office of the Rentalsman to which tenants could appeal landlord problems. In 1984, this method of tenant protection, as well as any kind of guideline increase limit, was replaced by the *Residential Tenancy Act*.

For Ontario tenants, the major points of interest in the B.C. system lie in its loopholes and in the fact that in the absence of rent controls, the private market still did not provide adequate rental housing for British Columbia's tenants.

The Tenants Rights Action Coalition, a tenants rights group similar to the Federation of Metro Tenants' Associations, described the difficulty of getting landlords to do repairs before the recent revisions of the *Residential Tenancy Act* (RTA):

In the absence of rent controls, many tenants are afraid to take their landlord to arbitration for repairs out of fear of retaliatory rent increases. Even those who do proceed through the arbitration system report that repairs are still not being done because the Residential Tenancy Branch (RTB) will not enforce repair orders.

The 1994 revision of the RTA continued to allow tenants to take their landlord to arbitration over repairs but still had a $35 application fee attached (which is paid by the loser of the hearing). It still did not allow the tenant to deduct the cost of the repairs from the rent prior to the ruling or the withholding of the rent because of disrepair. The "dispute resolution" process itself is three-fold:

1. *Clarification*: Following a request from one party, an RTB officer talks individually with the parties to clear up any misunderstanding. If no resolution arises from this then the process moves to:
2. *Reconciliation*: If both parties agree, the RTB sets up a meeting and tries to work towards a common understanding and a compromise solution. The RTB official stays neutral throughout.
3. *Arbitration*: An arbitrator reviews the facts and makes a decision that is binding on both parties.

When dealing with rent increases, tenants have only 30 days to apply for an arbitration hearing after they receive a rent increase notice. Once a date is set, the tenant must inform the landlord within three days.

A key point is that arbitration is dependent upon the tenant contesting the landlord's action. Although the arbitrator does have a criteria for determining what reasonable rent is, the landlord could issue any rent increase he thought reasonable and the onus would be on the tenant to challenge the increase.

However strange this may seem to Ontario tenants, the 1994 revisions are an improvement over the old arbitration system which, for one thing, did not allow tenants to remain in their premises until the claim is heard.

If B.C. becomes Ontario's new model then tenants must insist that the same loopholes do not exist here. We must show that under this system, rent increases far outpaced inflation, which is one of the key reasons for rent regulation.

The Tory dream of rent deregulation being the driving force behind an increased rental housing market is just that: a dream. The B.C. experience is just the opposite. The vacancy rate in Vancouver was similar to Toronto's in April 1995. Toronto had a rate of 1.0%, while Vancouver's was 1.3%. The B.C. government reported that from 1988-90, vacancy rates in Vancouver dropped below 0.5% and rents were increased by more than 30%. David Hulchanski pointed out that given high demand and the absence of rent control, the Vancouver rental scene should be fine. Canada Mortgage and Housing (CMHC) statistics show that the removal of rent control in 1983 has not resulted in increased private development. Hulchanski calls this situation "market failure."

In a 1989 study, he points out that the key is what he calls effective market demand. "Tenants simply cannot or will not pay the rents required to make private supply of rental stock economical. Once rent levels approach the monthly mortgage costs of a condominium or house, tenants with enough of a down payment have every incentive to choose the ownership option. Lower income renters have no choice and cannot pay higher rents." He goes on to say that developers are more apt to build condos than rental housing: "Condominium investors are always able to pay more for building sites than rental investors because condominium buyers can pay and are willing to pay more than renters."

The same market failure applies to the rental situation in Toronto. Condo development has provided increased housing stock at the high end of income levels at the same time private rental housing starts have declined, while demand for rental housing has been strong.

Thus the argument that the deregulation of the rental market will provide an improved situation for tenants as well as for landlords is false. The B.C. model has not helped tenants: it has not provided additional rental housing and it has not provided affordable rents. It has made some landlords very rich and it has increased the hardship for tenants.

A brief with respect to possible new tenant legislation

By the Federation of Ottawa-Carleton Tenants Association, 1996

It seems apparent that our government is going to terminate the third permanent rent law we have had in Ontario. They are going to terminate the *Landlord and Tenant Act* (LTA) which has served reasonably well for over 25 years. Also going is the *Rental Housing Protection Act* (RHPA), which has ensured that tenants have rights with respect to possible conversions, and the *Land Lease Act*, which has not been around long enough to offer much comment.

It appears that there will be a replacement law presumably known as the *Tenant Protection Act*. It will incorporate all tenant and landlord rights into one piece of legislation to be administered by a tribunal. These moves constitute a significant danger to consumer rights in rental housing and to the affordability of rental housing. Ironically, it was ten years ago that another government embarked on legislation that they termed a "delicate balance of interests" and which severely crippled rental affordability. Mercifully, it only lasted four years. Once again, we are hearing some fuzzy assurances that tenants will be protected and that there will be a balance of interests. Our skepticism is high, but we must attempt to help even this government so that the decisions that are reached are fair.

We will divide our discussion in terms of the potential law, the administrative system, and the underlying reasons for change.

A. The potential law

There are fundamental tenant concerns which must be adequately addressed in any legislation:
- Affordability
- Maintenance
- Security of tenure
- Supply

Affordability

Successive governments have caved in to landlords and awarded, as a matter of right, minimum rent increases which have outstripped inflation for ten consecutive years. Instead we should be looking at rent freezes and cuts with the same zeal that some governments pursue tax freezes and cuts. Unfortunately there still seems to be an attitude that tenants can pay more rent, and worse, that they should be paying more rent.

While tenants have been losing ground in the affordability race, landlords have been pocketing monies lawfully targeted for necessary capital expenditures. Citibank quotes the annual average yield for an apartment in Toronto as 10.08%.

Landlords want to squeeze every dollar they can from tenants (a market that is more captive than any other, since everybody needs housing and moving is never easy). They can get the last dollar if there is a constricted supply of affordable housing; if there is much discretion in deciding if maintenance gets done; if there is not real rent control, and if the ability of tenants to advocate is impeded. Unfortunately for tenants, landlords appear to be about to succeed in achieving all of these results.

The new approach favoured by the Ontario government is the British Columbia system. As we understand it, this system gives the tenant the right to appeal (for a $35 fee) an alleged unfair rent increase. An underlying assumption is that all rent increases are fair unless the government hears about it and determines the increase to be unfair. This system assumes that all tenants are capable of making an appeal, and that the relative abilities of landlords and tenants to advocate are equal. In the real world, there is a terrible imbalance between the two that will be exploited.

In such a system the majority of tenants will be excluded. This includes low-income people, the elderly, the illiterate, those with disabilities, non-English-speaking people, the uneducated, workers without the time (and often no ability to take the time off work), and the intimidated. As a result, a mild form of rent control will be available to the articulate tenant who has the time and energy — not to mention $35 — to use the system. Undoubtedly, there will be some successful cases which would enable the government to point out that tenants seem to be protected. But even these successful cases would be isolated. When a tenant in a highrise or a complex proves that their increase is unjustified, it is apparently assumed that no other tenant has been required to pay this increase.

Another problem with the B.C. system is that it does not permit a rent decrease. The lowest quality landlord is entitled to more rent!

For a further discussion of what an Ontario system must include please refer to the section on the administrative system.

Mike Harris did have one good idea during the election campaign when he suggested that the notice of rent increase be extended to six months. If there is to be an aspect of negotiation, an extended notice period would give the tenant adequate time to negotiate before having to give notice to vacate, which we trust will remain at 60 days.

Maintenance

Maintenance is a right paid for in the rent. Even with rent regulation and the *Landlord and Tenant Act*, some landlords have often failed to provide adequate maintenance to a reasonable standard. Some of these landlords have to occasionally face consequences, but more have profited. The challenge for the legislature is to find the best ways to remedy those situations where the customer does not get what they are supposed to get.

Currently, there are three avenues of remedy available to tenants. These are municipal property standards by-laws, abatements of rent and applications for reduction of rent.

Municipal property standards have been a victim (certainly in Ottawa) of municipal cutbacks. They are also almost entirely complaint-driven. It is up to the tenant to initiate inspections. This is a good example of why a tenant-initiated system is inadequate. In Ottawa-Carleton, a yearly average of $255 per establishment is spent to ensure that eating establishments are in compliance with all health and safety standards. On the other hand, less than $4 per year is spent on property standards per housing unit. People are safer in a greasy spoon than in an apartment.

Abatements of rent have been stifled by the need for tenants to work through the judicial system when they are unable to be represented. Represented tenants have often achieved good results as judges tend to understand that breaches of law should have meaningful consequences.

For the last three years, tenants have been able to apply to Rent Control for rent reductions. In Ottawa-Carleton, we have made this provision work to a certain degree. We have successfully advocated for adding parties to applications, which means all tenants have a chance for a rent reduction. We have often received orders freezing or reducing rents for tenants. We have generally found these reductions to be less than desirable but we are astounded as to how much better the overall results have been compared to other parts of Ontario. The system has lacked the courage to place adequate consequences on inadequate maintenance standards. The system has also been painfully and unnecessarily s-l-o-w!

The best result that we have observed with the current *Rent Control Act* is that landlords have improved their standard of maintenance. They have seen the consequence and they know that we have been able to present our cases well. Of course, this situation may be about to end.

Any new system will be judged on its results. Maintenance must be done and there must be consequences if it is not. For a further discussion of what the Ontario system must include, please refer to the section on the administrative system.

Security of tenure

It seems that a driving force behind the proposed changes is that some landlords want to be able to evict tenants more quickly and easily. They wish legislate homelessness. Every week in Ottawa-Carleton tenants are being evicted by the score. According to a study by the Metro Advisory Committee on Homeless and Socially Isolated Persons, the number of evictions has risen dramatically since the savage and unfair cutbacks to social assistance recipients.

These landlords wish to solve a phony problem. Any problems surrounding eviction are usually caused by uninformed and incompetent landlords and sometimes incompetent agents. In addition, there are the landlords who want to evict based on personal animosity or whimsy and not on just cause.

Obviously, it is vital that the current security of tenure found in the *Landlord and Tenant Act* remain. Additionally, protection against retaliatory evictions needs to be beefed up. Decision-makers must understand rules of evidence and whether the evidence warrants an eviction. The landlords' cases must be substantial. No innocent tenant should ever be evicted. If that means the occasional guilty one is not evicted — so be it. The provisions regarding relief from forfeiture must be kept.

The other major protection of security of tenure which is at risk is the *Rental Housing Protection Act*. This Act has ensured that the interests of tenants must be taken into account in any conversion application to a municipality. It has also deterred landlords from conversion attempts. Therefore, the Act has been achieving intended results.

It will be inconsistent with other government initiatives if the decision-making authority regarding RHPA applications is taken away from municipalities. For instance, the government believed municipalities should decide on the rights of owners to create accessory apartments.

During the enactment of the RHPA, we took the position that it was wrong to impose the administration on municipalities. If the responsibility returns to the province, the important question is whether it will permit large-scale conversions. In Ottawa, we have seen the increase in the vacancy rate lead to a number of conversion applications. Successful applicants can now sell off units and see their financial return quicker while continuing to rent the units they cannot sell. Another motivating factor is that units converted no longer have to pay the discriminatory multi-residential tax rates.

In Ottawa, the tendency has been to give conditional approvals to applications under the RHPA. These conditions commendably protect the interests of *in situ* tenants. However, this trend toward conversions will ultimately lead to a constricted supply of affordable housing. One such recent approval distresses us because it may have been a situation of "neglect and convert." The owners indicated that this is the only way they could afford to fix the places up, but no investigation was done. Therefore a signal may have been sent that could lead to reduced maintenance on rental properties.

Another trap is to treat the vacancy rate as gospel. The rate is up in Ottawa due to economic reasons — not because more units are being built. People who are not able to afford their own unit are doubling up or staying in the parental home longer. Therefore, conversions which seem to be non-threatening will lead to a constricted supply down the road.

One last issue on security of tenure: the government may be looking at using the lease as the protector of tenants. Leases are written by landlords for landlords. Who has ever heard of the tenant drawing up the lease? The ability of tenants to become monthly tenants is important to maintain mobility and to keep landlords on their toes. The government seems interested in making it easier for landlords to terminate tenancies and harder for tenants to do so. If that is indeed the case, tenants will be the least protected type of consumer in the land.

Supply

In 1986, the Liberal government tried to make rent review law in such a way as to produce an increased supply of rental units. They argued that more generous rent increases and an easier system would encourage landlords to build. They were wrong, and all that tenants got were massive rent increases. In 1992, the NDP brought in the *Rent Control Act* (RCA) and never tried to sell it as a supply measure. They were right, although even they gave in to the landlord lobby and permitted a high guideline in order to induce capital maintenance spending.

The point is that rent control is a consumer protection policy and not a supply policy. Supply for low and middle income renters is only possible through an effective non-profit housing program and a greater use of existing housing stock. Unfortunately, the current government has already gone the wrong way on both those fronts.

The goal of legislation should be to ensure fair and just treatment in existing rental stock. This means protection against arbitrary, unnecessary and exploitative rent increases as well as assurance that the customer gets what is paid for including maintenance and privacy. Increased supply is not going to be the result of this or any other legislation.

Other issues

If there is to be a major overhaul of legislation, the government should address the following issues which have been overlooked for too long:

Last month's rent

Why is it that tenants are the only consumers required to pay a deposit that is kept for the life of the tenancy? Even Bell Canada cannot charge such a deposit any more. The other major difficulty here is that when landlords fail to pay interest on this deposit, there is nothing a tenant can do that is practical.

It is time to end this anachronism. If landlords need to be protected from tenants who might not pay their rent, then permit them to collect a deposit for a limited period of one year. All current deposits can be returned to tenants to spend as they see fit. This is better than a tax cut.

After one year of tenancy, the tenant will have demonstrated that they will pay the rent. If not, a process for keeping the deposit may be in order. But it is ridiculous that this deposit is withheld from people who always pay their bills and whose credit worthiness is known.

Posting of information

Probably the most ignored provision of the current LTA is the requirement to post the name and address of the landlord and a summary of Part IV of the Act. Some tenants have brought this matter to the attention of the Justice of the Peace — only to be completely ignored. Buildings of any size should not have a problem complying with the posting provisions. Safety glass does exist. If a landlord does not post, the tenant does not have to pay rent. Now that would be meaningful.

Unlawful changes

Rent charges should continue to be all-inclusive except for parking and possibly utilities. Provisions against "premiums, fees, commissions, key deposits or other like charges" should continue. One issue that has been around for a long time is the charging of fees for subletting. Many years ago, the Divisional Court ruled clearly in *Geeves v. Keewatin* that these fees were unlawful. Yet they are still routinely charged. Charges for actual expenses are allowed, such as the cost of doing a credit check. A solution may be to allow for sublet fees to a maximum of $50 inclusive of all costs.

B. The administrative system

For years, people involved in the administration of successive rent regulation regimes have called for a tribunal system to deal with all tenant-landlord matters. Finally, they may be about to get that wish. Apparently, many landlords are arguing that they need quicker processes to deal with evicting tenants. Also, the Attorney General would like to reduce the costs of the justice system. The move to a tribunal worries many lawyers (and others) who believe that the courts are far superior in their abilities to determine evidence and act judicially. It is also argued that the LTA contains a complete set of procedures which can be relied upon in the courts — even by lay people.

We do not oppose a move to a tribunal system on principle. We believe a system can be devised which is just, fair, expeditious, and economical. Rather, our uncertainty lies in this government's willingness to work on developing such a system, as well as the track record of previous rent regulation regimes.

There have been three permanent rent laws in Ontario. These laws have had some differences and some similarities. One similarity has been the failure of the system of achieve timely results. The administration has needlessly delayed justice virtually at every turn. This organization can provide substantial evidence on this point. In general, cases which should take a few weeks from start to finish routinely take several months, often more than a year, and sometimes more than two years! Those landlords wanting quicker evictions could be sorely disappointed. Any proposed system must avoid the errors of the past.

Another scary prospect is one that would see a new system administered by unqualified political appointments. The current government appointed someone to the Social Assistance Review Board who has a record of vilifying social assistance recipients. This government would likely have a ready store of potential appointments who are demonstrably pro-landlord and anti-rent control. Therefore, the essential question is: who will mind the store? We suggest that new people, such as recently graduated students (including lawyers), are needed. We recommend that any people involved be result-oriented and are the type who do not get bogged down in lengthy paperwork processes. We strongly recommend that a tenant watchdog needs to be part of the system. Too often, we find that procedural and fairness problems are a result of closed door decisions made without adequate input from the tenant community.

Another thorny area concerns rights of appeal. This has traditionally been an area that has favoured bigger landlords because of their abilities to draw on legal resources. Without reviewing all of the history in this area, we recommend that there be an internal system of appeal based on questions of law. Appeals should not be for reviewing properly found facts. We recommend that appeals "stay" decisions respecting evictions or conversions, but not "stay" decisions respecting rents.

For an Ontario system to work fairly, the following must be included:
1. A published guideline at or below the rate of inflation.
2. A recognition of what is already built into the rents.
3. Actual rent as the starting point.
4. Tenant advocates.
5. Rent decreases permitted including retroactivity.
6. Building and complex-wide rent reductions.
7. An ability to order work to be done.
8. Meaningful consequences.
9. Penalties for landlords who charge tenants for routine maintenance. We recommend that tenants be compensated by rent reductions four times greater than the illegal charge.
10. Proactive building inspections.

11. A method of ensuring that all tenants have equal access to the system and that all parties have equal access to advocacy.
12. An ability at add parties to applications and to allow tenant associations to advocate for all the tenants in a complex.
13. A multilingual staff in the tribunal (including senior positions).
14. Adequate time lines and deadlines for steps in the process.
15. Evening hearings as a right.
16. Fees not to exceed $10.
17. Patterns of activities taken into account.
18. Quick decisions.
19. Penalties for retaliatory actions.
20. Plain language in all parts of the law.

C. The reason for change

It has been unusually difficult to prepare this submission because it is not clear what the driving force behind changing the system and the law is. Why is this a priority? What is the hurry? This is not to say that we do not have our theories or that we are completely surprised by these events. We know what landlords want. We know what was said by the Conservatives about "market rent control." We also know the political landscape respecting tenant legislation.

Landlords are on a ten year winning streak in that minimum rent increases have exceeded inflation. Lately, landlords have not been applying for above-guideline increases. In a startling number of cases, the regulated rent far exceeds the actual market rent. Evic-tions are way up since the draconian cuts to social assistance. Some balance has existed because of rent freeze and rent reduction provisions in the current RCA. Further balance has been achieved by the work of organized tenants and their federations. This has been a result of Community Partners Funding. In fact, there has been unprecedented peace the last couple of years.

We appreciate that we have had this opportunity to provide input at this time. Unfortunately, the current government seems to despise "special interest groups" (unless it is a business special interest group). The survival of organizations like ours is very much in jeopardy because of this government. Down the road we may not be here. The playing field will have tilted completely to the right. We believe that there is a possibility that some positive changes can be affected to make for an easier and fairer system. We worry that current and potential changes lead to a further erosion of rental affordability and a further erosion of tenant rights. Is that what this government wants?

The myth of landlord tenant law

- The current system does not work
- Because of the LTA, tenants can't be evicted
- Because of rent control there is no new rental housing being built
- Landlords are losing money
- Tenants have too many rights

The fact of landlord tenant law

- The current system needs improvement
- Tenants can't be evicted without just cause
- Rent control does not apply to new buildings. Even without rent control there will be no new buildings
- The average yield on a Toronto apartment is 10.08% — Citibank
- Landlords have the right to charge and collect rent in return for rights enjoyed by tenants, including security of tenure.

Eight myths about Rent Control in Ontario

From a pamphlet produced by the Tenant Advocacy Group (TAG), the Federation of Metro Tenants' Associations (FMTA) and Community Legal Education Ontario (CLEO), February 1996

1. Myth: Private landlords cannot afford to build new apartment buildings because of rent control.
Fact: It is true that in recent years, relatively few affordable rental units have been built in Ontario. This is not the fault of rent control.

Before 1985, units costing $750 a month or more were not rent controlled. Still, landlords did not build enough of this "high-end" rental housing. Even now, with a five-year exemption from rent control on new units, developers are not building.

David Hulchanski, a housing expert at the University of Toronto, points out that the private sector has not built enough affordable rental housing in provinces with no history of rent control.

2. Myth: Because of rent control, landlords cannot get a fair return on their investment.
Fact: Good landlords benefit from rent control. "Owners of high-rise properties who were serious about their real estate looked after their investment by providing good maintenance and were rewarded by capital appreciation and, more important, cash flow" (Ontario Association of the Appraisal Institute of Canada, 1994).

Developers have offered no proof whatsoever that rent control causes them financial hardship.

3. Myth: Landlords cannot afford maintenance and repairs because of rent control.
Fact: Your rent includes money for repairs and maintenance. The rent control guideline gives landlords an annual cost of living increase plus a two percent bonus.

In addition, landlords can get a rent increase above the guideline for major repairs (*Rent Control Act*, section 15).

4. Myth: Rent control discourages repairs and maintenance.
Fact: Rent control *encourages* repairs. If an apartment is not in good repair, then municipal or provincial inspectors can issue work orders to get repairs done. If there is an outstanding work order, the landlord is not allowed to increase the annual rent until the work is done (*Rent Control Act*, sections 34-38).

Tenants may apply for a reduction in rent if their apartment is not adequately maintained.

5. Myth: The market will provide a "fair rent for all."
Fact: A fair or affordable rent is not the same thing as the rent the market will bear.

British Columbia has not had rent control since the mid-1980s. The average annual rent increase was 27-29%, while the vacancy rate for the same period never went above 2.7% (CMHC statistics).

6. Myth: Rent control destroys market forces in private rental housing.
Fact: Supply and demand still set the rent for most units. Fred Dobbin of the Fair Rental Policy Organization (a major landlord group) has acknowledged that most rents under rent control now follow the market.

7. Myth: The rent control system is broken and tenants are unhappy with it.
Fact: An Environics poll published in April 1995 found that eight out of ten Ontario tenants strongly support the continued existence of rent control.

8. Myth: A "tenant-initiated dispute system" (like the one used in British Columbia) will protect tenants better than rent control does.
Fact: Under a tenant-initiated system, it will be up to the individual tenants to challenge their landlord's rent increase. This will put many tenants at a disadvantage.

When units become vacant, landlords will be able to raise the rent as much as they want. This will encourage them to force tenants out of their homes.

Chapter 9

Comparative study of apartment rent control laws in Ontario & Québec

by Alexander X.S. Sabharwal[1]

Introduction

This chapter critically compares Québec's rent stabilization system to Ontario's. The chapter begins with a history of national rent control, which was eliminated shortly after World War II and which was very protective of tenants. Also reviewed is Québec's history with rent stabilization and its present system, which has always been tenant-initiated, but which has been the subject of some progressive reform over time. In a tenant-initiated or *voluntary* system, as it is sometimes called, rent is only reviewed when a tenant sets the process in motion. A building can therefore effectively be exempted from controls if the review procedure is not invoked.[2] This chapter concludes with a critique of Québec's rent stabilization system and an explanation of why it cannot be productively transplanted into Ontario's very different apartment market, which at present has a mandatory system of rent control.

Compared to property owners, tenants are economically disadvantaged[3] and those most disadvantaged have always required rent control in order to afford reasonable accommodation. Rent control is increasingly becoming necessary to protect middle income, as well as low income, renters because housing is also moving out of their range.[4] This is a bad trend. Everyone has a right to good quality housing that is affordable.[5] Moreover, for several reasons including Ontario's low vacancy rate and Québec's high rate, transplanting Québec's system into Ontario would cause apartment rents to rise too high for tenants to afford. That said, however, rent control is no remedy for all ills. It cannot work alone to remedy the problems of not enough housing and too high rents. A real solution requires additional supply-oriented programs. Rent control is aimed at the demand side of the problem.[6]

Rent control in the federal jurisdiction

Rent control was first introduced into Canada during war time. It came in during World War I, and again during World War II.[7] Rent control was considered an important part of the almost total price fixing which was established by many countries during World War II.[8] The system was intended to prevent landlords from exploiting the conditions of a war-oriented economy in which residential construction was reduced to the barest trickle.[9] Order-in-Council P.C. 4616 dated September 11, 1940,[10] which was brought in under the *War Measures Act*[11] gave the federal Wartime Prices and Trade Board the power to control the price of rented housing.[12] The Board imposed rent freezes in 15 cities in September 1940.[13] The system was expanded by Order-in-Council 9029, which was approved on November 21, 1941.[14] P.C. 9029 gave the Board the power to set the maximum amount of rent that could be charged for any particular accommodation and services supplied by a landlord.[15] Based on the notion that security of tenure is essential for the enforcement of control on price,[16] the Order-in-Council also increased tenants' security of tenure over that which was provided by the common law and applicable statutes.[17] Provision was made for the appointment of officials to administer rent control across Canada, including a Rentals Administrator, Rentals Appraiser, Court of Rentals Appeals, and other officials.[18]

Under P.C. 9029, the rent chargeable on all real property in Canada that was subject to a lease on October 11, 1941, and for which a maximum rent had not previously been fixed by the Board, was frozen at the amount payable on October 11. And the maximum rent that could be charged for real property not subject to a lease on that date was the amount payable under the last lease in effect between January 2, 1940, and October 11, 1941. Between 1947 and 1951, landlords were granted several general rent increases.[19]

History of rent control in Québec

When the federal legislation expired in 1951, the Québec National Assembly passed *An Act to promote conciliation between lessees and property owners*.[20] This Act was not a part of more general price controls. Its purpose was limited to the protection of low-income tenants. Québec's history with rent stabilization has been evolutionary in that the system started out informal and has become increasingly more formal so as to better protect low-income tenants.[21] At the time of its passage, the Act was not one of general application "either in a geographic or an economic sense."[22] In the 1950s and 1960s, "there were a complex series of amendments to the Act, which produced variations in both the list of communities and the type of rented accommodation to which the Act applied."[23] As a result, by the early 1970s there was general confusion as to where rent stabilization applied.[24]

As of December 1, 1962, houses in Montréal (including dwellings and apartments but not rooming houses) for which the rent legally in force was more than $125.00 were given an exemption from the Act. In other municipalities, the figure was set at $100.00.[25] Under the Act, the National Assembly established a Rental Office with a Rental Administrator in each municipality and appeals were made to the Rental Commission.[26]

The basic scheme of the Act was tenant-initiated. At a specified period before the expiry of a term, landlords and tenants were supposed to bargain for the new rent and the renewal of the lease for another year. If no agreement was reached, the tenant could apply to the Rental Administrator for an extension of the lease and for the fixing of rent. If the tenant did not make an application and remained on the property, the tenant was required to pay whatever increase had been demanded by the landlord.[27] The Administrator only had the power to fix the amount at lower than what the landlord demanded where there was disrepair or where the tenants space or services were reduced.[28] To qualify for a reduction, the disrepair had to seriously reduce the rental value of the premises and could not be the tenants' fault.[29] Premiums, commissions and bonuses were forbidden and could be recovered by action.[30] The landlord was not allowed to get a higher rent from a new tenant than that received from the former tenant without the administrator's authorization.[31] At this stage in the development of the Québec system, it was possible to contract out of the protections in the Act.[32]

From the time that the Québec legislation was passed in 1951, it had a life of two years and had to be re-enacted every year. The re-enacting of the Act would also renew all leases for an additional year (but not necessarily at the same rent).[33] However, if the tenant broke a covenant in the lease or was in arrears for three weeks, the tenant could be evicted with the authorization of the Rental Administrator.

From July 1972 until December 1975, a number of bills were introduced in the National Assembly to make the system more tenant-protective, but most were withdrawn because of pressure from back-bench deputies and a powerful coalition of Québec lawyers and landlords. As a result, there was little change to the system except that the Act was expanded to cover all dwellings built before December 1, 1974.[34]

A task force was set up by the government in 1974 and it made its recommendations in 1976, one of which was that procedures and remedies be made more accessible to the public. It was also recommended that a new rent commission be set up and an immediate stop be put on conversions of apartments to condominiums. A stop on this practice was included in the December 1975 amendments.[35]

In 1979, the part of the Civil Code[36] dealing specifically with residential dwellings was revised.[37] *An Act to Establish the Régie du logement and to amend the Civil Code and other legislation*, in force since 1980,[38] changed the law already modified in the seventies to ensure further protection for lessees.[39] These changes and others are the subject of the next section of this paper.

The present system in Québec

Rent increases must be made in accordance with the *Code of Civil Procedure of Québec*[40] and *An Act respecting the Régie du logement*, which came into effect on October 1, 1980.[41] The Québec Ministry of Municipal Affairs Responsible for Housing is in charge of the rent stabilization system and processes the applications permitted by the legislation through the Régie du logement (literally translated as "the Housing Board").[42]

On October 1, 1980, the Régie du logement replaced the Commission des loyers, which administered the former *Act to promote conciliation between lessees and property-owners*[43].[44] The Régie is a specialized administrative tribunal of high calibre which deals with as many as one hundred different types of applications relating to almost every area of residential landlord and tenant law, including rent stabilization.[45] In addition to the substantive areas of law dealt with by the tribunal, it is responsible for:

1. informing landlords and tenants of their rights;
2. promoting conciliation between landlords and tenants;
3. conducting studies and gathering statistics on the housing situation; and
4. summarizing the decisions of the commissioners and publishing these summaries.[46]

The Régie's personnel are required to help draft applications for anyone who asks.[47] Also, at the beginning of a hearing the commissioner(s) must summarily tell the parties what the rules of evidence that apply are, and must give equitable and impartial assistance to each party during the hearing in order to make sure the substantive law is properly applied.[48] At the beginning of each year, the Régie announces what it considers is an appropriate average rent increase for the year.[49]

Persons (including tenants, landlords and cooperatives) are permitted to be represented at hearings by a lawyer where the amount at issue is over $3,000. Persons can also be represented by a lawyer where the claim is for $3,000 or less if the lawyer is exclusively employed by the person as a lawyer.[50]

The rent stabilization provisions of the Code and Act apply to all rental residential "dwellings." The term includes rooming houses, mobile homes placed on a *frame*[51] (with or without a permanent foundation) and land which is rented so that a mobile home can be put on it. The services, accessories and dependencies attached to the dwelling are also included in the definition.[52] The following types of apartments are not included in the definition of "dwelling":
1. a dwelling leased as a vacation resort;
2. a dwelling that is included in a lease with non- residential space (where the non-residential space makes up more than one third of the total area);
3. a room in a "hotel establishment";
4. a room in the "principal residence" of the landlord if
   a) the room does not have a separate entrance
   b) it does not have separate sanitary facilities and
   c) the owners do not rent out more than two rooms in the house;
5. a room in a health or social services institution (but, "low-income housing" is not considered a health or social services institution).[53]

The procedure for renewing and modifying leases is set out in Articles 1941 to 1946 of the Code.[54] Rent can be increased once a year.[55] As a general rule, leases for fixed terms are extended on the same conditions and for the same duration (unless the term was more than 12 months, in which case the lease is only extended for 12 months). However, landlords have the right, when a lease expires, to change the term or other conditions of the lease (including the rent). To do so, the landlord has to give the tenant a notice of rent increase, which sets out the rent presently paid, the increased rent (either in dollars or as a percentage of the rent paid), the date on which the increase will take effect, and (where the landlord proposes to alter the term of the lease) the term proposed for the extension. Where the lease that just ended lasted for 12 months or more, the notice must be given between the sixth and third month before the expiry of the lease. Where the lease is for an indeterminate term or for less than 12 months, notice must be given between the second and first month. Where the lease is for a room, the period is between 20 and 10 days.

Within a month of receiving the notice of increase from the landlord, the tenant must tell the landlord one of the following: (1) the tenant objects to the change but wants to stay;[56] (2) the tenant will vacate when the lease expires; or (3) the tenant agrees to the changes. If the tenant does not respond, the tenant is deemed to have consented.[57] Where the tenant chooses option one, the landlord has one month to apply to have the rent fixed by the Régie. Otherwise, the lease is renewed of right on the same conditions as were in the old lease.[58] After it receives an application from the landlord, the Régie sends the landlord two copies of the *Information Necessary for Fixing the Rent Form* (also referred to as the RN Form).[59] The landlord must file a completed copy of this form and its required receipts within 20 days of the date that the Régie mailed out the form.[60]

When a lease is made with a new tenant, the landlord must give the new tenant a notice specifying the lowest rent paid over the last twelve months or (if the rent has been fixed within that time) the amount that the rent was fixed at.[61] The new tenant may, within 10 days of making the lease, or (if the lessor fails to provide the tenant with the notice) within two months of the start of the lease, apply to have the rent revised if the new tenant pays more rent than either the lowest rent paid for the last 12 months of the old lease or (if the rent has been fixed by the Régie within that time) the amount fixed.[62] The same rule applies to sublessees, and the relevant date is the date on which the sublease was made.[63]

A tenant can apply for a reduction of rent if the noise level in the building is so high that it prevents the tenant from fully enjoying the dwelling, a tenant's comfort and well-being in the apartment are affected because the landlord has not carried out some necessary repairs, the landlord makes a tenant vacate so that the landlord can make repairs, or the landlord cuts out some service or reduces the quality of one or does not provide an appliance or appurtenance that the landlord is supposed to.[64]

A lease can also provide its own formula for calculating rent increases. While this kind of lease does not violate the Code or Act, it is virtually useless (assuming the tenant has the knowledge, resources and inclination to bring a challenge) because all the specific rules in the Code relating to leases[65] are considered to be "of public order" and thus cannot be contracted out of.[66] A lease also cannot provide for an increase more often than every 12 months.[67] Within a month of an increase for which a formula is provided in a particular lease, either a tenant or a landlord is allowed to contest the increase on the basis that it is inadequate or excessive.[68]

Settlement/mediation

The Régie du logement, like certain Ontario tribunals such as the Ontario Labour Relations Board, uses staff conciliators who attempt to settle every case without the need for a formal hearing.[69] In a study on the Québec rent control system prepared for the Commission of Inquiry into Residential Tenancies, Professor François Des Rosiers of Laval University, who is an economist with a Masters degree in urban planning and a doctorate in urban and regional planning from the London School of Economics, described the Québec system as follows:

> The basic philosophy that prevailed to the establishment of the Régie rests upon the principle that harmonious relationships between landlords and tenants will emerge from better information on their respective rights and duties and that, where this cannot be achieved, the Régie will help them settle their disputes in a fair and just manner and in the best possible atmosphere.
> ...Thus, the Régie is actually a tribunal with the double mandate of deciding on claims submitted to it and, where possible, bringing landlords and tenants together. It should be stressed that the mandate of the Régie is not to set rent universally or globally, but to favour above all negotiation [sic] and private settlement between the two parties. Consequently, it intervenes only in a limited number of cases accounting for between 5 percent and 10 percent of the rental market and operates on a case by case basis; even then, only a fraction of all claims presented before the Régie will actually be settled through a decision by the tribunal.[70]

Criteria for fixing rent

The criteria the Régie applies are set out in the *Regulation Respecting the Criteria for the fixing of rent*.[71] The criteria set out apply to all "dwellings" as earlier defined, as well as to attached services,[72] accessories and dependencies.[73] The Regulation provides that, in arriving at the proper amount to be charged for a particular apartment, the charges that follow are to be added to the base rent (i.e., the rent already being paid) in the proportion that they are attributable to that apartment.[74] In applying the following formula, the Régie must exercise some discretion and cannot apply it rigidly[75]:

1. any change in the cost of property tax and municipal services;
2. the change in cost of fire and homeowner liability insurance;
3. the percentage which is set out in Schedule 1 of Québec Reg. c. R-8.1, r. 1.01 for the following charges:
    a) cost of electricity;
    b) fuel;
    c) maintenance;
    d) service;
    e) management fees;[76]
4. management fees at 5% of income or (if supporting documents are provided) up to 10% of income;
5. the full cost of any new service, appliance or appurtenance;
6. the percentage set out in Schedule 1 of:
    (a) capital expenditures[77] and
    (b) revenue but, the included amount of a capital expenditure cannot be more than the amount borrowed for the capital expenditure minus the amount payable of the interest and capital that is guaranteed or granted by a public authority.

The application of Québec's *Regulation Respecting the criteria for the fixing of rent*, then, is not intended to produce a figure that is the fair level of rent for a particular apartment. Rather, it represents the amount by which the existing rent can be fairly increased. The only exception to this rule is where, at the end of a lease, the rent is "preferential" (a defined term).[78] In such cases, the Régie must determine the proper amount to be charged by looking at the rent usually paid for similar dwellings.[79] Québec, then, cannot really be considered a *rent control* system because it does not fix or determine rents. Rather, because it is only concerned with the rate of increase of rents, and is better described as a *rent stabilization* system.[80]

Application fees

There is a $41 fee payable for all applications filed with the Régie, including applications for the fixing of rent.[81] This fee is not refundable by the Régie, even if an application has been withdrawn or an agreement has been reached before a hearing — even where Régie personnel assist the parties in arriving at a settlement.[82] Only people who establish that they are receiving benefits under a last resort assistance program under the *Act respecting income security* need not pay this fee.[83] This fee is payable by the applicant tenant if the tenant files an application to reduce the rent because of noise or any other reason.

As well, even where the landlord makes the ordinary application to fix the rent, the tenant may at the end of the hearing be required to pay the $41 fee by the Régie Commissioner presiding at the hearing.[84] The case law gives individual commissioners the discretion to allocate payment of the application fee as they see fit. In most cases, the commissioners have not made reference to the allocation of the fee, with the result that the applicant landlord was not reimbursed by the tenant. However, the case law is apparently changing. According to a Régie official, the law is moving towards a 50-50% split. In other words, the Régie will reallocate the fee to the tenant(s) in approximately 50% of the cases.[85] This fee is often large since a separate application must be filed for each unit that the tenant objects to an increase of rent for — this is the case even though the applications may be joined by the Régie for a common hearing. Thus, there will be a $41 fee payable for each unit assessed. Where, for example, applications are filed for 25 apartments, the fee which may be charged back to tenants is $1,025.[86]

Revision and appeal

Generally speaking, an appeal lies to the Court of Québec (formerly called the Provincial Court) from Régie decisions. But, decisions concerning an application, the sole object of which is the fixing or revision of rent, are exempted from this right of appeal. Decisions regarding rent increases may, though, be reviewed within a month of the date of the decision.[87] A decision rendered pursuant to a motion for review cannot be appealed to the Court of Québec.[88]

Analysis of the Québec system

In summary, the basic features of Québec's rent control system that are relevant in comparison to Ontario are as follows:

168 | Rent control laws in Ontario and Québec

1. Québec has no rent registry;
2. Québec has a tenant-initiated, rather than universal system;
3. Québec's system makes significant use of conciliators;
4. Québec has a large application fee and this is increasingly passed on to tenants;
5. Québec does not prescribe a maximum limit to which rent can be increased;
6. Québec has a rent stabilization rather than a rent control system.

As is discussed below, these characteristics have created certain difficulties for tenants in Québec due to the universality of the phenomenon of unequal bargaining power in the landlord-tenant relationship. However, notwithstanding this basic similarity, the problems caused by Québec's weaker regulatory system are somewhat offset by other features of its rental industry.[89] The President of the Federation des Associations de Locataires du Québec, Simon Langlois, recognized the differences between Québec and other parts of the country:

> What strikes me (and the other participants from Québec) is how unique Québec's housing problems are. Of course the degree to which Québec is different has often been observed by Canadians but when it comes to rents this is especially obvious for, as I have already said, Québec is a land of tenants.[90]

For instance, for the past several years Québec has had a high vacancy rate.[91] Statistics compiled by the Canada Mortgage and Housing Corporation (CMHC) regarding vacancy rates in privately initiated residential apartments of six units and over demonstrate this trend (see table on the facing page).

In contrast, the vacancy rates for various Ontario cities as of October 1995 is as follows: Metropolitan Toronto, 0.8%;[93] the City of Toronto, 0.9%; Etobicoke, 0.9%; City of York, 1.0%; Borough of East York, 0.8%; Scarborough, 0.5%; City of North York, 0.8%; Mississauga, 0.6%; City of Brampton, 1.1%; Town of Oakville, 0.5%; York Region, 1.6%; Pickering and Ajax, 0.5%.[94] The national average vacancy rate is 4.2%.[95] In 1987, the vacancy rate in Toronto was 0.1%.[96]

In addition to Québec's high vacancy rate, owners of apartment buildings in Québec tend to be smaller and more likely to live in the buildings they rent than do building owners in Ontario, which —

Vacancy rates in privately initiated residential apartments per year[92]

Metropolitan Areas	1987 Apr.	1987 Oct.	1988 Apr.	1988 Oct.	1989 Apr.	1989 Oct.	1990 Apr.	1990 Oct.	1991 Apr.	1991 Oct.	1992 Apr.	1992 Oct.	1993 Apr.	1993 Oct.	1994 Apr.	1994 Oct.	1995 Apr.	1995 Oct.
Chicoutimi-Jonquière	8.9	10.5	7.2	7.7	5.3	5.1	3.6	6.2	5.7	6.9	5.5	7.5	6.5	6.9	5.4	6.9	5.7	6.9
Montréal	1.7	3.6	3.9	4.0	3.8	4.9	4.6	5.9	5.6	7.8	6.8	8.4	6.7	8.2	6.8	7.5	6.2	6.8
Hull	7.7	10.7	7.2	4.5	3.5	3.2	3.9	4.2	5.5	4.9	4.1	3.8	3.8	5.1	5.2	6.9	6.0	8.7
Québec City	3.0	5.6	5.2	5.2	4.0	4.6	4.3	6.1	4.7	5.7	5.2	6.7	5.3	6.2	5.9	7.1	5.6	6.2
Sherbrooke	4.8	6.5	6.6	8.6	7.6	9.4	7.8	10.5	9.8	10.7	9.3	10.0	8.9	8.4	6.7	8.5	6.5	6.8
Trois Rivières	6.1	9.0	6.9	6.2	5.8	5.6	6.2	8.1	7.6	9.0	8.1	7.4	7.1	7.0	6.6	7.8	7.5	7.8

especially in the Metropolitan Toronto Area — tend to be large corporations.[97] For instance, in Québec as of June 30, 1991 the average number of units per privately-initiated residential building are 8.54. The figure for the metropolitan area of Montréal is 8.36; for Québec City, 9.97 units; for Hull, 8.88 units; for Sherbrooke, 10.25 units; for Trois-Rivières, 7.45 units; and for Chicoutimi-Jonquière, 6.66 units. In contrast, the average number of units per privately-initiated building in 1991 was 37.17 units for the metropolitan area of Toronto; 22.34 units for London; and 22.15 units for Ottawa.[98]

Moreover, in comparison to Ontario, Québec's Régie du logement is much more involved in public legal education.[99] For instance, the Régie publishes numerous pamphlets and guides for both landlords and tenants, and it provides specific advice and guidance to landlords and tenants both by telephone and in person at local Régie offices on quite a large scale.[100] The impact of the information provided by the Régie is strengthened by the fact that, in Québec, the vast majority of leases expire at about the same time each year (i.e., June). This makes the information provided more effective because the Régie targets its education drives for this time period and because people tend to listen more to information that is directly relevant.[101]

For the reasons discussed above, even though Québec's system is weaker than Ontario's, grave injustice has not resulted in that province.[102] However, given the marked differences between Ontario and Québec, it likely would cause serious hardship for tenants if Québec's system was transplanted into Ontario.

(1) Tenant initiation

A tenant-initiated system is of concern to tenants because it is less protective of tenants than is a mandatory/automatic system. The reason is that because of the vulnerable position of tenants relative to landlords, tenants need the assistance of remedial legislation to put them in a position where they can make effective use of whatever legal rights they are given.[103] And a system whose operation requires initiation by one of the parties (especially if the party who must pull the trigger is the more vulnerable one) will result in less actual reviews than a system that is mandatory and is constantly operating.[104] When it comes to rent control, a useful remedial measure would be an automatic/mandatory system.[105] Therefore, the experts have roundly concluded that a mandatory/automatic system is more desirable than is a tenant-initiated one.[106] The federal government has also recommended that the provinces introduce a more comprehensive system, rather than the system that presently exists in Québec.[107]

While cautioning against a "moralistic approach to law reform" and carefully avoiding an approach that would "ascribe particular blame or bestow praise upon either landlords or tenants,"[108] the Ontario Law Reform Commission in 1968 recognized the inequality of bargaining power inherent in the landlord-tenant relationship and the lack of freedom of contract in any meaningful sense.[109] Although this disparity of power is particularly pronounced where there is a shortage of housing,[110] the Commission concluded that "landlords' *standard forms* of lease do not change appreciably during periods of greater availability of rental accommodation."[111] Thus, "the principle of freedom of contract must be flexible enough to yield where experience has shown it to be a pious hope and an unrealistic assumption."[112]

The problem with a tenant-initiated rent control system, then, is that, while apparently recognizing that rent control is a worthy goal, it does not provide a system which is effective in achieving this goal. Much of the effectiveness of the regime is thus negated. The Ontario Law Reform Commission expressed this problem in a different context in the following terms:

> An examination of efforts to effect changes in the landlord and tenant laws demonstrates the need to create effective procedures so that the intention, inherent in the changes, can be realized. If new rights are created, they must be capable of being enforced speedily and with a minimum of expense. If procedures are slow, costly and difficult to follow, the remedy which they are intended to achieve will not be realized in the manner intended. In some cases an ineffective procedure can destroy the intent of the legislature.[113]

Similarly in a classic article titled "Protecting the Interests of the Indigent Tenant: Two Approaches," Professor Shier said:

> As a general matter, parties to a contract establish reciprocal rights and duties through the accepted medium of arm's length bargaining. Thus, in the ideal circumstance, where the parties meet on equal

terms to establish their obligations under the agreement, the prospective landlord offers the premises and certain services, and the prospective tenant offers to pay a price felt to be in accord with the going rate. When all terms have been agreed to by both sides, the exchange is concluded and the parties consider themselves bound. Of course, ideal circumstances are foreign to the poor tenant. [The tenant does not bargain with the landlord, for the tenant cannot] meet the landlord on anything approximating equal terms. Without bargaining strength [the tenant must] accept the landlord's offer as to duration, price and services."[114]

In another non-ideological study that was "not intended as a justification of one policy or another,"[115] Jeffrey Patterson and Ken Watson of the Canadian Council on Social Development concluded that it is a compelling argument against tenant initiative that, under such a system, many tenants in need of protection may remain unprotected. The reason is that tenants would fail to take initiative. The authors found that a disproportionate amount of those who would not take the initiative would likely have low incomes since low-income tenants tend to be more easily intimidated by landlords and government bureaucracy than more affluent ones. They also tend to be less knowledgeable concerning their rights.[116]

Moreover, Patterson and Watson felt that tenant-initiated systems exacerbate landlord-tenant relationships since tenant initiative often shifts the wrath of landlords from the bureaucracy to tenants — especially in the case of small landlords who are more likely to be personally familiar with their tenants.[117] As the authors stated, given that "landlord and tenant have to fight each other individually before a hearing officer, conflicts and bad feeling may be increased."[118] Thus, many commentators (including Québec government officials) have observed that Québec's system is the most damaging one in the country to landlord-tenant relations.[119]

A tenant-initiated system can result in incongruous results because reviews will not necessarily be taken with any consistency. A survey conducted by Professor Des Rosiers found that significant discrepancies exist between rents charged for identical units.[120]

In a system which relies on tenant initiation, the most vulnerable tenants are likely to suffer most from unfair rent increases.[121] The most vulnerable tenants include older people, pensioners and others who have lived in the same neighbourhood for a long time; students; single mothers (especially those on social assistance); persons with disabilities; low-income individuals, and immigrants (especially those with limited language skills).

Québec's rent stabilization system is not purely *tenant-initiated*. Rather, it is a *hybrid* system. Some applications which give rise to modifying the rent are tenant-initiated, but this is not entirely the case for the main application for the fixing of rent. That said, however, the application for the fixing of rent is tenant-initiated in the sense that a crucial first step in the process of getting the Régie to fix the rent is started by the tenant.[122]

The statistics available on the Québec system do seem to bear out the concerns that there will be few applications in a tenant-initiated system and that those most vulnerable will suffer the most. For instance, the Régie du logement has estimated that, at present, the tribunal only fixes the rent increase of slightly less than one half of one per cent of the total stock of dwellings.[123] Similarly in 1981, only 2.9% of the apartments in Montréal were subject to rent control,[124] and only 4.6% of the Québec City metropolitan area was subject to rent control.[125] This is the case even though the majority of the population in the Montréal region[126] and Québec generally[127] are tenants. At the time rent control was enacted in 1951, 82% of people in Montréal were tenants, 84% of those in Verdun, 80% in Québec City, 75% in Sherbrooke and 70% in Trois-Rivières.[128] In 1972, 70% of Montréal and 56% of the province were tenants.[129]

Further, the statistics show that recipients of a Québec government program called the "Logirente" shelter allowance (all of whom are senior citizens) were subjected to rent increases almost two times as high as renters generally.[130]

Moreover, the use of the system by tenants appears to be in decline while its use by landlords, who tend to know more about residential tenancies law than do tenants, is on the rise. Compared to other applications made to the Régie, applications regarding rent increases rose by 57% between 1981 and 1982 and accounted for 44% of all claims. However since then, they have experienced a steady decline, with the number of claims falling to nearly half their 1982 level. At the same time, 1982 was characterized by numerous requests for significant rent rises by landlords.[131] This is likely the case because the rent stabilization program in Québec has been constructed so as to compensate landlords for increases in their operating and maintenance costs.[132] Patterson and Watson concluded that "rent control provisions can [thus] be said to affect ultimately a quite limited portion of the rental market..."[133]

(2) Québec has no rent registry

Québec has no rent registry. Because tenants do not have access to reliable information about rents previously charged in the absence of a registry, the Act's potential for protecting low-income tenants is weakened by the absence of a registry. As was said above, landlords are supposed to give new tenants a notice setting out the lowest rent. If the tenant discovers a falsehood, the tenant can then apply to have the rent fixed. However, without a rent registry that keeps track of the rents charged, tenants have no way of knowing if the information provided by the landlord is true. Certainly, few tenants would have the ability to track down old tenants and find out how much rent they paid.[134] Further, this defect is likely to impact hardest on those tenants who are most vulnerable (i.e., those who have the least ability to find out what the last charged rent was).

The lack of a registry would also likely impact most upon disadvantaged groups living in the inner-city since nearly all housing in these locations is second hand — that is, tenants tend to move into apartments that were lived in by someone else before them more often than in more affluent areas of the city.[135]

Professor Des Rosiers has pointed out that in practice the landlord can easily frustrate the Act by keeping the dwelling unoccupied for a couple of months so as to avoid contact between the previous and the new tenant.[136] Indeed given the imbalance of power between landlords and tenants, what likelihood is there that even if the tenant discovers a lie, he or she will bring it to the attention of the Régie? Or what chance is there that the landlord will even provide the tenant with the required notice? Jeffrey Patterson and Ken Watson of the Canadian Council on Social Development found that conformity on the part of landlords with these and other notice requirements "is far from universal." Accordingly, they concluded that a system without a registry would be virtually ineffective.[137] A rent registry corrects the prejudice to tenants of not knowing what rents they should pay.[138] Patterson and Watson highlighted the incongruity of a province not having a rent registry along with its regime of rent control in the following terms:

> In many provinces we require the registration of overnight facilities for tourists and travellers — it

would be a blow to tourist promotion if too many tourists were subjected to inferior rooms or unscrupulous inn keepers —but we do not require the registration of dwellings in which families spend their lives and nurture their children. We often have tourist information kiosks, maintained at public expense, but there are few information centres for families seeking a home. For these reasons, the registration of rented dwellings and their rents should be required of both private and public landlords.[139]

William Gray, former executive director of the Hamilton Ontario Apartment Board has stated that "A system of licensing is essential to set standards and keep check on the whole system of rentals."[140] Another expert has found that new tenants do not use their right to request a rent decrease to the level paid by the previous tenant.[141]

Patterson and Watson have found that an added advantage of a registry is that, from the government's perspective, it is relatively simple, clear and cheap. As well, it decreases uncertainty so that landlords and tenants know in advance where they stand. This will head off conflicts between landlords and tenants.[142] Further, a rent registry provides a useful source of information for the government should it decide to monitor the rents tenants pay in order to prevent what is referred to as rent gouging.[143] Moreover, even if the government does not actually monitor the rent registry in detail, the mere fact that the landlord is required to mail its notice of increase to a government body likely will discourage landlords from charging usurious rents.

(3) Québec's system makes significant use of conciliators

A system of mediation adds one more step to the process for applicant tenants and given the resources of tenants compared to those of landlords, it is likely that unrepresented tenants would engage in settlement discussions with landlord lawyers. This lack of assistance combined with the already unequal bargaining power of landlords, prejudices tenants.[144] Moreover, the Act essentially provides that in the case of a claim of $3,000 or less, individual tenants cannot be represented by lawyers. Landlords are really not subject to the same restriction. Landlords who are affluent enough to employ lawyers to act solely as in-house counsel, can be represented by those lawyers in all proceedings regardless of the amount of money that is at issue.[145] Even where the landlord is not represented, one can assume that a large apartment complex owner would be familiar with the system and able to represent itself before the tribunal. The tenant, in contrast, is likely to be facing this situation for the first time and may be intimidated from the start.[146]

Moreover, mediation unavoidably brings other matters into consideration when the only point that is at issue is whether the rent increase that the landlord wants is too high or whether the landlord has made illegal rent increases. As the Thom Commission said:

> It may be asked whether mediation is a suitable approach to tenants' problems when they involve rent. Questions such as whether the landlord has breached an obligation to keep the premises in a good state of repair or has interfered with the tenant's enjoyment of the premises are frequently as much a matter of feelings or opinion as of fact, and it is understandable that a resolution of those difficulties by mediation would be preferable to a hearing before a Commissioner. However, the determination of what rent a tenant should have paid in the past or should be paying now involves essentially matters of fact that could be resolved by a study of the relevant records. If mediation is useful for dealing with rent problems, particularly those arising under section 129 regarding alleged illegal rents, it is because the Act is deficient in not defining lawful rent and how it should be determined and because, without a rent registry, information on past rents is sometimes difficult to obtain.[147]

The Commission continued:

> The landlord could offer concessions on matters that were relatively [unimportant to the landlord but that] were important to the tenant for the enjoyment of the premises [the tenant occupied] and might thereby induce the tenant to forego [the tenant's proper] claim to a lower rent or to the recovery of excess rents.[148]

The Commission thus concluded that negotiated rent arrangements between landlords and tenants are incompatible with the idea of limiting landlords' unilateral power to decide what rents will be charged for apartments.[149]

Another problem with mediation relates to the institutional concerns it tends to foster. That is, when a system of mediation has been put in place by a tribunal for some time, institutional pressure may develop for more cases to be settled through mediation and less to be settled by formal tribunal decision. Tenants may therefore in some cases feel pressured to compromise in settlement negotiations when there is no justifiable reason (other than a concern for public resources) why they should compromise.

(4) Application fee

Québec's constantly increasing application fee and the increasing possibility that it could be passed on to tenants have been described above. The fee likely acts as a deterrent to low-income tenants. Although tenants who receive benefits from last resort assistance programs under the *Act respecting income security*[150] do not have to pay the fee, this exemption does not go far enough. There are numerous other types of social assistance in Québec, and many people who receive these other forms of assistance do not have a higher income than do recipients of the last resort assistance program. Moreover, Canada has a growing number of people who have been described as "the working poor"[151] Those who fall within this group do not have expendable income which could be spent on rent review applications.

(5) Québec does not prescribe an annual tent cap

The lack of a prescribed maximum increase inevitably brings some ambiguity into the process of setting rent. Although it is true that a formula is set out in the *Criteria Regulation*,[152] terms like "capital expenditure" are vague and in fact have been the subject of literally hundreds, if not thousands, of applications.[153] Given the steep application fee described above it seems likely that the ambiguity in the calculation may deter low-income tenants from contesting rent increases.[154] A tenant who has little or (in the case of applicants receiving a different type of social assistance than "last resort assistance") no disposable income is unlikely to be willing to gamble on the chance that they will win the application at the end of the day.[155]

(6) Rent stabilization rather than rent control

As mentioned above, Québec's system is designed to regulate rent increases, rather than the absolute level of rent. The base level of

178 | Rent control laws in Ontario and Québec

rent (i.e., the rent that existed prior to the application) is implicitly assumed to be a fair one.[156] Even if the rent was unfairly high or low,[157] the Act does not give the Régie the authority to reduce it below the base level.[158] The nature of this system, then, means that if there is a discrepancy, it may be perpetuated indefinitely. The result is that a rent stabilization system simply cannot ensure a fair level of rent unless it is assumed that the base rent is already a fair one.[159] If it was the case that base rents were fair, rent review would not have been introduced in the first place.

NOTES

1. LL.B.and member, Tenant Advocacy Group. T.A.G. is the working group of the Metropolitan Toronto legal aid clinics' landlord and tenant case workers. T.A.G. participates in law reform, case work and tenant organizing. T.A.G. has worked for progressive reform of landlord-tenant and rent review legislation with Liberal, New Democrat and Progressive Conservative Party governments in Ontario. Thanks to all members of the Legislative Reform Subcommittee of T.A.G., including R. Carey, K. Hale, L. Abramowicz, J. Buncel, T. Burton, J. McNally, G. Stevenson, H. Tessler and T. Young. Thanks also to A. Bennett of Services d'animation teninform, P. Chapman LL.B., and P. Marchand of Régie du Logement. The author's views are not necessarily those of T.A.G. nor of anyone thanked.
2. R.A. Muller, "Ontario's Options in the Light of the Canadian Experience with Decontrol" in R.J. Arnott & J.M. Mintz, *Policy Forum on Rent Controls in Ontario* (Policy Forum Series No. 13) (Kingston, Ont.: John Deutsch Institute for the Study of Economic Policy, Queen's University, 1987) 21 at 22. See also: Ontario, *Report of the Commission of Inquiry into Residential Tenancies*, vol. 2 (Toronto: Queen's Printer, 1987) [dated April 1987, but released 28 January 1988] (Chair: S. Thom) at 72-77.
    At the time this chapter went to press, Ontario's conservative government was considering removing tenant protections and moving to a tenant-initiated system (H. Tessler, "The Tenant Protection Program: What Tenants Should Expect" *The [FMTA] Tenants' Bulletin* (Winter 1995-1996) 1 at 1 & 8; City of Toronto, Commissioner of Housing & Commissioner of Planning and Development, *Potential Impacts of the Removal of Rent Control and Rental Housing Protection Legislation* (Toronto: City of Toronto, 8 February 1996). See also: Ontario, *Consultation Paper: Rent Control Regulations* (Ontario: Government of Ontario, December 1995) and the reason seems clear. A 1975 government paper stated that if policy-makers decided the current system should be relaxed, one way to do so would be to make the system tenant-initiated (Ontario, Ministry of Consumer and Commercial Relations, *Policy Options for Continuing Tenant Protection* (Green Paper) (Ontario: Ministry of Consumer and Commercial Relations, 10 February 1978) at 42).
3. J.D. Hulchanski, *Rental Housing Trends in the City of Vancouver* (CHS

Research Bulletin) (Vancouver: UBC Centre for Human Settlements, April 1989) at 6 & 8; Ontario, [Royal] Commission of Inquiry into Residential Tenancies, *The Rent Control System in Québec* (Research Study No. 25) by F. Des Rosiers (Toronto: The Commission, December 1985) (Chair: S.D. Thom); Federation of Metro Tenants' Associations, *Report to the Standing Committee on General Government on Bill 121* (Toronto: F.M.T.A., 26 August 1991) at 1; Federation of Metro Tenants' Associations, *Fact Sheet on Rent Control* (Toronto: F.M.T.A., undated) at 1; Federation of Metro Tenants' Associations, *Facts on Tenants and Tenant Issues* (Fact Sheet) (Toronto: F.M.T.A., May 1990) at 1.

4. A.B. Comick, "Rent Control: The Facts Vancouver Should Know" (1993) 4 W.R.L.S.I., 91 at 93.

5. Social Planning Council of Metropolitan Toronto, Community Review and Research Group, *Rent Controls: Why We Need Them: What Kind? How Long? A Background Analysis* (Toronto: Social Planning Council, October 1975) at 2; D. Donnison in Canadian Council on Social Development, *Is there a Case for Rent Control? Background Papers and Proceedings of a Canadian Council on Social Development Seminar on Rent Policy* (Ottawa: C.C.S.D., 1973) at 155; Ontario, Thom Commission, *supra*, note 1 at 228 & 382; F.M.T.A., *supra*, note 3; Federation of Metro Tenants' Associations, *Rent Control: We Still Don't Have It* (Fact Sheet on Bill 4) (Toronto: F.M.T.A., undated) at 1; *Green Paper, supra*, note 1.

6. Comick, *supra*, note 3; *Interim Report of the Ontario Law Reform Commission on Landlord and Tenant Law Applicable to Residential Tenancies* (Toronto: Ontario Department of the Attorney General, 1968) at 63; J. Patterson and K. Watson, *Rent Stabilization: A Review of Current Policies in Canada* (Ottawa: The Canadian Council on Social Development, 1976). See also: Ontario, Ministry of Housing, *Rental Housing Protection Act: Future Directions* (Ontario: Ministry of Housing, 6 April 1988). This is not to say that more demand-oriented policies are not also needed.

7. Ontario, Commission of Inquiry into Residential Tenancies, *Government Intervention in Housing Markets: An Overview* (Research Study No. 29) by E.B. Adams et al. (Toronto: The Commission, April 1986) at 9 (Chair: S. Thom).

8. Patterson and Watson, *supra*, note 6 at 5. Indeed, rent control was considered so important that any offence against a regulation, order or requirement of Order-in-Council 9029 was deemed to be a criminal offence (*Regulations Respecting Leasehold Rights and Obligations in Time of War, infra*, note 14, ss. 2(2) & 6-9).

9. Ontario Law Reform Commission, *supra*, note 6 at 63-64; SI/12-1, P.C. 4616, C. Gaz. 1940.LXXIV.977 at paras. 1-5; P.H. White, in C.C.S.D., *supra*, note 5 at 135, para. 2.

See also Patterson and Watson, *supra*, note 6 at 12: "When housing supply fails to keep pace with demand, the scarcity value of the existing rental housing stock becomes a powerful force for reallocating income in favor of landlords. Rent stabilization or control can, in the short-run at least, frustrate this undesirable change in the distribution of income. [Its object is not the redistribution of income to tenants.] In this sense of protecting the status quo and frustrating undesirable income redistribution, rent control is a conservative instrument." Further, the pure and massive transfer of income from tenants to the landlord population which would result from a market where no construction was taking place due to a shortage of building materials would not be justified by any increase in landlord costs. The sole reason for the transfer would be the unique market position of landlords as owners of a scarce commodity that is not only in high demand but is also a basic necessity. "Since the proportion of tenant income spent on housing is substantial, this shift would be an enormous burden upon the tenant population (*Id.*, at 13)." Allowing the market to operate freely, then, would cause a regressive income redistribution (J.D. Hulchanski, *supra*, note 3 at 6).

10. *Id.*
11. R.S.C. 1927, c. 206.
12. In peacetime, rent control falls within the provinces' authority under "property and civil rights" (L. Ross in "Seminar on Rent Policy: Proceedings" in C.C.S.D., *supra*, note 5 at 114 citing *Constitution Act, 1867* (U.K.), 30 & 31 Vict., c. 3).
13. M. Audain and C. Bradshaw, "Rent Regulation: Sketches of Various Schemes" in C.C.S.D., *supra*, note 5, 13 at 27; Adams et al., *supra*, note 7 at 9.
14. *Regulations Respecting Leasehold Rights and Obligations in Time of War*, SI/22-1, P.C. 9029, C. Gaz. 1941.LXXV.1820.
15. *Id.*, s. 3; Ontario Law Reform Commission, *supra*, note 6 at 63-64; Audain and Bradshaw, *supra*, note 13; Adams *et al.*, *supra*, note 7 at 9.
16. Ontario Law Reform Commission, *Id.* at 64; W.F. Spence, "Rental Control in Canada" in Law Society of Upper Canada, *Refresher Course Lectures*, vol. 1 (Toronto: L.S.U.C., 1945). See also, more generally, M.J. Radin, "Residential Rent Control" (1986) 15, *Philosophy & Pub. Affairs,* 350 at 372; Hulchansky, *supra*, note 3 at 6; Patterson and Watson, *supra*, note 6 at 92-93; Social Planning Council of Metropolitan Toronto, *supra*, note 5 at 2 & 15; G. Yee, "Rationales for Tenant Protection and Security of Tenure" (1989) 5, *J.L. & Soc. Pol.*, 35 at 56-57; M. Gorsky, "Seminar on Rent Policy: Proceedings" in *C.C.S.D.*, *supra*, note 5 at 97; Adams *et al.*, *Id.* at 10; Ontario, Ministry of Consumer and Commercial Relations, *supra*, note 2 at 22; B. Bucknall, "Rent Review in Ontario: Policy, Politics and the Well Paved Road" (1977) 8(2), *Housing and People,* 8 at 10: "Rent control is, in theory, inseparable from a regime of security of tenure. As in the Ontario program, even where the control is placed upon the unit rather than upon the tenancy agreement, landlords may find some advantage in forcing tenants to move so that covert rent increases can be taken. A scheme whereby tenants can be evicted from the units only upon cause and with due procedure is essential to avoid this sort of evasion."
17. *Regulations Respecting Leasehold Rights and Obligations in Time of War*, *supra*, note 14, s. 3. Section 3 gave the board the power to prescribe the grounds on which and the way in which leases could be terminated.
18. Ontario Law Reform Commission, *supra*, note 6 at 64.
19. Adams *et al.*, *supra*, note 7 at 10-11; Patterson & Watson, *supra*, note 6 at 5; Ontario Law Reform Commission, *Id.* at 64.
20. R.S.Q. 1977, c. C-50. See: Audain and Bradshaw, *supra*, note 13 at 31; Adams *et al.*, *Id.*, at 42. See also: L. Ross in C.C.S.D., *supra*, note 5 at 115, which said that "It was necessary to bring in this measure since so many

landlords were unable to control themselves."
21. Patterson and Watson, *supra*, note 6 at 53; S. Langlois in C.C.S.D., *Id.* at 134.
22. Ontario Law Reform Commission, *supra*, note 6 at 66. See also: Social Planning Council of Toronto, *supra*, note 5 at i.
23. Patterson and Watson, *supra*, note 6 at 50-51.
24. Ontario Law Reform Commission, *supra*, note 6 at 66; Social Planning Council of Metropolitan Toronto, *supra*, note 5 at i.
25. Act to promote conciliation, *supra*, note 20, s. 35a; L. Ross in C.C.S.D., *supra*, note 5 at 116-117. These dwellings were considered luxury apartments and therefore the tenants were not in need of protection. In theory, such an exemption is justifiable since more wealthy tenants do not need to be protected by rent control. However, it may be that in some markets the resulting incentive to landlords to own luxury apartments will in fact have prohibitive side effects on the poor (Radin, *supra*, note 16 at 378). As well, difficulty arises in establishing a standard above which apartments are considered luxurious. For instance in today's market, at first glance, a rent of $950 may seem luxurious, but it is not hard to imagine a parent with four children spending this much on an apartment that is not luxurious.
26. Ontario Law Reform Commission, *supra*, note 6, at 66-67.
27. Patterson and Watson, *supra*, note 6 at 9; Adams *et al.*, *supra*, note 7 at 42; British Columbia, Inter-departmental Study Team on Housing and Rents, *Housing and Rent Control in British Columbia* (Vancouver: Inter-departmental Study Team on Housing and Rents, Minister of Housing & the Attorney General, 20 October 1975) at 383 (Chair: K. Jaffary); Social Planning Council of Metropolitan Toronto, *supra*, note 5 at i; L. Ross in C.C.S.D. *supra*, note 5 at 115.
28. *Act to promote conciliation*, *supra*, note 20, s. 26.
29. *Id.*
30. *Id.*, s. 28.
31. *Id.*, s. 29.
32. L. Ross, *Id.*, at 116 & 119.
33. Patterson and Watson, *supra*, note 6 at 41 & 49; Social Planning Council of Metropolitan Toronto, *supra*, note 5 at i; Audain and Bradshaw, *supra*, note 13 at 31; L. Ross, *Id.* at 115.
34. Patterson and Watson, *Id.* at 41, 49 & 51.
35. *Id.*, at 41-42.
36. *Infra.*, note 40. Québec has a civil law rather than a common law system, which is derived from the law of France. In a civil law jurisdiction, the legal rules, including the laws of lease and contract (which are the two areas which govern landlord-tenant law) are codified in the Civil Code (M. Casavant, "The Quebec Law of Lease" in C. Bentley, J. McNair and M. Butkus, William and Rhodes: *Canadian Law of Landlord and Tenant*, vol. 2, 6th ed. (Toronto: Carswell, 1988), 30A.1 at 30A.1) [Chapter 30A updated to 1994].
37. M. Franklin, D. Franklin and R. Des Rosiers de Lanauze, *Introduction to Quebec Law*, 3d ed. (Toronto: Copp Clark Pitman Ltd., 1984) at 160.
38. *Loi instituant la Régie du logement et modifiant le Code civil et d'autres dispositions legislatives*, L.Q. 1979, c. 48 [sanctionnee le 7 novembre 1979].

39. Franklin et al., supra, note 37 at 170; Patterson and Watson, supra, note 5, at 51.
40. C.c.Q. (new).
41. R.S.Q., c. R-8.1 [en. S.Q. 1979, c. 48]. There are also rules of procedure: *Rules of Procedure of the Régie du logement*, R.R.Q. 1981, c. R-8.1, r. 5.
42. The Régie is composed of commissioners, including a chair and two vice-chairs (*An Act Respecting the Régie, Id.*, s. 6). Applications are generally heard and decided by one commissioner who must be either a lawyer ("advocate") or a judge (*Id.*, s. 29, para. 1 & s. 30; M. Franklin et al., *supra*, note 37 at 160). However, the Act provides that the chair or the vice-chair designated for that purpose can increase the number to up to five. Where this is the case, one of the judges or advocates must be designated to preside (*Id.*, s. 29, para. 2). The Act also says that a Régie employee can be appointed as a "special clerk" and given the power, among other things, to fix the rent in the same way that a commissioner would (*Id.*, ss. 30.1 & 30.2(3). Where a special clerk decides a case, the tenant can have the decision reviewed by a commissioner if the application for review is made within 10 days of the date of the decision (*Id.*, s. 30.3). The special clerk can refer any matter to be decided to a commissioner that the clerk considers necessary in the interests of justice (*Id.*, s. 30.4).

    Disputes arising out of commercial leases are not dealt with by the Régie, but by the regular courts (M. Franklin et al., *supra*, note 37 at 179).
43. S.Q. 1975, c. 84.
44. M. Casavant, "Notes on the Quebec Law of Lease: The Residential Lease" in M. Butkus et al., *supra*, note 36 at 30.12 [Chapter 30 updated to 1992]; Adams et al., *supra*, note 7 at 44; Ontario, Thom Commission, *supra*, note 2 at 8. Section 4 of *An Act respecting the Régie, Id.*, establishes the Régie du logement and s. 138 replaces the Commission des loyers with the Régie.
45. Interview with P. Marchand, l'Agent de recherche, Research Department, Régie du logement (21 February 1996); M. Franklin et al., *supra*, note 37 at 171; Des Rosiers, *supra*, note 3 at 8.
46. *An Act respecting the Régie, supra*, note 41, s. 5.
47. *Id.*, s. 21.
48. M. Casavant, *supra*, note 44 at 30.20 *citing An Act Respecting the Régie, Id.*, s. 63, paras. 2 & 3.
49. Letter from Régie du logement Vice-presidente C. Hovington to Federation of Metro Tenants' Associations Tenant Organizer H. Tessler (25 October 1995) at 1 [this letter is available from the author of this Chapter]; Interview with P. Marchand, *supra*, note 45.
50. Section 73 of *An Act respecting the Régie, supra*, note 41, says that this is the case "Notwithstanding the Charter of human rights and freedoms (c. C-12)." See also: s. 72; Des Rosiers, *supra*, note 3 at 9.
51. I.e., a "chassis"
52. C.c.Q. (new), Art. 1892, paras. 1 & 2.
53. *An Act respecting the Régie, supra*, note 41.
54. C.c.Q. (new). This procedure is summarized below. For a more in-depth treatment of the issue, see: Casavant, *supra*, note 44 at 30.55-30.57 & 30.81-30.84.
55. *An Act respecting the Régie, supra*, note 41, s. 133.

56. Tenants living in certain types of dwellings are not allowed to object to a proposed increase. They must therefore vacate if the changes requested by the landlord are not agreed with. These types of dwellings are: (1) dwellings built under *An Act to authorize the Members of the Council of the City of Montréal to carry out a plan for the elimination of slums and the construction of sanitary housing*, S.Q. 1956-57 (1st Sess.), c. 23 [assented to 19 December 1956], and the *Act to further Facilitate the carrying out of a Plan for the Elimination of Slums and the Construction of Sanitary Housing in the City of Montréal*, *Id.*, c. 53 [assented to 21 February 1957]; (2) dwellings leased by housing cooperatives to their members (C.c.Q. (new), Art. 1955, para. 1); and (3) dwellings that are less than 5 years old or which have undergone a change of use less than 5 years ago (*Id.*, at para. 2). In order to qualify for one of these exemptions, however, the restriction must be mentioned in the lease (*Id.*, at para. 3). Dwellings in "low-rental housing" (a defined term) are also exempted from this rent stabilization procedure (*Id.*, Arts. 1956, 1984 & 1992-1994). A separate procedure is set out elsewhere in the Code for low rental housing. The same goes for dwellings which have been subleased (*Id.*, Art. 1940).
57. The tenant also has the right to demand that the time within which he or she has to respond be extended (Casavant, *supra*, note 44 at 30.57 *citing Turenne v. Gagne*, [1981] D.R.L. 267 (Prov. Ct.) & *Harper v. F.D.L. Compagnie Ltee*, J.L. 83-123 (Prov. Ct.), J.L. 88-102 (Régie). See also: *Societe imobiliere Parc Samuel Holland Inc. c. St. Pierre*, [1988] R.J.Q. 1100 (Prov. Ct.))
58. C.c.Q. (new), Art. 1947.
59. *Rules of Procedure*, *supra*, note 41, s. 8.
60. *Id.*, s. 9, paras. 1 & 2.
61. C.c.Q. (new), Art. 1896. This notice does not have to be provided if the apartment is in a co-op., a recently renovated/erected/converted dwelling or one that is in "low rental housing" (*Id.*).
62. Franklin *et al.*, *supra*, note 37 at 177. If the notice contains a false declaration, the tenant can apply for a rent fixing within two months of discovering the lie (C.c.Q. (new), Art. 1950).
63. *Id.*
64. C.c.Q. (new), Arts. 1863, para. 1 & 1865; *Regulation respecting the Criteria for the Fixing of the Rent*, R.R.Q. 1981, c. R-8.1, r. 1.01, s. 8; Québec, Ministry of Municipal Affairs Responsible for Housing, Régie du logement, *Noise* [Pamphlet] (Québec: Régie, February 1994) at 3; Québec, Ministry of Municipal Affairs Responsible for Housing, Régie du logement, *Rent Reduction* [Pamphlet] (Québec: Régie, February 1994) at 1-2.
65. Namely, C.c.Q. (new), Book V, Title II, Chapter IV, Section IV.
66. C.c.Q. (new), Art. 1893.
67. *Id.*
68. *Id.*, Art. 1949. Where the increase is contested, the Régie will determine the rent using the criteria provided in the *Criteria Regulation* (*Id.*), which are described below.
69. Des Rosiers, *supra*, note 3 at 7-9; Gouvernement du Québec, Régie du logement, *Conciliation: A Service worth asking for!* [Pamphlet] (Québec: Régie, February 1994); Inter-departmental Study Team, *supra*, note 27 at 388.

Section 31 of the Act, *supra*, note 41, provides the Régie with the authority to use conciliators to settle cases.
70. Des Rosiers, *Id.* at 7 as quoted in Ontario, Thom Commission, *supra*, note 2. See also: Québec, *Se Loger au Québec: une analyse de la realite un appel a l'imagination* [On Accommodation in Québec: An Analysis of the Reality and an Appeal to the Imagination] (Québec: la Direction generale des publications gouvernementales du ministere des Communications, 1984); Québec, Ministre des Affaires municipales et ministre d'Etat au developpement des regions, Régie du logement, *Régie du logement: Rapport annuel 1994-1995* (Sainte-Foy: Les Publications du Québec, juin 1995).
71. R.R.Q. 1981, c. R-8.1, r. 1.01. See also C.c.Q. (new), Art. 1953; *Act Respecting the Régie*, *supra*, note 41, s. 5.
72. "Services" is defined to mean only those services that the tenant does not have to pay for upon each use or on a unit basis (*Criteria Regulation, Id.*, s. 1). In other words, the term "service" refers to those services which, at least notionally, are already included in the rent which the tenant has been paying each month.
73. *Id.*, s. 2. The same rules regarding the fixing of rent apply to rooms, mobile homes and land intended for the installation of a mobile home, with such modifications as the circumstances require (*Id.*, s. 10).
74. *Id.*, ss. 3, 4.1 & 5, para. 1. The proportion attributable to a particular apartment is equal to the proportion its rent is of the total of: the rent actually received from all tenants in the building plus the "estimated rent" for the building (*Id.*, s. 5, para. 1). "Estimated rent" is the total of the following estimates: (1) the rent that would have been charged for apartments that are vacant if they were not vacant and; (2) the rent that would have been charged for apartments that are used for operating the building or by the lessor, the lessor's family or a janitor or superintendent if those apartments had been rented to regular tenants (*Id.*, s. 1). If capital expenditures, electricity, fuel costs or taxes for services apply only to certain units, these amounts are only applied to the rents and estimated rents of the dwellings concerned (*Id.*, s. 5, para. 2). Neither a share of an expenditure that relates to non-residential premises nor the net income from the operation of those premises can be considered in calculating the rent of other apartments (*Id.*). Section 11 provides that, notwithstanding s. 5, the share attributable to a room, mobile home or land intended for the installation of a mobile home shall be calculated by allowing for the margin of profit earned on the operating expense or capital expenditure concerned, where this profit can be determined. Section 12 provides that, in the case of a room located in a dwelling, the tribunal will take into account the rent of the house in proportion to the value of the room.
75. *Commission des loyers c. Cedar Investment Inc.*, [1981] R.P. 244, [1980] D.R.L. 108 a la p. 246, M. le juge Bisson.
    Section 15 of the *Criteria Regulations*, *Id.*, provides that, where information required for determining the rent under this Regulation is lacking, the Régie can make up for this by relying on any relevant information at its disposal. On the other hand, the Régie has held in a number of cases that it may not rule on an application to fix the rent where there are no supporting vouchers (M. Casavant, *supra*, note 44 at 30.84 *citing La societe de gestion*

Acmon Ltee c. Wasserman, J.L. 87-107; *Couturier c. Corporation de gestion Sylvia Kasner*, J.L. 87-108 & *Pearson c. A & F Investments Inc.*, J.L. 89-161).

76. Schedule 1, *Id.*, provides that, for leases expiring between April 1, 1995 and March 31, 1996 and for contestations of adjustment of rent to take effect between April 2, 1995 and April 1, 1996, the rates to be used are as follows:

Percentage applicable to the cost of electricity subject to the:	
domestic rate (D or DM)	0.1%
domestic dual energy rate (DT) -	0.5%
general small power rate (G)	0.2%
all other rates	0.1%
Percentages applied to the cost of fuel:	
heating oil	10.4%
gas and other forms of energy	5.3%
Percentage applicable to the cost of maitenance:	1.3%
Percentage applicable to the cost of providing services:	1.1%
Percentage applicable to management costs:	1.1%
Percentage applicable to capital expenditures:	8.3%
Percentage applicable to net revenue:	0.5%

Schedule 1 also provides that where the percentage set out above for the cost of electricity and fuel is not accurate, the board (where it has the necessary information) shall take those costs into account by proceeding in the manner provided for in s. 4, para. 2. Section 4, para. 2, states as follows: "In the case of fuel and electricity, the tribunal shall apply the percentage change in the unit cost between the period considered and the preceding period to their cost for the period considered. In the case of taxes and insurance premiums, this variation is equal to the cost difference between the two periods." Section 14 of the Regulation, *Id.*, provides that where the electricity rate changes part way through the year, the Régie shall calculate this factor so that the two (or more) rates will be used for the periods of time to which they relate.

77. "Capital expenditure" is defined by s. 1a of the *Criteria Regulation, Id.*, as "spending on a building for major repairs and renovations or the offering of a new service" minus: (1) any subsidy towards the expenditure by the federal, provincial or municipal government or a public utility and minus (2) any compensation from any third person as consideration for or for the loss that caused the expenditure. This definition has been further clarified by a number of decisions of the Régie.

The Québec system accepts any major expenditure whatever its nature and does not question whether it is necessary to have spent the money or not (Letter from Régie du logement, *supra*, note 49 at 2). In contrast, Ontario extracts over a number of years an amount from the rent pertaining to major expenditures (*Id.*).

That an unrestricted percentage of capital expenditures are included in the fixed rent without justifying that they were necessary is a cause of concern. What if the tenant is relatively immobile, has been in the building for a long time and has a genuine difference of opinion with the landlord as to whether the repairs are necessary? What if the tenant is a pensioner? And even if we assume the outlay was necessary, it does not necessarily follow that the landlord should be able to reimburse the outlay through rent. It could be argued that the expenditure is simply an investment in the property which will eventually pay off should the owner decide to *cash-in* the property (see also, more generally, F.M.T.A., *supra*, note 3 at 6-7).

78. Under s. 1, *Id.*, the rent for a particular unit is "preferential" if it is less than what is usually charged for a comparable dwelling and the reason why is one of the following: (1) the tenant is the lessor's relative, associate or employee; (2) the lessor supports or supported the tenant; (3) the apartment is located in a building that was inherited and the amount of the rent is attributable to bad management by the deceased; or (4) the lessor is a department or agency of the Government of Québec. The "support" referred to in the definition of "preferential rent" has been held to not be limited to financial support (*Terrasses Greenfield c. Lamer*, J.L. 87-118 (Régie); M. Casavant, *supra*, note 44 at 30.85). Incongruously, the rent rise determination process does not account for expenses incurred by tenants for major repairs and improvements to their dwelling. Since the landlord directly benefits from such expenses which will eventually translate into higher rents and a higher building value, tenants should be systematically reimbursed or have their rent — or the rent rise — reduced accordingly (Des Rosiers, *supra*, note 3 at 79-80, para. b).

79. *Criteria Regulation, Id.*, s. 6.
80. Patterson and Watson, *supra*, note 6 at 7 & 52.
81. Interview with P. Marchand, *supra*, note 45. Originally, no application fee was charged by the Régie (L. Ross in C.C.S.D., *supra*, note 5 at 118). Starting on April 1, 1982, a $20 fee was charged for all applications other than those relating to the fixing of rent (*Regulation respecting fees payable to the Régie du logement*, O.C. 630-82, 17 March 1982, G.O.Q. 1982.CXIV.930, s. 1). Later, the fee rose to $25 (O.C. 740-88, 18 May 1988, G.O.Q. 1988.CXX.2141, s. 1(1)) and was later increased to $35 (M. Casavant, *supra*, note 44 at 30.21-30.22; O.C. 1433-91, 23 October 1991, G.O.Q. 1991.CXXIII.4107, s. 1(1)) and again to $40 for all applications, including applications regarding rent increases (O.C. 1578-92, 4 November 1992, G.O.Q. 1992.CXXIV.4877, s. 1(1)). The last amendment to the Regulation provided that the amount of the fee shall thereafter be adjusted on November 1st of each subsequent year according to the C.P.I. for that year, rounded off to the nearest dollar (*Id.*, s. 1).
82. *Noise Pamphlet*, *supra*, note 64 at 3; Québec, Ministry of Municipal Affairs, Régie du logement, *Rent Payment* [Pamphlet] (Québec: Régie, June 1995) at 6.

This was not always the case. Under O.C. 603-85, 27 March 1985, G.O.Q. 1985.CXVII.1402, s. 1, the Régie was required to refund fees where (1) a copy of the settlement agreement was submitted prior to or during a hearing; (2) the fee was paid for submitting a motion to make a correction and the motion was granted or; (3) the fee was paid for submitting an application for revocation that was granted. Under O.C. 1054-90, 18 July 1990, G.O.Q. 1990.CXXII.1975, s. 2, refunds were no longer required for

the reason set out in No. 1, but were still required for those set out in Nos. 2 & 3. See also: Des Rosiers, *supra*, note 24, at 9.
83. R.S.Q., c. S-3.1.1 as cited in O.C. 1433-91, *supra*, note 71, s. 2. See also: Des Rosiers, *Id.*
84. Noise Pamphlet, *supra*, note 64 at 3.
85. Interview with P. Marchand, *supra*, note 45; Interview with A. Bennett, Services d'animation, Teninform Inc. ("tenant information") (February 1996).
86. *Id.*
87. *An Act respecting the Régie, supra*, note 41, ss. 90, para. 1 & 91, para. 1; Franklin *et al.*, *supra*, note 37 at 179; Casavant, *supra*, note 44 at 30.37.

Some procedural rules that apply to applications for revisions follow: When an application is made, the chair or designated vice-chair decides how many commissioners will hear the application. This number must be larger than the number of commissioner(s) and special clerks who originally heard the case. The commissioner(s) who sat at the initial hearing cannot sit on the review panel (*Rules of Procedure*, *supra*, note 22, s. 47). Unless provisional execution is ordered, the application for review will suspend the execution of the decision (*Id.*, s. 90). However, the Board may, on a motion, either order provisional execution where it has not been ordered, or bar or suspend it where it has been ordered.
88. Casavant, *Id.*, note 44 at 30.07; *An Act respecting the Régie, Id.*, s. 91(1).
89. Interview with P. Marchand, *supra*, note 45.
90. S. Langlois in "Seminar on Rent Policy: Proceedings" in C.C.S.D., *supra*, note 5, 87 at 166.
91. Interview with P. Marchand, *supra*, note 45. Generally, economists consider 4% to be a comfortable vacancy rate (*Id.*).
92. Canada Mortgage and Housing Corporation, *Toronto Rental Market Survey* (Toronto: C.M.H.C., 1990) at 32; Ontario, Ministry of Housing, *Rental Housing Protection Act: Future Directions* (Ontario: Ministry of Housing, 6 April 1988) at 43.
93. C.M.H.C./S.C.H.L., *Rental Market Report: Vancouver CMA* (Vancouver: C.M.H.C., October 1985) at 6 & 8.
94. Canada Mortgage and Housing Corporation, *Rental Market Report - Toronto C.M.A.* (Toronto: C.M.H.C., October 1995).
95. British Columbia, Ministry of Housing, Recreation and Consumer Services, *Rental Housing Trends in British Columbia* (Housing Research Reports Series) (B.C.: M.O.H., undated) at 2.
96. G. Yee, *supra*, note 16 at 38 citing "Toronto's vacancy rate lowest in nation at 0.1%" The [Toronto] *Globe and Mail* (27 November 1987) B9. In fact, the vacancy rate may actually be even lower than the figures suggest: See *infra*, note 115.
97. The relevance of size of buildings to our analysis is established by Prof. Des Rosiers (*supra*, note 3 at 54). Des Rosiers statistically demonstrates that larger buildings (defined as those with twenty-one or more units) account for a growing proportion of claims in Québec, at the expense of small buildings (defined as having three units or less) (*Id.*). As well, notice may be taken of the fact that larger landlords are more legally sophisticated than smaller ones.

98. Interview with P. Marchand, *supra*, note 45; Canada Mortgage and Housing Corporation, *Dwelling Statistics in Canada* (C.M.H.C., 1991). The average number of units per building for the Province of Québec = 593,436 Bldgs. o/o 69,499 units;

Montréal = 461,325 o/o 55,177; Québec City = 68,110 o/o 6,830; Hull = 17,712 o/o 1993; Sherbrooke = 22,980 o/o 2,242; Trois-Rivières = 15,303 o/o 2,055; Chicoutimi = 8,006 o/o 1,202; Toronto = 296,769 o/o 7,984; London = 40,322 o/o 1,805; Ottawa = 62,272 o/o 2,811. In the Province of Québec 42.7% of buildings had between 6 and 19 units and 27.7% had less than 6; in Montréal 42.6% had between 6 and 19 and 22.2% had less than 6; in Québec City 42.2% had between 6 and 19 and 18.3% had less than 6; in Hull 34.5% had between 6 and 19 and 22.5% had less than 6; in Sherbrooke 39.8% had between 6 and 19 and 16.5% had less than 6; in Trois-Rivières 58.8% had between 6 and 19 and 22.0% had less than 6; in Chicoutimi-Jonquière 54.4% had between 6 and 19 and 34.3% had less than 6; in Toronto 43.5% had between 50 and 199 and 33.6% had more than 200; in London 58.4% had between 50 and 199 and 7.1% had over 200; in Ottawa 40.2% had between 50 and 199 and 29.0% had over 200.

99. David Donnison, Director of the Centre for Environmental Studies in London, England, has stated that "...A rent regulating system must be actively staffed and administered by officials employed to advise people and ensure they get their rights, as well as fix rents. If you simply pass laws and leave it to people to seek their rights in the courts, those who need help most will not benefit. Indeed, they will probably suffer, by being squeezed into [illicit] markets on the fringes of the regulated sectors (D. Donnison in C.C.S.D., *supra*, note 5, at 154)."

The President of the Federation des Associations de Locataires du Québec criticized the earlier legislation for not trying to educate tenants of their rights: "The first [problem] is lack of public education. [If the law] is to really work, they must first and foremost be made aware of [their rights]. Under the...legislation, Québec tenants often have not sought their rights simply through [lack of knowledge of the legal avenues open to them]. So in implementing the new rent code the Québec government must first of all vigorously undertake the job of educating tenants of their rights and not rely on existing tenants' associations to do this for them (S. Langlois in C.C.S.D. *Id.* at 132-133)."

100. In the 1994-1995 fiscal year, for example, persons working at the Régie's 28 offices provided information to more than 785,000 callers and provided information in-person to more than 200,000 visitors (Québec, Ministre des Affaires municipales, *supra*, note 70 at 16-17, Tables 2 & 3. See also Letter from Régie du logement, *supra*, note 49 at 1-2). These numbers include questions relating to rent increases as well as other questions. That said, however, rent stabilization is one of the things that the public asks most about (interview with P. Marchand, *Id.*).

In terms of the quality of advice provided, in 1993 and 1994, 43.2% and 39.6% of callers reported that they were very satisfied ("tres satisfaite"), and 49.2% and 50.9% said that they were satisfied ("satisfaite") (Québec, *Id.*, note 70 at 20, Figure 6).

101. Interview with P. Marchand, *Id.*; Patterson and Watson, *supra*, note 6 at 54;

Inter-departmental Study Team, *supra*, note 27 at 385.
102. Interview with P. Marchand, *Id.* Patterson and Watson have noted, *Id.* at 75, that as of 1971 "Montreal, whose older stock [of apartments] has been under rent control since 1940, has the lowest rents of Canada's major cities even after income levels are considered. Rent per room was 3.8 per cent of income in 1971. Only smaller cities such as Saint John, New Brunswick and Québec City had lower rents in 1971."

However, mobilized tenants are aware of the limitations of the Québec system, as compared to other provinces, and feel that the system does not work for them. A survey of tenants in one of the largest tenant unions in Montréal, Cote des Neiges provided evidence of this dissatisfaction (Des Rosiers, *supra*, note 3 at 78-81). Professor Des Rosiers pointed out that his survey was not analytically rigorous enough to justify very much reliance on it (*Id.*). However, Professor Des Rosiers is an expert on the Québec system and to some extent his opinion stands on its own.
103. That tenants require assistance to level the playing field is demonstrated by studies that show a disproportionate avoidance of the adjudicative system by tenants (Yee, *supra*, note 16 at 57 citing S.R. Fodden, "Landlord and Tenant and Law Reform" (1974) 12 *Osgoode Hall L.J.* 44 & D.L. Martin, "Civil Remedies Available to Residential Tenants in Ontario: The Case for Assertive Action" (1976) 14 *Osgoode Hall L.J.* 65 at 91). As Mr. Yee, former Director of Toronto's Metro Chinese and Southeast Asian Legal Clinic and an expert on tenant law, said: "Fodden's article presents a detailed look at landlord and tenant actions commenced in Ontario [between 1970 and 1973]. The lack of access by tenants is demonstrated in the statistic that under 1 per cent of these actions were initiated by the tenant and 2/3 of the actions involved no appearance by the tenant (*Id.* at 57)." See also, more generally: F.M.T.A., *supra*, note 3.
104. The statistics show that it would be better for tenants if more cases are actually dealt with by the Régie. Statistically in Québec between 1979 and 1983, rent increases requested by landlords varied from a low of 15% in 1984 to a high of 26% in 1982, whereas increases allowed by the board varied from 6% in 1984 to 15% in 1982 (Des Rosiers, *supra*, note 3 at 56).

M. Gorsky in "Seminar on Rent Policy: Proceedings" in C.C.S.D., *supra*, note 5, 87 at 120: "The low level of rent complaints...may point[] to the responsibility of the legislators to provide more information for those people, so they will pursue their rights."
105. Automatic in the sense that the system would automatically kick in without initiation by either party. Mandatory in the sense that the mechanism will, generally speaking, be binding unless either the landlord or the tenant challenges the decision.
106. See authors cited, *infra*
107. Patterson and Watson, *supra*, note 6 at 45.
108. Ontario Law Reform Commission, *supra*, note 6 at 9.
109. *Id.* at 11-12 & 68-69.
110. *Id.* at 13.
111. *Id.* at 11.
112. *Id.* Accord: M. Cassidy in C.C.S.D., *supra*, note 5 at 140. See also Yee, *supra*, note 16 at 41: "...Unequal bargaining power also characterizes the

relationship between the landlord and... prospective tenants, especially if the vacancy rates is low [sic.]. However, even without a low vacancy rate, the prospective tenant interested in a certain apartment usually wants it much more than the landlord wants that particular tenant. The landlord's interest is mainly, if not solely, economic while the tenant's interest is largely psychological. It has been noted that the housing market is very heterogeneous with many different types of accommodation; there is no single market. Therefore, the supply available to each tenant is actually much more limited than the vacancy rate would suggest. The tenant has very limited possibilities for substitution [footnotes omitted]." See also Yee, *Id.*, at 42.

113. Ontario Law Reform Commission, *supra*, note 6 at 12. Professor Gorsky made a similar statement at a national conference on Rent Control: "Any procedures developed to enforce rights must...be cheap, quick and accessible" (M. Gorsky in "Seminar on Rent Policy: Proceedings" in C.C.S.D., *Id.*, 87 at 97). *Accord:* D. Donnison in "Seminar on Rent Policy: Proceedings" in C.C.S.D., *Id.*, 87 at 107: "Simply passing laws and leaving it to people to find their way to court is wholly inadequate."

114. C. Schier (1966) 54 *Calif. L. Rev.* 670 at 673. See also: R.S. Schoshinski, "Remedies of the Indigent Tenant: Proposal for Change" (1966) 54 *Georgetown L.J.* 519 at 552.

115. Patterson and Watson, *supra*, note 6 at 3. See also D. Donnison in "Seminar on Rent Policy: Proceedings" in C.C.S.D., *Id.*, 87 at 106; M. Gorsky, *supra*, note 5, 87 at 97: "As for the 'bad tenant' and 'bad landlord,' all I can say is that such discussion merely confuses the issue. The state first determines what rights and duties the tenant and landlord should have. Then court or administrative procedures are established to deal with breaches of these rights."

116. Patterson & Watson, *Id.* at 11. See also: Ontario, *supra*, note 2 at 42; Des Rosiers, *supra*, note 3 at 79, para. e. See also: C. Dagneau as cited in Ontario, *supra*, note 5 at 75; F.M.T.A., Report, *supra*, note 3 at 5-6.

117. *Id.*

118. *Id.* at 59. See also: *Id.* at 76: "The system may be socially undesirable because of the degree of tenant initiative required to contest a rent increase, which naturally brings the tenant into direct conflict with the landlord."

119. *Id.* at 77. Ironically, one reason the National Assembly enacted the type of system it did is to try to bring landlords and tenants closer together (Québec, *Se Loger au Québec*, *supra*, note 70 at 59).

120. Des Rosiers, *supra*, note 3 at 78-81. See also: L. Ross in "Seminar on Rent Policy: Proceedings" in C.C.S.D., *supra*, note 5 at 116. As well the current system is confined to dealing with rent increases, rather than the full amount of the rent (see section 6 of this paper). Discrepancies between the base rent charged for similar units are thus ignored and perpetuated over time (Des Rosiers, *Id.* at 78 & 79, para. a). A mandatory system of rent control would help surmount these inconsistencies.

121. P.C. Oxendine, "Tories face heat in attempt to remove rent control" [York University's] *Excalibur* (6 March 1996) 1 at 1; D. Donnison, "The Regulation of House Rents: Some Background Notes" in C.C.S.D., *Id.*, 3 at 11. More vulnerable groups tend not to know their rights and consult legal advisors and they have more difficulty finding alternative housing.

122. Namely, the tenant must give notice that the tenant wants to stay, but does not agree to the amount demanded.
123. Letter from Régie du logement, *supra*, note 49 at 1; Interview with P. Marchand, *supra*, note 45.
124. Des Rosiers, *supra*, note 3, at 51. Des Rosiers cited statistics compiled by the Régie du logement and Canada Mortgage and Housing Corporation. Even these low figures are an overestimate because they refer to *rent-related claims*, a larger category than *rent control-related claims*. See also Patterson and Watson, *supra*, note 6 at 75; Social Planning Council of Metropolitan Toronto, *supra*, note 5 at ii.
125. *Id.*
126. Franklin *et al.*, *supra*, note 37 at 160.
127. S. Langlois in "Seminar on Rent Policy: Proceedings" in C.C.S.D., *supra*, note 5, 87 at 124; L. Ross, *Id.* at 114; Inter-departmental Study Team, *supra*, note 27 at 385. In each of 1931, 1941, 1951, 1961, 1966 and 1971, the majority of the province's population were tenants (Patterson and Watson, *supra*, note 6 at 17).
128. L. Ross, *Id.*
129. Interdepartmental Study Team, *supra*, note 27 at 38.
130. Québec, *Se Loger au Québec*, *supra*, note 70 at 70. The fact that elderly people pay larger rent increases than do other tenants is especially troubling given that a disproportionately high number of tenants are elderly. For instance, in his 1985 study for the Thom Commission, *supra*, note 3 at 69-70, Prof. Des Rosiers found that nearly 25% of tenants were retired.
131. Des Rosiers, *Id.* at 50.
132. Patterson and Watson, *supra*, note 6 at 75.
133. *Id.* at 53.
134. See also: Des Rosiers, *supra*, note 3 at 41 & 80.
135. D. Donnison, "The Regulation of House Rents: Some Background Notes" in C.C.S.D., *supra*, note 4, 3 at 5.
136. Des Rosiers, *Id.*, note 3 at 41n. As the Thom Commission stated, "Even if there is no formal policy of vacancy decontrol, an optional system of rent regulation will tend to decontrol rents when there are vacancies (Ontario, Thom Commission, *supra*, note 2 at 72). See also: Tenant Advocacy Group, Federation of Metro Tenants' Associations & Community Legal Education Ontario, *8 Myths about Rent Control in Ontario* (Pamphlet) (Toronto: T.A.G. & F.M.T.A., February 1996) at 5 [chapter 8 in this book].
137. *Supra*, note 6 at 93.
138. Ontario, [Royal] Commission of Inquiry into Residential Tenancies, *Report*, vol. 1 (Toronto: Queen's Printer, 1984) (Chair: S. Thom).
139. *Id.* at 94. Emphasis in the original.
140. In C.C.S.D., *supra*, note 4 at 139.
141. L. Ross, *supra*, note 128 at 116-117.
142. *Supra*, note 6.
143. Ontario, Thom Commission, *supra*, note 138 at 28. See also: Bucknall, *supra*, note 16 at 12.
144. *Id.* at 195. As Brian Bucknall, a partner in the Toronto law firm of Osler, Hoskin & Harcourt and a former Professor at Osgoode Hall Law School, pointed out in an article, "...Concern has been expressed that if any rent

abuse this right and intimidate tenants into accepting wholly unjustified increases (*Id.*)."
145. Although cooperatives technically have the same advantage, the symmetry is more apparent than real. Few co-ops, even large ones, have the resources to have in-house counsel.
146. As well, the tenant may be unfamiliar with legal proceedings and feel overwhelmed by procedures lawyers would consider simple (S. Langlois in C.C.S.D., *supra*, note 4 at 133).
147. Ontario, Thom Commission, *supra*, note 138 at 194.
148. *Id.* at 195.
149. *Id.*
150. *Supra*, note 83.
151. See, for e.g.,: Canada, Library of Parliament/Bibliotheque du Parlement, Research Branch, *Poverty in Canada* (Current Issue Review) by V. Shalla (Ottawa: Minister of Supply and Services Canada, 14 March 1995) at 4-5; D.P. Ross, *The Working Poor: Wage Earners and the Failure of Income Security Policies* (Canadian Institute for Economic Policy Series) (Toronto: James Lorimer & Company, Publishers, in association with the Canadian Institute for Economic Policy, 1981); D.P. Ross, E.R. Shillington and C. Lochhead, *The Canadian Fact Book on Poverty - 1994* (Ottawa: The Canadian Council on Social Development, 1994) at 75-87.

The number of working poor households, as the term was defined in *The Canadian Fact Book on Poverty*, increased between 1981 and 1991 by 30% for families and 57% for unattached individuals (*Id.* at 76, Table 6.1). As of 1981, there were more than 600,000 Canadian families living in poverty, as the term was defined by David Ross in *The Working Poor*, and almost half of these were families whose major income was derived from wages. With the addition of the one-quarter million unattached individuals in the same situation, there were more than one-half million wage-earning poor in Canada in 1981 (*Id.* at xiii).
152. *Supra*, note 71.
153. See, for example: Casavant, *supra*, note 44 at 30.58.
154. Indeed, the very requirement of making an application may deter applicants:see section 2 of this chapter.
155. Indeed, a commissioner can require you to pay the application fee even if you win the application.
156. Des Rosiers, *supra*, note 3 at 10-11, 41 & 44.
157. This feature of the system is not just a disadvantage for tenants, but it is also a disadvantage for landlords where, for e.g., the apartment building is an old one with an artificially low rent. In a city like Toronto, which has a relatively large number of old residential buildings, the costs to landlords of having a *rent stabilization system* is not likely to be insignificant.
158. The only exception to this rule is where the tenant applies to have the rent reduced on the basis that the landlord failed to ensure the tenant's quiet enjoyment of the premises. However, even then, the rent reduction redresses the tenant's lack of enjoyment of the premises. It does not redress the possibly unfair rent that the tenant is paying. The tenant continues to pay a rent which is at odds with what a fair rent would be.
159. Des Rosiers, *supra* at 11 & 41.

Chapter 10

Rental housing trends in the City of Vancouver

by Vanessa Geary and Leslie Stern, 1996

Vanessa Geary recently graduated from the School of Community and Regional Planning at the University of British Columbia, where she focused on issues relating to affordable housing, gender and international development.

Leslie Stern is a former student of Dr. David Hulchanski at the School of Community and Regional Planning at the University of British Columbia. She has been a housing advocate and development consultant for more than 15 years, and has actively participated in many non-profit housing initiatives in the Lower Mainland.

This study was made possible through the sponsorship of the Centre for Human Settlements and the Tenants' Rights Action Coalition (TRAC).[1]

In 1989 at the height of an affordable housing crisis in the City of Vancouver, Dr. J. David Hulchanski, then Director of the Centre for Human Settlements at the University of British Columbia, issued a research bulletin entitled "Rental Trends in the City of Vancouver." At the time, Dr. Hulchanski determined that the rental housing market was at risk of failure, due to escalating land costs, increasing housing prices and the inability of lower-income earners to pay "market" rents. Thousands of good rental units were being lost each year and a demand for affordable rental housing was not being addressed. This update reviews some of the activities, initiatives and changes in housing policy over the last five years and their impact on the supply and affordability of rental housing in the City of Vancouver today.

Since 1989, crisis has become endemic in Vancouver's rental housing economy. The City now vies with Toronto for the highest rents and lowest vacancy rates in Canada. International market forces and the dynamics of growth have led to escalating property values and increased pressure on rental housing. New construction is geared heavily towards single family dwellings and condominiums. Social housing and purpose-built rental accommodation are being constructed in much smaller numbers than needed to meet the City's rental housing needs. Tenants in Vancouver face increasing insecurity as their housing options narrow, and more and more are forced into condominiums, secondary suites or shared accommodation. A comprehensive strategy for provision of affordable rental housing is required to meet the present and future housing needs of Vancouver's tenant households.

1. Who rents in the City Of Vancouver?

With the City of Vancouver at its centre, the Vancouver Metropolitan Area is the fastest growing major metropolitan area in Canada[2] (see Table 1). The population of the City itself grew by approximately 41,000 between 1986 and 1991: from 431,100 to 471,844, an increase of almost ten percent.

Unlike the province and the country as a whole, the majority of households in the City of Vancouver rent. The 1991 Census found approximately 118,000 renter households in the City, or 59 percent of Vancouver's 200,000 occupied dwellings. Between 1986 and 1991, the number of renters grew by ten percent, the number of owners by only five percent.

Changing patterns in household[3] size, family structure, age distribution and in-migration determine the City's housing needs. During the 1970s and 1980s, the number of households grew at a faster rate than the number of people, with the formation of more single-parent families and single-person households and the growing tendency toward fewer children per family unit. According to the 1991 Census, 76,600 houshholds in Vancouver (approximately 40 percent) consisted of one person.

Renters are a diverse population including young people, seniors, recent immigrants, students, and families. Renters usually live in smaller households with lower incomes than those of owners. Renting may be a temporary phase for many household types, however in Vancouver fewer tenants can afford to purchase a home than in most other Canadian cities.[4] In any case, for the following groups renting is more likely to be long-term.

Lone Parents

According to the 1991 Census, lone parent families[5] represent 25 percent of the City's 66,000 households with children. Of these, approximately 83 percent were headed by women. Single parent families have the lowest incomes, and spend the highest proportion

Table 1.
Population and Housing Stock

		1986		1991
Population		431,100		471,844
Occupied Dwellings		185,800		199,540
Renter Households	58%	108,000	59%	118,055
Owner Households	42%	77,800	41%	81,480
Single Detached Houses	38%	70,200	34%	67,480
Condominiums			14%	28,000

Source: 1986 &1991 Census data

Note: Number of renter households may have been understated for 1986, because 1986 Census data excluded non-permanent residents while 1991 Census data include them.

Figure 1: Owners and Renters in Vancouver

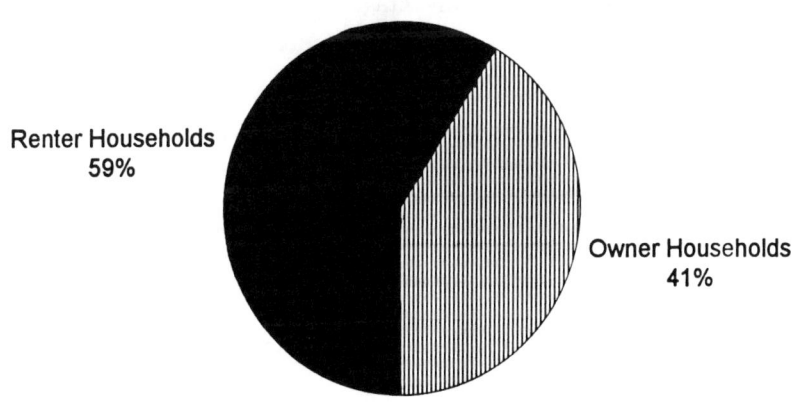

Renter Households 59%

Owner Households 41%

of income on shelter. Seventy percent of single parent households are renters, and half of these households experience "core housing need" (pay more than 30 percent of household income for shelter and/or live in substandard conditions, or both).[6]

Seniors

In 1991 there were 60,225 persons over the age of 65 in the City of Vancouver, with 21,295 of these senior citizens living alone. Women over the age of 65 considerably outnumber their male counterparts (138 females for every 100 males over 65 in Canada) and most have very limited income. More elderly women than men live alone in rented premises.

People with Special Needs

There is a broad spectrum of people with particular housing needs which are often unmet. These needs may be both financial and physical in nature, and likely linked to the provision of services. Discussions about special needs too often result in a list of labels rather than strategies to accommodate people with these needs. Special attention must be given to the housing requirements of people with disabilities; mental illness; chronic physical illness, particularly HIV+/AIDS; the homeless or hard to house; women in crisis; and the frail elderly. These people have in common the likelihood of limited income which limits their access to appropriate housing, resulting in a layering of disadvantage.

Income levels

Table 2 compares income levels for various household types in 1985 and 1990 in the Vancouver Census Metropolitan Area (CMA).[7] As previously noted, households dependent on one income are apt to be at a severe disadvantage in the housing market and, due to limited resources, most likely to rent. In B.C. in 1990, the average household income for renters was 59 percent of the average for owners, or $32,817 compared to $55,731 (see Table 3). Renters in every category are likely to pay a higher percentage of income for shelter; overall, renters are nearly three times as likely as owners are to pay more than 30% of their income on shelter.

Households with limited incomes have the least choice when it comes to housing. Income Assistance (welfare) recipients, for example, have incomes well below the medians by household type. Shelter allowances paid under the Guaranteed Available Income for Need (GAIN) program fall far short of average Vancouver rents. If a tenant's rent is higher than the allowance, the household must dip into

Table 2.
Household Incomes
Vancouver Census Metropolitan Area

	1985	1990
Average Incomes		
Individual Income	$25,020	$25,905
Males	31,221	31,943
Females	17,805	19,176
Family Income	51,473	57,100
Single Parent Families		
Male-headed	43,763	49,184
Female-headed	25,649	30,385
Median Incomes		
Individual Income	21,976	22,335
Males	29,365	29,041
Females	15,773	17,379
Family Income	45,547	49,595
Single Parent Families		
Male-headed	38,090	40,275
Female-headed	20,487	25,061

Source: Statistics Canada; The Nation, Table 6, 93-331, pg 167.

its support allowance, which is meant to cover food, clothing, transportation and all other expenses.

Rental rates

Across Canada in 1991, shelter costs for renters were highest in British Columbia and Ontario and among metropolitan areas, Vancouver had the second highest rental rates.[8] By 1994, Vancouver's rental rates had climbed to be the highest in Canada.[9] In Greater Vancouver it is estimated that close to 25 percent of tenant households pay more than 50 percent of their income on rent.[10]

Table 3. Household Income by Tenure
British Columbia, 1991
Based on 20% Sample Data

Household Type	Number of Households		Average Income		Per cent paying more than 30% of Income*	
	Owner	Renter	Owner	Renter	Owner	Renter
All private households	769,450	438,115	$55,731	$32,817	14.4%	39.7%
One maintainer	450,925	314,810	$50,012	$28,069	15.7%	45.0%
Two maintainers	311,235	110,815	$63,534	$43,487	12.6%	26.4%
Three or more maintainers	7,290	12,495	$76,282	$57,829	14.6%	25.9%

Source: Statistics Canada; the Nation, Cat. No. 93-330, Table 11, p. 207; Table 12 p. 220
* *Refers to total average monthly payments to secure shelter. Owner's major payments include monthly mortgage payments, utilities such as electricity, heating fuel, water and municipal services, property taxes, and as of 1991, condominium fees. Gross rent includes monthly cash rent and utilities as above.*

Table 4.
Rents, Incomes and Consumer Inflation

Rents for City of Vancouver; Incomes and CPI for B.C.

Year	1 Bedroom	2 Bedroom	Consumer Price Index	Average Weekly Earnings
1987	$447	$637	103	$457
1988	488	704	107	467
1989	531	779	112	498
1990	568	854	118	515
1991	605	842	124	535
1992	611	872	127	549
1993	629	909	.132	561
1994	643	930	134	577
Increase	44%	46%	30%	26%

Sources: CMHC, Trade Union Research Bureau

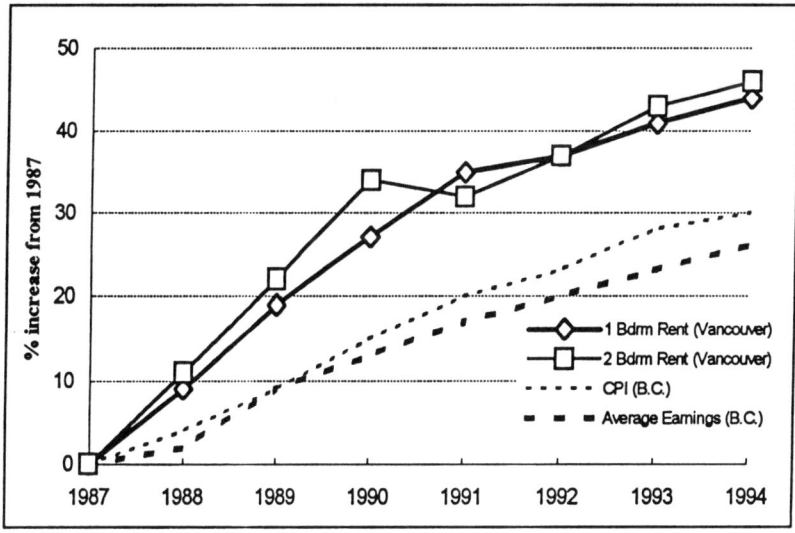

Figure 2. Average Rents, Incomes and Consumer Inflation

Table 4 provides an overview of rental rates in purpose-built, multi-unit developments in Vancouver between 1987 and 1994, with a comparison to the overall inflation rate as well as average earnings. As the Table shows, rents increased over this period by 44 to 46 percent,[11] while average weekly earnings increased by only 26 percent.[12] Though rent increases were more moderate from 1991 to 1994, incomes still have not caught up with the large average rent increases experienced between 1987 and 1991.

2. The existing rental stock

In his 1989 study, Dr. Hulchanski identified five major categories of rental housing stock: (1) purpose-built apartment buildings, (2) secondary suites, (3) social housing, (4) rooming houses and residential hotels, and (5) condominiums and houses. Table 5 provides a breakdown of the rental stock by type in 1994. The numbers are based on information from Statistics Canada, Canada Mortgage and Housing Corporation (CMHC) and the City of Vancouver.[13]

Census data probably underestimates the number of rental units in the City. Many secondary suites, rooming house units, and housekeeping rooms are likely to have been missed by the census as they are not easily identified. However, these types of accommodation are an important part of Vancouver's affordable housing supply and are at risk under current development pressures.

In 1989, Dr. Hulchanski found that purpose-built rental apartments, secondary suites in some neighbourhoods and the rooming house stock were particularly threatened. A study subsequently commissioned by CMHC to compare rental markets in five Canadian cities discovered a major shift unique to Vancouver from purpose-built rental accommodation to condominium development.[14]

Apartment buildings

Privately-owned purpose-built rental apartments are the largest component of rental housing in Vancouver, comprising over 57,000 units, or nearly 50 percent of the City's total rental stock.[15] However, the long-term viability of this housing is in doubt. The issues identified by Dr. Hulchanski in 1989 continue to be serious concerns: "The stock is aging. Few new units are being added and many buildings are being lost to demolition and conversion."

Table 5.
Rental Housing Stock by Type
City of Vancouver

Conventional Rental	
Apartments	55,573
Townhouses	2,274
Total	57,847
Secondary Suites	
Total Estimate	20,000
Registered	2,525
Social Housing Units	18,739
Residential Hotels & Rooming HouseUnits	
Downtown	7,431
Total Estimate	10,000
Condominiums for Rent	11,000
Detached Houses for Rent	5,000

Sources: CMHC Rental Market Reports and Housing Activity Reports; City of Vancouver.

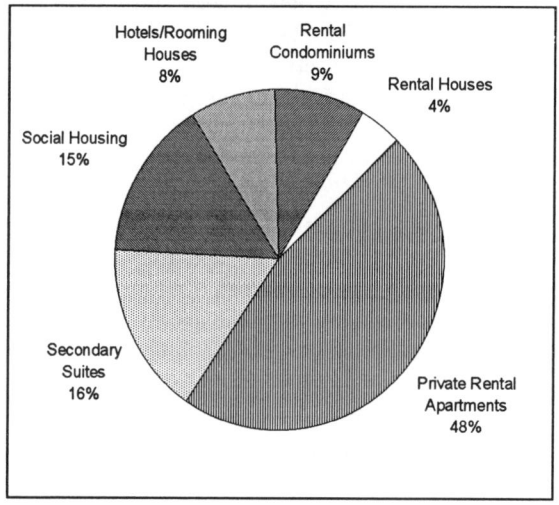

Figure 3. Rental Housing Stock by Type

Secondary suites

Secondary suites are the second largest component of the City of Vancouver's rental housing stock, estimated at between 18,000 and 26,000 units. Secondary suites represent 15 to 20 percent of the City's total rental stock and a substantial portion of its affordable rental housing. With 70 percent of Vancouver's land base zoned for single detached houses and up to one third of such houses containing a suite, secondary suites impact the affordability of housing for both owners and renters, affecting up to 50,000 households at any one time.

The debate over regulation of secondary suites has been one of the most controversial in the City's recent history. For fifty years, a house containing a suite with its own kitchen contravened the municipal "RS-1" zoning bylaw regulating single family neighbourhoods.[16] In spite of this, the City's practice of non-enforcement from 1976 to 1986 led to a proliferation of "illegal" secondary suites. These suites increased the affordability of ownership for many households and provided low cost accommodation in neighbourhoods from which renters might otherwise have been excluded. They also reflected the change in demographics toward smaller families. However, the proliferation of secondary suites led to claims in some neighbourhoods that the "character" and services of single family neighbourhoods were being compromised.

The City embarked on a review of secondary suites in 1988. The review process consisted of a city-wide vote and neighbourhood by neighbourhood surveys. See section 3 for a discussion of the impact of the review process and the City's attempts to register and regulate suites.

Social housing

The next largest component of the City's rental accommodation is social housing. Developed over the last fifty years under a number of federal and provincial government housing programs, this stock includes all public housing, non-profit rental housing, and government subsidized housing cooperatives. At 18,739 units, social housing comprised 9.4 percent of all housing and 15.9 percent of rental housing in Vancouver in 1994. Social housing is the only component of rental housing which provides long term affordability and stability, free from the impacts of inflation, speculation and rising land costs.

Residential hotels and rooming houses

It is estimated that there are approximately 10,000 residential hotel and rooming house units throughout the City, with the majority located in the downtown core. Most single room occupancy (SRO) units consist of a 10' by 10' room in a residential hotel, where residents share common washroom facilities. Some of the units have cooking facilities (most likely a hot plate), while others have none or share a common kitchen. Most SRO units are rented on a monthly basis, with the vast majority at the maximum Income Assistance shelter allowance of $325 per month. Though these rents seem low, in fact, residential hotels cost more per square foot than many luxury apartments and single family houses.

The SRO stock is particularly vulnerable. Most of it is old, run down and threatened by redevelopment and gentrification. Though substandard, this stock represents the only housing available and the last step before homelessness for many individuals.

Condominiums

The *Condominium Act*, introduced to B.C. in 1967, allows for individual ownership of apartments or townhouses through a process called strata-titling. Between 1971 and 1991 the number of condominium or strata units in the City of Vancouver grew from 250 to over 28,000.[17] A strata council (the body governing the condominium owners' common affairs) may pass a by-law to restrict rentals if approved by a majority of owners. However, under the *Condominium Act*, the developer has the right to rent any unsold apartments; this right passes to the first purchaser. Though geared for owner-occupancy, it has been suggested that over 40 percent of strata units are likely to be rented to tenant households[18] comprising almost 10 percent of the City's rental stock.

Tenants renting in condominiums face greater insecurity of tenure than those living in other forms of rental housing, as well as weaker protection of their rights under the *Residential Tenancy Act*. The strata council, as well as the owner, may exercise the rights of the landlord in relation to eviction. In addition, amendments to the strata rules are binding on the tenant, even if they contradict the terms of the existing tenancy agreement between the tenant the individual owner.

Live-work studios

The City has recently adopted zoning that permits "live-work

204 | Rental housing trends in Vancouver

Figure 4. Residential Hotel. Approximately 10,000 Vancouverites live in Single Room Occupancies — residential hotels and rooming houses. Living conditions vary from tolerable to grossly inadequate, but for many tenants this form of housing is the last step before homelessness.

Figure 5. At a typical rent of $325 for a 10-by-10-foot room, Single Room Occupancies tenants pay more per square foot than many tenants in luxury accommodation. Some SRO residents stay a short time; others live in the same hotel room for 20 years or longer.

studios" in some commercial and industrial areas. Intended for practicing artists, this form of housing is proving attractive to developers due to its lower land and finishing costs. The impact on the rental market is uncertain at this point.

Detached houses

The 1991 Census found 67,480 detached houses in the City of Vancouver, down from 70,200 in 1986. An important component of the rental housing stock for both families and students, it is difficult to determine the number of houses which are tenant-occupied at any given time. Much depends on market conditions. At times of high market activity, houses are likely to be sold to new owner-occupiers or to developers, and units may or may not remain rental. Like condominiums, this form of rental housing is particularly insecure.

3. The loss of existing units

Rental housing in Vancouver has been lost through demolition, conversion, and government regulation. Table 6 shows units lost to demolition between 1986 and 1994. Table 7 shows the impact of the secondary suite review program. Tables 8 and 9 trace the conversion of rental housing to condominiums.

Table 6.
Housing Units Demolished

Year	Total Units	Rental Units
1986	1,289	372
1987	1,777	514
1988	1,718	374
1989	2,327	502
1990	1,689	767
1991	1,140	427
1992	1,704	425
1993	1,610	436
1994	1,825	704

Source: City of Vancouver

	Suites registered for phase-out		Suites registered for permanent occupancy			Family suites
	2028		772			74
	In RS-1 zones	In RS-1S zones	Existing suites	New suites in existing houses	Suites in new houses	Registered in RS-1 zones
Total	**561**	**1467**	**415**	**94**	**263**	**74**
Point Grey	66	15	2	1	1	7
Kitsilano	19	133	44	10	14	2
Dunbar	30	2				23
Marpole	29					3
West Riley Park	9	25	12	5	14	1
Riley Park	57	142	39	6	7	7
Sunset	4	291	70	11	47	2
Kensington/Cedar Cottage		382	97	12	82	3
Victoria/Fraserview	129	31	6	2	4	10
Renfrew/Collingwood	96	123	21	11	32	11
Joyce Station	86	76	34	4	10	4
Hastings Sunrise	30	247	72	18	49	
Other	6		18	14	3	1

Source: City of Vancouver Secondary Suite Program

Demolitions

Between 1989 and 1994, there was a loss to demolition of 3,261 rental units, including units in multi-resident rental buildings, "legal" secondary suites or other designated rental accommodation. These preliminary City figures represent a minimum estimate due to possible errors, omissions, and under-reporting. It is particularly difficult to track the loss of "illegal" secondary suites in single family dwellings, but it is possible, based on the city-wide ratio, that up to a third of demolished houses contained unreported secondary suites.

According to City development permit records, in some neighbourhoods up to 10 percent of detached houses were demolished between 1988 and 1993. Eighty percent of these were replaced by larger, more expensive houses, while the remaining 20 percent were likely replaced by duplexes and townhouses.

Gentrification/upgrading

Gentrification refers to the process of affluent, middle-class households moving into areas which were formerly working class or lower income. Gentrification begins with the renovation, upgrading or demolition of existing rental housing which is then converted for owner-occupancy or luxury rental with significantly higher rents. Rent increases between 30 and 40 percent are not uncommon in these circumstances, and increases of up to 150 percent have been reported on occasion. In most cases "displacement" of the original tenants occurs. This phenomenon is familiar to most large North American cities. In Vancouver, a number of older neighbourhoods are being transformed by gentrification, including Mount Pleasant, Grandview Woodlands, Strathcona and the Downtown Eastside. While gentrification and upgrading do not necessarily result in the loss of rental stock, both result in the erosion of affordable rental housing.

Loss of SROs

Dr. Hulchanski identified this in 1989 as one of the most threatened segments of the rental housing stock. Since then, approximately 400 SRO units per year have been lost in the City.[19] Hotel room stock in the downtown core is particularly at risk as redevelopment and gentrification encroach from Yaletown, the waterfront and the Concord Pacific projects on False Creek.

Loss of secondary suites

The results of the secondary suite review program launched in

208 | Rental housing trends in Vancouver

Figure 6. Effect of Secondary Suites Program

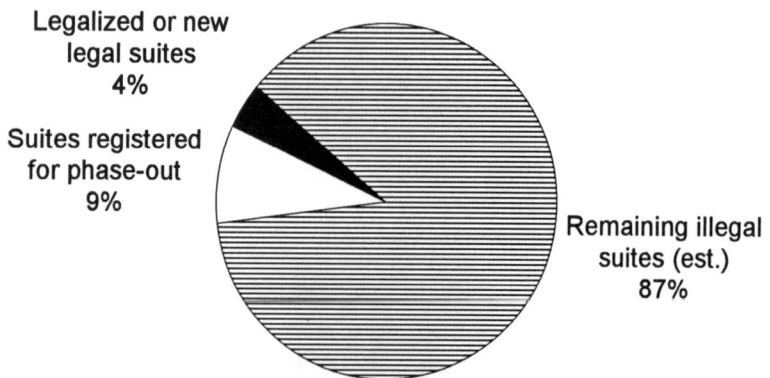

1988 have been ambiguous at best. A reported $2.5 million has been spent on the program, yet the City has reverted to a system of voluntary registration, with enforcement only on the basis of complaints. The vast majority of suites continue to be illegal.

After review, 53 percent of single family properties retained their RS-1 zoning, which allows secondary suites for immediate family members and caretakers only. Under the bylaw, all other suites in RS-1 areas are illegal, and must be closed immediately or upgraded and phased out over 10 years. The remaining 47 percent of properties, located predominantly on the East side, were rezoned to RS-1S, allowing for one legal revenue suite per house. Suites in RS-1S areas can become legal once they are registered and upgraded to meet building code standards.

The cost of upgrading suites has acted as a deterrent to registration. The requirements for permanent suites in RS-1S areas include sprinklers, two off-street parking spots, and 6'10" ceiling heights. The costs of these upgrades can be as high as $6,000, and considerably more if the house must be raised to accommodate the ceiling height. While these upgrades increase safety and amenity standards for tenants, many homeowners either avoid registration or register for "phase-out."

Since the program began, a total of 2,874 suites have been registered, representing only 11 to 16 percent of the City's secondary suites. Worse, 2,028 of those registered are phase-out suites, including 1,467 in RS-1S areas. Only 489 existing suites have been made permanent, and 357 new permanent suites have been added to the stock.

Condominium conversions

There are two types of condominium conversions. Conversion from purpose-built rental apartments registered under one title to separately titled (strata-titled) condominiums requires City Council approval under the Condominium Act. The sale of apartments which were strata-titled at construction but operated initially as rental buildings does not require City approval. These "silent" conversions are uncontrolled because legally they represent only the sale of existing condominiums.

Table 8 traces the loss of purpose-built rental housing to condominium conversion with City Council approval since 1979. In response to public concern about the loss of affordable rental housing, the City has regulated condominium conversions since 1986. Current guidelines require written consent from two-thirds of tenants in the building before a rental conversion can be approved by Council. Between 1979 and 1993, a total of 2,125 rental units were converted this way.

Over the past two decades almost all new market rental housing has been strata-titled by developers at the time of construction, and thus has not been subject to City approval when converted to condominium use. Table 9 traces the recent loss of strata-titled units in the City of Vancouver, which came on the market as rental housing but were subsequently sold as condominiums. These units may be purchased by an owner-occupier or an investor landlord, making it difficult to trace the distinction between owner and renter after the initial transaction. Many of these units re-enter the rental market, but often at increased rental rates and with significantly less security of tenure. According to CMHC figures, more than 4,000 strata-titled apartments in the City of Vancouver were removed from CMHC's rental database between 1991 and 1994 as the buildings they were in moved from primarily rental to individually-owned units. This represents nearly 14 times the number of condominium conversions approved by City Council during the same period.

Table 8. Condominium Conversions Approved by City Council
City of Vancouver

Year	Count
1979	41
1980	140
1981	163
1982	244
1983	160
1984	119
1985	110
1986	358
1987	231
1988	142
1989	49
1990	23
1991	76
1992	65
1993	122
1994	40
1995	

Source: City of Vancouver
Note: Conversions of buildings strata titled at construction are excluded.

Table 9. Condominiums Removed from CMHC Database
City of Vancouver

Year	Count
1991	458
1992	2,323
1993	911
1994	440
TOTAL	**4,132**

Source: Canada Mortgage and Housing Corporation
Note: Buildings are deleted when the number of rental units managed by a single property manager falls below 3 units or 50% of total units.

Figure 7. Inner City Gentrification. Gentrification threatens tenants in many older buildings in inner-city neighbourhoods. Tenants in this West End building struggled for many years with successive owners to improve conditions in the building, only to be forced out by large rent increases in 1993.

Figure 8. Condominium Conversion. Conversion of rental buildings to condominium ownership continues to erode Van-couver's rental supply. Approximately 90% of total conversions do not require City approval.

Zoning for secondary suites, City of Vancouver, 1995

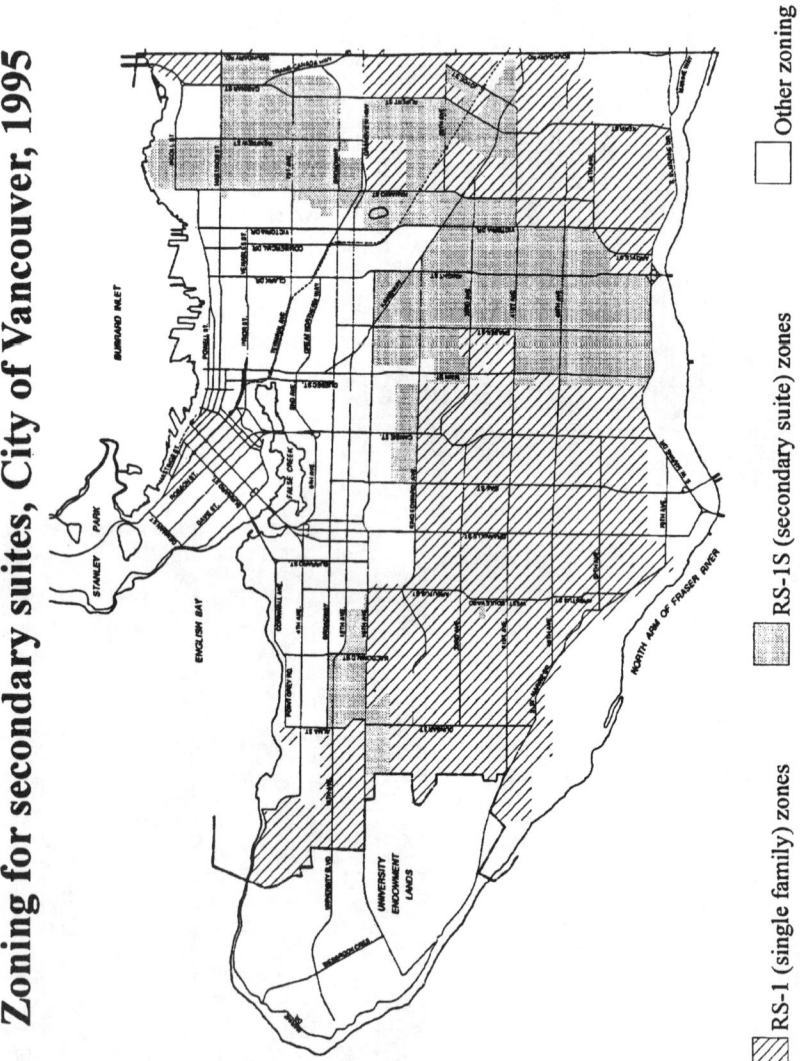

4. Supply of market rental units

Tables 10 and 11 reflect vacancy rates and housing costs in Vancouver. Tables 12 through 14 provide an overview of private housing starts between 1989 and 1995. Table 12 shows that only 3,316 conventional rental apartments were constructed between 1989 and 1995. Table 13 indicates that 18,534 condominium units were built during this time, and it is estimated that over 40 percent will be available as rental accommodation for some period of time. Table 14 shows that 9,250 units of single and semi-detached houses were started, with an unknown number on the market as rental.

Private rental

There has been only one non-subsidized rental development completed in Vancouver in recent years. This 216-unit development in the downtown core targets a luxury high-rise market niche.

Megaproject development

Four major developments are underway in the Downtown Peninsula with a projected total of 12,680 units of housing. Under the City's inclusionary zoning policy, each of these developments contains a 20 percent allowance for "non-market" housing. However, achieving affordable housing on these sites is dependent on programs and funding from senior levels of government (see discussion in section 5 below). In addition, there may be small numbers of market rental units built in exchange for increased density for the developers. The vast majority of the housing on these sites, however, will be upscale condominiums. Many will be sold to non-resident investors who may choose to offer them on the rental market on an interim basis.

Secondary suites

Despite the problems associated with Vancouver's suite review, there remains a broad consensus that secondary suites are the most cost effective and efficient method of producing affordable rental housing without significant expenditure to government.[20] In order to encourage and support secondary suites, the Provincial Commission on Housing Options recommended in 1993 that the *Municipal Act* and *Vancouver Charter* be amended to provide one additional residential dwelling in detached houses "as a right," provided that special

Table 10.
Vacancy Rates, City of Vancouver

Date	Private Rental Apts. Total	Vacant	Vacancy Rate
1989 Apr	53,244	282	.5%
Oct	54,418	174	.3%
1990 Apr	54,360	538	1.0%
Oct	53,874	389	.7%
1991 Apr	54,551	1,115	2.0%
Oct	55,966	1,024	1.8%
1992 Apr	56,611	1,546	2.7%
Oct	55,982	767	1.4%
1993 Apr	55,486	1,193	2.2%
Oct	55,573	506	.9%
1994 Apr	55,430	767	1.4%
Oct	55,482	381	.7%
1995 Apr	55,362	561	1.0%
Oct			.8%

Source: CMHC Rental Market Reports

Table 11.
Housing Costs, City of Vancouver

Average Apartment Rents

	Studio	1-Bdrm	2-Bdrm
1991	$476	$599	$830
1992	486	611	872
1993	498	629	909
1994	521	643	930
1995	546	661	945

Source: CMHC Market Survey

Median House Prices

	East Side	West Side
1989	$207,000	$435,500
1990	200,000	405,000
1991	220,000	455,000
1992	255,000	525,000
1993	295,000	568,000
1994	313,000	644,500

Source: Real Estate Board

Median Condominium Prices

	East Side	West Side
1989	$82,000	$160,500
1990	110,000	172,500
1991	118,000	183,500
1992	128,500	184,000
1993	139,500	170,500
1994	134,700	188,500

Source: Real Estate Board

Table 12.
Private Sector Rental Starts
City of Vancouver

Year	Apartment	Row	Total
1989	230		230
1990	547	81	628
1991	433	97	530
1992	659		659
1993	360	12	372
1994	598	4	602
1995	295		295
Total	3,122	194	3,316

Source: CMHC Housing Activity Reports

Table 13.
Condominium Starts
City of Vancouver

Year	Apartment	Row	Total
1989	1,803	109	1,912
1990	1,573	68	1,641
1991	1,775	87	1,862
1992	1,987	72	2,059
1993	3,683	121	3,804
1994	3,560	121	3,681
1995	3,351	224	3,575
Total	17,732	802	18,534

Source: CMHC Housing Activity Reports

Table 14.
Single and Semi-Detached Starts
City of Vancouver

Year	Single	Semi-Detached	Total
1989	1,559	166	1,725
1990	716	88	804
1991	1,021	181	1,202
1992	1,382	138	1,520
1993	1,360	130	1,490
1994	1,168	130	1,298
1995	1,075	136	1,211
Total	8,281	969	9,250

Source: CMHC Housing Activity Reports

safety regulations are met. In addition, as a further means of encouraging secondary suites, the commission recommended that the province provide assistance to homeowners for upgrading suites.

To date, no action has been taken on these recommendations. This is due in part to continuing resistance from municipal councils, some of which regard provincial legislation on secondary suites as an encroachment on their jurisdiction.

Federal government incentives

Since the early 1970s, most purpose-built rental units have been developed only in conjunction with government incentives. Between 1975 and 1985, a total of 7,817 rental units were built under three federal rental incentive programs: Multiple Unit Residential Building Program (MURB), the Assisted Rental Program (ARP), and the Canada Rental Supply Program (CRSP). These programs provided either substantial tax benefits or interest write-offs to investors willing to develop housing which would remain rental for an agreed period of time. With 85 percent of the units stratified at the time of construction, by now, many of these projects have been converted to privately-owned condominiums. When the federal programs were discontinued in the mid-1980s, the development of private rental housing ground to a halt until the province introduced its own Rental Supply Program.

B.C. rental supply

The B.C. Rental Supply Program (RSP) was introduced in 1989 to stimulate private sector investment in new rental housing for seniors and families, replacing the earlier federal incentive programs. Interest costs were to be reduced on projects that met program requirements and would remain rental for a specified period of time. The program has not had a significant impact on construction in Vancouver. Of 2,219 Vancouver apartments either approved or applied for between 1989 and 1993, 86 percent were developed by Vancouver Land Corporation, which had the additional benefit of City incentives.

Vancouver Land Corporation

In 1989, at the initiative of the City, the Vancouver Land Corporation (VLC) was established to develop multi-family residential rental housing. VLC received an exclusive option to lease $48 million of City-owned property for a period of 80 years, in return for building and maintaining moderately-priced rental accommodation throughout the term of the lease. VLC was expected to produce rental accommodation at 80 to 120 percent of low end of market rates, with increases limited to the Consumer Price Index (CPI).

Originally VLC projected building 2,000 units by the end of 1990, and 1,500 to 2,000 units annually thereafter.[21] However, by April 1994, a total of 652 units had been completed. Under agreement with the City, no payments will be made on the land-lease until the projects produce a positive cash flow. Though rents are relatively high, by the end of 1994 no payments on land had been made. Having established itself as a developer on the strength of the City leases, VLC has recently changed its name to Greystone Properties and moved into the condominium market.

Smaller suites

In January 1993, City Council voted to reduce the City's allowable minimum suite size from 320 to 275 square feet, acting in response to an initiative by a private developer. Previously, special approval had been granted for small suites in a few social housing projects and one VLC project then under construction. While developers and the majority of City Council promoted this as a measure to create more affordable housing, opponents viewed the decision as a reduction in housing standards and a threat to livability for low-income households.

Municipal planning mechanisms

The province has amended the *Municipal Act* and the *Vancouver Charter* to encourage the provision of affordable rental housing in B.C.[22] All municipalities must now include policies on affordable, rental and special needs housing in their official community plans. Municipalities also have a number of new mechanisms to facilitate provision of affordable housing. These include: zoning specifically for rental accommodation; density bonusing for rental housing or other affordable initiatives; and, allowing restrictive covenants or housing agreements to be registered with the land title to control future changes in use. In addition, they give greater power to municipalities to enforce standards of maintenance for rental housing.

The City of Vancouver has taken some of these approaches under its existing Charter. However, these amendments emphasize the City's role and responsibility in the provision of affordable housing.

Table 15.
Co-op and Non-Profit Housing Starts
City of Vancouver

Year	Apartment	Row	Total	
1989	554	27	581	
1990	230		230	
1991	331	43	374	*
1992	177	120	297	**
1993	152	15	167	
1994	237	19	256	
1995	152	39	191	
Total	**1,833**	**263**	**2,096**	

Source: CMHC Housing Activity Reports
*(includes 150 Apt ILM co-op Units)
**(includes 106 Row ILM Co-op Units)

5. Supply of non-market/social housing

Table 15 shows that the annual construction rate for social housing units in Vancouver declined by 70 percent between 1989 and 1993. In May 1995, the B.C. Housing Management Commission waiting list for subsidized housing in the Lower Mainland included 5,900 families and 8,800 households in total. These numbers were up by 40% and 33% respectively from one year earlier.

Federal policy

Beginning in the 1940s, the federal government took a leadership role in the development of social housing. Innovative Canadian housing programs such as non-profit cooperatives and community-sponsored non-profit rental have received international recognition. However, since the late 1980s the federal government has increasingly divested itself of its responsibility for social housing. In 1992 the Conservative government cancelled the Cooperative Housing Program altogether, and cut back the Non-Profit Housing Program. In 1993, federal funding for new construction under the Non-Profit Housing Program was eliminated, maintaining budget commitments only for operating subsidies of existing units. The Liberal government elected in the fall of 1993 has not restored funding for housing programs.

Provincial policy

Beginning in 1986, the province entered into a cost-sharing agreement with the federal government for the provision of social housing units. Since the 1991 election, the provincial New Democratic government has maintained its share of funding for social housing at 1991 levels, retaining a limited construction program despite the withdrawal of federal funds. In 1994, the Ministry of Housing announced a new, fully provincially-funded housing program. In addition, the province has adopted a "housing first" policy for development of provincially-owned land. However, total funding for social housing programs in B.C. currently equals less than one-half of total spending by both governments in the past.

City policy

Approximately one third of all social housing in Vancouver has been built on City-owned land. The current policy is to lease sites for 60 years at 75 percent of the value of outright purchase. This is considered a fair market value lease.[23] The City also operates a housing portfolio for seniors and special needs households.

The City has a long history of facilitating the inclusion of non-profit housing in major developments within Vancouver. Notable examples of this include the south shore of False Creek, Champlain Heights, and the Fraser Lands. Comprehensive development guidelines for the south shore of False Creek attempted to reflect the actual income mix and household composition of the City as a whole. Under these guidelines, on land leased by the City, 55 percent of the housing built was either non-profit cooperative or low cost rental for families and seniors.

The non-profit sector advocated a continuation of this comprehensive zoning policy for all major development projects, including those on privately-owned land. But in the late 1980s Council reduced the requirement to 20 percent for "core need" households. In the spring of 1994, the City further weakened this policy. Citing the current lack of federal funding and the direction of provincial housing programs, the target of the 20 percent inclusionary zoning policy shifted from core need to "non-market" housing, which can encompass a wide range of incomes and household tenures including ownership.

In the past, the City has relied heavily on senior government programs to provide social housing for low-income households. As programs shrink and demand increases, new approaches will be necessary.

The City Plan approved in 1995 after a two-year consultative process recognizes the need for affordable housing in the City, but offers no clear strategies to replace the senior government funding withdrawn from the social housing sector. The Plan advocates a continuing or increasing reliance on the market to meet the City's housing needs.

6. Affordability/effective demand

The experience in Vancouver over the past ten years clearly demonstrates that the private market is either unable or unwilling to provide new, secure and affordable rental housing for low- and moderate-income households. As Dr. Hulchanski reported in 1989, however, the problem is not a lack of demand but a lack of "effective market demand." Tenants' incomes are lower than those of owners. Because many tenants cannot pay rents high enough to make private construction of new rentals profitable, lower-income renters "create social need which the market cannot respond to."[24] When investors have the choice between building rental or condominium units, most choose the quick return and greater investment flexibility offered by condominiums.

Rent legislation

Recently the provincial government adopted amendments to the *Residential Tenancy Act* to give tenants the right to appeal "unjustified" rent increases. The new system, introduced in early 1995, does not impose rent ceilings, but will instead allow tenants to dispute rent increases on an individual basis. Rent increases on vacant units will be uncontrolled.

In 1989, Dr. Hulchanski outlined four rationales for rent regulations: security of tenure; maintenance of the affordability of existing rental stock; prevention of the unfair redistribution of income from tenants to landlords; and, balancing the power relationship between tenants and landlords, especially around the issue of rental rates.

Conservative arguments against rent regulation claim that it interferes with the normal functioning of the "free market," and discourages investors from building rental housing. Yet in British Columbia, when rent controls were weakened considerably after

1975 and removed entirely in 1983, the market did not deliver sufficient supply of rental housing despite strong demand.[25]

In any case, the primary intention behind the new legislation appears to be to protect tenants' security of tenure, especially in tight rental markets. It will not protect long-term affordability of the rental housing supply, and is not expected to have a significant impact on private sector rental housing construction.

7. Where To next? The future of rental housing

Income and the distribution of income are the keys to who owns and who rents in the City of Vancouver.[26] On average, renters earn 60 percent of what owners earn, and economically disadvantaged groups tend to be the City's tenants. For many thousands of households, tenancy is a lifelong housing situation.

The hope that market forces will ensure provision of adequate housing is misplaced. As Dr. Hulchanski pointed out in 1989, those with lower incomes do not create "effective market demand" in a housing economy dominated by spiralling land values and speculative investment. Vancouver's tenants are increasingly subject to the pressures of the marketplace; the supply of affordable rental housing is in a precarious balance. Especially vulnerable are young people, senior citizens, single parent households (usually headed by women), recent immigrants, people with disabilities, the unemployed and underemployed, and low wage earners.

After fifty years of active support for new affordable housing, the federal government has stepped back from this role, downloading responsibility for housing policy and funding onto lower levels of government. The provincial government has been forced to take a larger role in the development and implementation of housing policy, but has been unable to fill the funding gap for social housing left by the federal withdrawal. The City of Vancouver has shown some leadership in the use of municipal powers to support social housing. However, in a development climate heavily oriented towards home ownership, the City has had difficulty protecting and expanding the supply of rental housing.

The resulting trends are leading to increased insecurity for the City's tenants. Several important policy areas require attention.

Renewed support for social housing

Social housing is vital in Vancouver's housing economy because it is the only rental housing that is truly secure in the long term. The federal government must renew its commitment to social housing, and follow British Columbia's example of utilizing public land for affordable housing. At the same time, given the continuing pressures on rental housing in the Lower Mainland, it is critical that the provincial government maintain and expand its financial commitment to social housing programs. The City may be forced to expand its activity in this sector, moving from a facilitative role to one of active development and funding.

Retention and expansion of purpose-built rental housing

Purpose-built rentals have been a mainstay in Vancouver's housing economy since the 1950s. This stock, however, is subject to deterioration, demolition and condominium conversion, and little is being done to replace the loss. Past federal and provincial programs to promote construction of rental housing have been short-sighted, leading to the ongoing problem of "silent" condominium conversions. Imaginative approaches and long-term strategies are required to retain a supply of secure rental housing into the next century.

Better protection of tenants renting condominiums

As the predominant choice among developers and investors, by default, condominiums will continue to grow in importance in the City's rental economy. However, even if affordable, condominium rentals leave tenants vulnerable to eviction and possible mismanagement. The solution lies in better legislative protection for tenants renting condominiums, and less reliance on condominiums to fill the rental housing gap.

Retention and replacement of residential hotel accommodation

The City's stock of Single Room Occupancy (SRO) accommodations in the downtown core and the Downtown East side is increasingly threatened by development pressures from surrounding areas. Strategies to protect and ultimately replace the City's decaying SRO stock could include rehabilitation of hotels through direct investment, acquisition of SROs in partnership with non-profit management, and replacement with self-contained housing.

Legalization and encouragement of secondary suites

Secondary suites will continue to be an important part of the rental supply in Vancouver. They offer affordable ground-oriented housing and can increase population density without widespread demolition. Their full potential will only be realized, however, if they are legalized with appropriate building and fire codes, and encouraged in all neighbourhoods.

Better use of planning tools

The planning tools available to City Council enable the City to influence the direction of new development. In addition to acquiring sites for public sector housing, the City can influence form of tenure and affordability in private-sector development. The City could benefit from the experience of American cities, such as Seattle and San Francisco, which have pioneered creative approaches to promote retention and construction of rental housing without senior government funding.

Toward the 21st century...

Dr. Hulchanski warned in 1989 that renter households may be pushed out of the City or into increasingly crowded and inadequate accommodation. Seven years later, market forces continue to cater to those who can compete in an inflated real estate market, providing diminishing housing options for low- and moderate-income households. Left on its own, the market response to demand for affordable housing will lead to continuing erosion of housing standards, smaller units, and increasing homelessness. We face the spectre of a 21st-century city increasingly home to the very rich and the very poor.

Current policies affecting rental housing in the City are a patchwork of short-term strategies, inadequate programs, and overreliance on market mechanisms. The rental and non-profit sectors must be strengthened if the City's future housing needs are to be met. A coherent housing strategy must involve coordinated efforts among federal, provincial and municipal governments, as well as the active participation and vigilance of the community.

NOTES

1. The authors wish to thank Dr. J. David Hulchanski for developing the original analysis for this paper and allowing us the opportunity to update and build upon his framework.

    We also want to acknowledge the initiative of Tom Durning of the TRAC who initiated this update as a small part of his efforts to preserve rental housing in Vancouver.

    Thank you to Dr. Aprodicio Laquian, Director of CHS, who acted as advisor, and to Mike Walker, coordinator at TRAC, for his editing. Thanks also to Christine Evans of CHS for her patient efforts in the production stage.

Staff at Vancouver City Hall and at the Vancouver office of CMHC provided much valuable information and showed good humour in answering all of our questions.

2. This paper focuses primarily on the City of Vancouver rather than the Vancouver Census Metropolitan Area which includes all municipalities west of and including Langley in the Fraser Valley.
3. According to Statistics Canada the term "household" refers to a person or group of persons who occupy the same dwelling. It may consist of a family group with or without other non-family persons, several families who share a dwelling, a group of unrelated persons, or one person living alone. The number of households equals the number of occupied dwellings.
4. CMHC, Oct. 1994.
5. The term "lone parent" is used interchangeably with the term "single parent" throughout this paper. The Census definition of "family" includes all heterosexual couples, both with and without children, as well as single-parent households.
6. CMHC, Oct. 1993: 1,2.
7. Median incomes are used here because they more accurately reflect the actual income mix in the City.
8. Statistics Canada 1993:1.
9. CHMC, 1994.
10. City of Vancouver, 1993, Section 4, Part 5:2.
11. CMHC Rental Market Reports.
12. Trade Union Research Bureau, 1995.
13. It is recommended that efforts be made to standardize data for consistent and easily accessible information. For example, a row house for one agency is a town house for another. Housekeeping rooms may be a room in a house or a unit in a single room occupancy (SRO) hotel.
14. Clayton, 1991.
15. CMHC's definition of rental apartments includes purpose-built rentals, apartment hotels, and rented condominiums in structures where more than 50 percent of the units are rented under the management of a single property manager.
16. Even if living in an "illegal" suite, tenants have full protection under the *Residential Tenancy Act*, which is governed and administered by the province.
17. City of Vancouver, 1993, Section 4, Part 4:2.
18. Hamilton, 1991: 8.
19. Green and Hay, 1994.
20. Audain and Duvall, Executive Summary, 1993: 13.
21. City of Vancouver, 1989, Appendix A.
22. See Bills 20 and 57 (1993) and Bill 31 (1994).
23. Housing and Properties c. 1992: 9.
24. Hulchanski, 1989: 6.
25. See Clayton Research Associates' 1991 study for a detailed discussion of rental supply dynamics in Vancouver in the 1980s.
26. Baxter, 1994: 3.

Bibliography

Audain, Michael and Elain Duvall. 1992. *New Directions in Affordability: The Report of the Provincial Commission on Housing Options*. (Victoria: Ministry of Municipal Affairs, Recreation and Housing).

Baxter, David. 1994. *Notes for an address to the GVRD Social Issues Committee*. May 25, 1994.

Canada Mortgage and Housing Corporation. *Rental Market Report*. Vancouver CMA (Vancouver: CMHC), reports dated April 1990 to October 1994 were utilized.

Canada Mortgage and Housing Corporation. *Housing Market Activity*. Vancouver CMA/Fraser Valley (Vancouver: CMHC) reports from 1990 to 1994.

City of Vancouver. 1995. *CityPlan: Directions for Vancouver draft*. February, 1995.

City of Vancouver. 1994. *The State of Social Housing in Vancouver*. Policy report to City Council, April 6, 1994.

City of Vancouver. 1993. *CityPlan Tool Kit: People and Housing*.

City of Vancouver. 1993. *Vancouver Trends*.

City of Vancouver. 1993. *Survey of Low-Income Housing in the Downtown Core*. A report prepared by the Housing Centre, Housing and Properties Department, March 1993.

City of Vancouver. 1989. *City Manager's Report*. Appendix A, Report to Council, August 11, 1989.

Clayton, F. 1991. *Rental Housing: A Study of Selected Local Markets*. A report prepared for Canada Mortgage and Housing Corporation and British Columbia Housing Management Commission by Clayton Research Associates Ltd. in association with Jules Hurtubise and City Spaces consultants.

Green, Jim and Monica Hay. 1994. *Single Room Occupancy Research and Discussion Paper*. (Victoria: Ministry of Housing, Recreation and Consumer Services and British Columbia Housing Management Commission).

Hamilton, Stanley. 1991. *Metropolitan Vancouver Condominium Rental Study*. (Vancouver: Canada Mortgage and Housing Corporation).

Hulchanski, David. 1989. *Rental Trends in the City of Vancouver*. (Vancouver: Centre for Human Settlements, University of British Columbia).

Ministry of Housing, Recreation and Consumer Services. 1995.

Straight Facts for B.C.'s Consumers: Buying an Undivided Interest.

Non-Profit and Community Based Housing Network. 1993. *Non-Profit Housing: Is There a Future?* Workshop proceedings.

Statistics Canada. 1993. *Housing Costs and Other Characteristics of Canada Households, The Nation, 1991 Census.*

Trade Union Research Bureau. Personal communication, 1995.

Appendix

Tenant information on the Internet

CANADA

Ontario
- "Landlord Remedies," by Nicholas F. Ferguson
http://www.niagara.com/northland/cc/pubs/landrem.nff
- Ontario Government Website
-Appeals from Decisions Made by Rent Review Services
http://govonca3.gov.on.ca/MBS/english/FOI/HOU1278.html
- *Metro Toronto Housing Authority*
http://govonca3.gov.on.ca/MBS/english/programs/HOU1306.html
- *Ontario Court (GEN DIV), Central Office*
http://govonca3.gov.on.ca/MBS/english/programs/ATG1797.html
- *Ontario Court (GEN DIV), General Office*
http://govonca3.gov.on.ca/MBS/english/programs/ATG0584.html
- *Ontario Court (GENERAL DIVISION)*
http://govonca3.gov.on.ca/MBS/english/programs/ATG0846.html
- *Ontario Legal Aid Plan*
http://govonca3.gov.on.ca/MBS/english/programs/ATG0841.html
- *Rent Control Programs*
http://govonca3.gov.on.ca/MBS/english/programs/HOU0680.html
- *Rent Registry*
http://govonca3.gov.on.ca/MBS/english/programs/HOU1018.html
- *Rent Registry*
http://govonca3.gov.on.ca/MBS/english/FOI/HOU1277.html
- *Rent Review Hearings Board*
http://govonca3.gov.on.ca/MBS/english/programs/HOU0641.html
- *Rent Supplement*
http://govonca3.gov.on.ca/MBS/english/programs/HOU0216.html
- *Rent Supplement Program*
http://govonca3.gov.on.ca/MBS/english/programs/HOU1124.html
- *Submission from Landlords or Tenants Respecting Proposed Orders*
http://govonca3.gov.on.ca/MBS/english/FOI/HOU06262.html

Ottawa
- Federation of Ottawa-Carleton Tenants Associations
http://www.ncf.carleton.ca/freeport/community.associations/focta/menu
- *About the Tenants Federation* (focta/brochure)
- *Tenants' Questions, Answers & Discussion*
- *Federation Services for Tenants* (focta/services)
- *Tenant Tips* (focta/tips/menu.tips)
    - *Maximum Rent* (focta/tips/maxrent)
    - *Property Standards* (focta/tips/propstds)
    - *Heat* (focta/tips/heat)
    - *Inadequate Maintenance and Reductions of Rent* (focta/tips/maintenance)
    - *Records* (focta/tips/records)
    - *Spending Your Own Money* (focta/tips/organize)
    - *Organizing* (focta/tips/organize)
    - *Subletting Your Apartment* (focta/tips/sublet)
    - *Tenants and Municipal Councillors* (focta/tips/council)
    - *Recycling and Tenancy* (focta/tips/recycling)
    - *Personal Fire Safety* (focta/tips/fire)
    - *Last Month's Rent* (focta/issues/lastmois)
    - *Dollar a Month Campaign* (focta/issues/dollar)
- *September 95 Newsletter* (focta/summer95.txt)
- *January 95 Newsletter* (focta/jan95)
- *Upcoming Events* (focta/events.txt)
- *How to Contact Us* (focta/contact)

United States

California
- Eviction Defence Network
http://www.iww.org/housing/edn/a0.html
"Holiday evictions stopped as tenants get together, fight back." (Case of Casa Costanzo, a residential hotel in North Beach).

***

- Landlord's newsletter, published by Ernest F. Gilbert, Attorney at Law
barrister @ lawref.com

***

- Nolo Press - Legal Briefs
http://gnn.com/gnn/bus/nolo/briefs.html
- Articles taken from the "Nolo News." Articles on landlord-tenant issues include "Keeping Your Home Safe for the Holidays," "Nolo's Fast Facts: A Landlord's Right of Entry" and "How to Get Neighbours to Turn Down the Volume."
- Nolo Press - California Editions
http://gnn.com/gnn/bus/nolo/category/housing/html
    - *For Sale by Owner*
    - *How to Buy a House in California*
    - *Homestead Your House*
    - *The Landlord's Law Book - Vol. 1: Rights and Responsibilities*
    - *The Landlord's Law Book - Vol. 2: Evictions*
    - *Nolo's Law Form Kit - Leases and Rental Agreements*
    - *Tenants' Rights*
    - *The Deeds Book*
- Nolo Press - National Editions
http://gnn.com/gnn/bus/nolo/category/housing/html
    - *Neighbour Law: Fences, Trees, Boundaries and Noise*
    - *Safe Homes, Same Neighbourhoods: Stopping Crime Where You Live*
    - *Law on the Net*

Massachusetts
- "Landlord vex Newton officials - Multiple-unit dwellings become a multiple court-battleground," by Tom Moroney, Boston Globe
http://asylum.sf.ca.us/pub/u/tim/jaffe.html
- "The Tenant's Commandments," published by Executive Office of Consumer Affairs, State of Massachusetts
http://www.consumer.com/consumer/TENANTS.html

Minnesota
- Plain-Person's Guide to Minnesota Landlord-Tenant Law, by Michael Olenick, Olen Publishing, 1604 Dayton Ave., St. Paul, MN 55104, (612) 644-0029, E-mail michael@winternet.com
http://www.olen.com/rentlaw/index.html
- Landlords and Tenants - Rights and Responsibilities - From the Office of Hubert Humphrey III, Minnesota Attorney General
Landlords and Tenants - Rights and Responsibilities - Table of Contents
http://www.olen.com/rentlaw/handhead.html#top
- Selected Landlord-Tenant Laws of Minnesota, Section 504

http://www.olen.com/rentlaw/504.html/#504
• Selected Landlord-Tenant Laws of Minnesota, Section 566
http://www.olen.com/rentlaw/566.html#566.18
• Selected Landlord-Tenant Laws of Minnesota, Miscellaneous Statutory Provisions
http://www.olen.com/rentlaw/miscstat.html#misc
• Frequently asked questions about Minnesota landlord-tenant law
http://www.olen.com/rentlaw/faq.html#faq
These questions concern damage deposits, late fees, notice of moving, etc.
• Resource Directory of Minnesota Landlord-Tenant Law
http://www.olen.com/rentlaw/resource.html#resource
• New Minnesota Landlord-Tenant Laws
http://www.olen.com/rentlaw/newlaw.html#newlaw

Minnesota's Kari Koskinen Manager Background Check Act:

Requires that owners of property run background checks on prospective building managers. If the manager has been convicted of a serious crime (murder, rape, stalking, etc.) the owner may not hire the manager or must discharge the manager if the manager has already been hired. If the manager was already working as of July 1, 1995, and the owner knows the manager committed a serious crime, the owner must notify all tenants. If the tenants wish, they have the right to give two weeks notice and quit their lease. [A tenant] exercising this option is treated as if they had given the proper amount of notice before leaving. The rule was named after Kari Koskinen, a woman murdered by her building manager. The manager had a previous criminal record that was not disclosed to her.

The *Tenant's Right to Privacy Act* "prohibits landlords from entering an apartment unless they give proper notice and have a reasonable reason for entering. Managers found entering for an illegitimate reason are subject to a $100 fine for each unreasonable entry which is paid to the tenant. The rule also requires managers or owners to leave a note informing the tenant they have entered the apartment. The statute contains a list of reasonable reasons to enter an apartment.

Minnesota landlords are responsible for utility bills in apartment buildings that do not have separate meters for each individual unit. "If there is a utility dispute, the landlord is responsible for settling the dispute, so the utilities cannot be disrupted."

- Minnesota Multi Housing Association Sample Lease
http://www.olen.com/rentlaw/mha.html
- "The purpose of this project" - by Michael Olenick
http://www.olen.com/rentlaw/purpose.html#purpose

New Jersey

Rutgers Info
- Landlord-Tenant Disputes (Rentals, Renters, Tenants, Housing)
http://info.rutgers.edu/Directories/OutsideRolodex/Card.153.html

New York

CTRC

The Community Training Resource Center (CTRC) is a New York not-for-profit organization that "champions the rights of modest- and low-income tenants and promotes the preservation, improvement and expansion of affordable housing. CTRC provides training and technical assistance for neighbourhood housing groups, community based organizations, legislative staffs and social service providers. CTRC produces fact sheets on tenants' rights, develops and publishes research reports, and provides a written guide to New York City government processes. CTRC advocates on budget policies that affect housing and related services in low-income neighbourhoods. CTRC has led the campaign for the improvement and expansion of the city's Housing Maintenance Code inspection and enforcement services.
- Publications are available by mail order from CTRC. Ordering information can be obtained on the Internet at:
gopher://ursula.blythe.org:70/00/pub/TenantNet/Rights/CTRC/publist

CTRC's mailing address is:
47 Ann Street, NY 10038
Tel: (212) 964-7200
Fax: (212) 227-1125
- *Rent Regulation in New York City: A Briefing Book*, by September Jarrett and Michael McKee, 50 pages, $5.00
- *Unravelling the Myths: Co-op Conversion in New York City 1987-1990*, by Jocelyne Chait, 131 pages, $10.00
- *Housing Court, Evictions and Homelessness: The Cost and Benefits of Establishing a Right to Counsel*, published by CTRC and the City-Wide Task Force on Housing Court, 38 pages, $2.50

Tenant information on the Internet

Tenants' Rights Fact Sheets

Fact sheets can be mail ordered from CTRC or consulted free of charge on the Internet by substituting the appropriate code for "publist" in the Internet address.

gopher://ursula.blythe.org:70/00/pub/TenantNet/Rights/CTRC/publist
- *Statutory Rights of Tenants*: ctrcf001
- *Warranty of Habitability*: ctrcf002
- *Unlawful Eviction Law*: ctrcf003
- *Private Unregulated Housing*: ctrcf004
- *Rent Payment* (how and to whom): ctrcf005
- *Security Deposits*: ctrcf006
- *Tenants' Right to Pets*: ctrcf007
- *Landlord Discrimination and Harassment*: ctrcf008
- *Anti-Retaliatory Eviction Law*: ctrcf009
- *Leases and Lease Renewals*: ctrcf100
- *New Equipment Rent Increases*: ctrcf101
- *Rent Overcharges:* ctrcf102
- *Current Lease Renewal Guidelines*: ctrcf103
- *Past Lease Renewal Guidelines*: ctrcf104
- *Unlawful Fees*: ctrcf105
- *Minimum Base Rent Increases*: ctrcf106
- *Personal Use Evictions*: ctrcf107
- *Succession* (family may remain in apartment): ctrcf108
- *Complaints to NYS Division of Housing and Community Renewal*: ctfcf109
- *Rent Reductions for Lack of Services*: ctrcf110
- *Petition for Administrative Review*: ctrcf111
- *General Complaint Form*: ctrcf200
- *Heat and Hot Water Complaints*: Fact Sheet #201
- *Code Enforcement*: Fact Sheet #202
- *Housing Court Overview*: Fact Sheet #300
- *Organizing and Negotiating*: Fact Sheet #401

• A Guide to Housing Part Actions
gopher://ursula.blythe.org:70/00/pub/TenantNet/Rights/CTRC/hpaction
• Rent Regulation in New York City, by Stanley Panesoff and Kevin Ryan (1995)
gopher://ursula.blythe.org:70/00/pub/TenantNet/Rights/CTRC/rentreg
• Research and Resources: Fact Sheet #400
gopher://ursula.blythe.org:70/00/pub/TenantNet/Rights/CTRC/tresourc

***

Appendix | 233

Heat Sheet
* Heating Requirements for New York City in effect October 1 to May 31
http://ursula.blythe.org/TenantNet/Court/Howcourt/heat/html
  Compared to Québec, where the courts have required a minimum indoor temperature of 70°F, the rules in New York City seem grossly inadequate: as low as 55°F between 10 p.m. and 6 a.m., and 68°F between 6 a.m. and 10 p.m.

***

* Housing Court Decisions: Cases of interest
http://www.housingcourt.com/cases.html
* "Tenant allowed to recover legal fees in successful defense..."
Novick, Edelstein, Lubell, Reisman, Wasserman & Leventhal, P.C.
http://www.housingcourt.com/highlights.html
  Cases on multiple dwelling registration, warranty of habitability, recovery of legal fees, illegal activity in tenant's dwelling, landlord's notice of non-renewal, non-signatory of lease.

***

* How to handle problems with a co-op's board of directors: questions and answers. G. Oliver Koppell, New York State Attorney General (1994)
gopher://ursula.blythe.org:70/00/pub/TenantNet/Rights/atgcoop
* How to handle problems with a condominium's board of managers: questions and answers
G. Oliver Koppell, New York State Attorney General (1994)
gopher://ursula.blythe.org:70/00/pub/TenantNet/Rights/atgcondo

***

Lenox Hill Neighbourhood Association
Tenant Organizing Manual
http://ursula.blythe.org/TenantNet/Organize/Lenox/lh-toc.html
  This manual contains chapters on the right to organize, the how-to's of organizing, strategies to improve conditions, harassment and demolition.

***

234 | Tenant information on the Internet

Noise
• General statement and list of sources
http://ursula/blythe.org/TenantNet/Rights/Noise/index.html
• "Quiet Please!", by Stephen A. Newman, *New York Magazine,* August 29, 1983
http://ursula/blythe.org/TenantNet/Rights/Noise/noise1.html
• "Music vs. Noise - Your Legal Right to Practice at Home — Within Reason", by Mort Cohen, *Allegro Magazine*, September 1989
http://ursula/blythe.org/TenantNet/Rights/Noise/noise2.html
• "Foolproof Ways to Tune Out Your Neighbours", by Isabel Forgang, *New York Daily News* (date unknown).
http://ursula/blythe.org/TenantNet/Rights/Noise/noise3.html
• "New York Quiet? Never. Quieter? Maybe. Listen Up", by N.R. Kleinfeld, *New York Times* (date unknown)
http://ursula/blythe.org/TenantNet/Rights/Noise/noise4.html

***

• NYC Rent Guideline Board Orders
gopher://ursula.blythe.org:70/00/pub/TenantNet/RentLaws/RGBOrders/rgbtoc

Orders for each year (1968-70, 1970-71, etc. up to 1995-1996) can be looked up by substituting the numbers 01 to 27 in the Internet address. For example, Rent Guidelines Board Order 27 (1995-1996) can be found under:
gopher://ursula.blythe.org:70/00/pub/TenantNet/RentLaws/RGBOrders/rgb27
• Questions and answers about tenants' rights by Assemblyman Dick Gottfried (1989)
gopher://ursula/blythe.org/TenantNet/Rights/Noise/index.gottf

***

THE RENTER'S HANDBOOK
by Senate Minority Leader Manfred Ohrenstein (April 1990)
Described by TENANTNET as "a comprehensive and succinct primer for tenants and tenant leaders and a good starting point for further investigation of tenant issues."
gopher://ursula.blythe.org:70/00/pub/TenantNet/Rights/renters

***

Appendix | 235

Tenantnet

"TENANTNET is an on-line project of TENANT WATCH, a coalition of tenant leaders and advocates. TenantNet offers information to the two million rent regulated tenants in New York State, limited counselling and referrals and advocacy."

The following paragraphs are from the TenantNet home page:

"These are trying times for tenants. Landlords have mounted intense public relations campaigns filled with inaccuracies and misrepresentations about hard-won tenant protections and rent regulation. Tenants are losing basic services and being price-gouged at alarming rates. There is a very real chance tenant protections will be repealed in 1997, leaving over 2.4 million New Yorkers at risk."

"It is a mistake to think this is all new. Even before the political winds changed in 1994, basic tenant protections were undermined and gutted to no more than a shell by those running regulatory agencies, by politicians who maintained a fiction of being for tenants' rights and by tenants themselves who lost sight of the value of stable communities."

- New York State Rent Stabilization Code
gopher://ursula.blythe.org:70/00/pub/TenantNet/Rent Laws/rsccode
- New York City Housing Maintenance Code
gopher://ursula.blythe.org:70/00/pub/TenantNet/Other Laws/HMC/hmc
- Emergency Tenant Protection Act of 1974
gopher://ursula.blythe.org:70/00/pub/TenantNet/Rent Laws/etpa
- Emergency Housing Rent Control Law (adopted in 1946, amended in 1961).
gopher://ursula.blythe.org:70/00/pub/TenantNet/Rent Laws/ehrc61
- Local Emergency Housing Rent Control Act (1962)
gopher://ursula.blythe.org:70/00/pub/TenantNet/Rent Laws/lehrca62
- New York City Rent Stabilization Law (1969)
gopher://ursula.blythe.org:70/00/pub/TenantNet/Rent Laws/rsl
- New York State Rent Regulation Reform Act (1993)

This law severely weakened rent protection for all rent regulated tenants in New York State, particularly by gutting the rent registration system. The politicians sold these changes to the public by focusing on decontrol of high-income and high-rent apartments and measures to help small landlords.
gopher://ursula.blythe.org:70/00/pub/TenantNet/Rent Laws/reform
The Effect of the 1993 Late Registration Amendment in Determining Lawful Rents. Analysis by Andrea T. Novick
gopher://ursula.blythe.org:70/00/pub/TenantNet/Rent Laws/novick

236 | Tenant information on the Internet

• Tenant's Rights, State of New York (1987). Issued by Attorney General Robert Abrams
gopher://ursula.blythe.org:70/00/pub/TenantNet/Rights/atgrent

Washington State
• Washington - Housing - Landlord & Tenant Laws
gopher://leginfo.leg.wa.gov:70/00/pub/rcw/title 59

Also published by

BLACK ROSE BOOKS

PRIVATE INTEREST, PUBLIC SPENDING
Balanced-Budget Conservatism and the Fiscal Crisis
William Scheuerman and Sidney Plotkin

Extremely informative about the political trends that exist and about the political economic system of business dealing with government.
The Activist

280 pages, index
Paperback ISBN: 1-895431-98-0 $19.99
Hardcover ISBN: 1-895431-99-9 $48.99

THE CANADIAN CITY
Kent Gerecke, ed.

...a heady mix of thought-provoking essays examining this country's urban evolution (or devolution) over the past two decades... must reading for citizens' groups willing to face the big guns at City Hall.
Canadian Book Review Annual

281 pages
Paperback ISBN: 0-921689-92-6 $19.99
Hardcover ISBN: 0-921689-93-4 $48.99
L.C. No. 91-71474

THE LIMITS OF THE CITY
2nd revised edition
Murray Bookchin

Valuable for its historical perspective and its discussion of the effects on the individual of the modern city.
The Humanist in Canada

194 pages, index
Paperback ISBN: 0-920057-64-0 $17.99
Hardcover ISBN: 0-920057-34-9 $46.99

URBANIZATION WITHOUT CITIES
The Rise and Decline of Citizenship
revised edition

To reverse the city's dehumanization, social thinker Bookchin here advocates an agenda for participatory democracy... It is significant.
Publisher's Weekly

340 pages, index
Paperback ISBN: 1-895431-00-X $19.99
Hardcover ISBN: 1-895431-01-8 $48.99
L.C. No. 91-072980

DYING FROM DIOXIN*
A Citizen's Guide to Reclaiming Our Health and Rebuilding Democracy
Lois Marie Gibbs

It's in our food. It's in our water. It's in our bodies. And it's making us sick. According to recently released studies, widespread exposure to dioxin is destroying the health of the people. In *Dying from Dioxin*, Lois Marie Gibbs and grassroots activists at the Citizen's Clearinghouse for Hazardous Waste describe the alarming details of this public crisis, and explain how citizens can organize against this toxic threat.

200 pages, index
Paperback ISBN: 1-55164-084-8 $19.99
Hardcover ISBN: 1-55164-085-6 $48.99

TRIUMPH OF THE MARKET*
Essays On Economics, Politics, and the Media
Edward S. Herman

Who lubricates the machine that controls trade and finance on a global scale? What force keeps us money-hungry and always waiting for the next sale? In this book, Edward S. Herman reveals the power-magnet market operators who dictate how economic life is organized the world over.

A disturbingly blunt warning about the clear and present dangers to democracy, economic rationality, national sovereignty, global economic stability and progress, and international peace.
Samori Marksman, WBAI-FM, Pacifica Radio

286 pages, index
Paperback ISBN 1-55164-062-7 $19.99
Hardcover ISBN 1-55164-063-5 $48.99

POLITICS OF SUSTAINABLE DEVELOPMENT
Citizens, Unions and the Corporations
Laurie E. Adkin

The attitudes and actions of citizen's groups, unions and corporations reflect not only their stakes in protecting particular interests, but also the limits of their abilities to envision, or mobilize support for, alternatives to the prevailing mode of economic growth. Growing public concern about toxic chemical and industrial pollution issues coincide with a peak in environmental activism and government initiatives. These challenges are then set alongside the complex problem of labour movement responses.

250 pages, photos, maps, illustrations
Paperback ISBN 1-55164-080-5 $19.99
Hardcover ISBN 1-55164-081-3 $48.99

BEYOND HYPOCRISY*
Decoding the News in an Age of Propaganda
Including a Doublespeak Dictionary for the 1990s
Edward S. Herman

Illustrations by Matt Wuerker

In a highly original volume that includes an extended essay on the Orwellian use of language that characterizes U.S. political culture, cartoons, and a cross-referenced lexicon of doublespeak terms with examples of their all too frequent usage, Herman and Wuerker highlight the deception and hypocrisy contained in the U.S. government's favourite buzz-words.

This spirited book offers abundant examples of duplicitous terminology, ranging from the crimes of free enterprise to media coverage of political events.

Rich in irony and relentlessly forthright, a valuable resource for those interested in avoiding 'an unending series of victories over your own memory'.
Montréal Mirror
Makes us think and thinking is what protects our minds, otherwise we are going to join Orwell's characters.
Times-Colonist
Edward Herman starts out with a good idea and offers a hard-hitting and often telling critique of American public life.
Ottawa Citizen

239 pages, illustrations, index
Paperback ISBN: 1-895431-48-4   **$19.99**
Hardcover ISBN: 1-895431-49-2   **$48.99**

BANKERS, BAGMEN, AND BANDITS
Business and Politics in the Age of Greed
R.T. Naylor

A collection of articles from the shadowy underworld of business, the shady side of politics, and the twilight zone they share.

Based on Naylor's widely read column, this book is designed to give the news behind the news, to put back into the stories the 'awkward' details the main stream media find more convenient to omit.

An eminently readable book, with outré insights into the corrupt underside of world affairs in each chapter.
Canadian Book Review Annual
Without exception, the essays make very interesting reading... Naylor's book is an exhilarating if sometimes frightening roller coaster ride through the real world.
The Alternative Voice

250 pages
Paperback ISBN: 0-921689-76-4   **$18.99**
Hardcover ISBN: 0-921689-77-2   **$47.99**

COMMUNITY ACTION
Organizing for Social Change
Henri Lamoureux, Robert Mayer and Jean Panet-Raymond

trans. by Phyllis Aronoff and Howard Scott

...a thoroughly readable and immensely useful work...required reading for community activists.
Quill & Quire

248 pages, bibliography
Paperback ISBN: 0-921689-20-9 $16.99
Hardcover ISBN: 0-921689-21-7 $45.99

FIGHTING FOR HOPE
Organizing to Realize Our Dreams
Joan Newman-Kuyek

This book finds the common threads in activism and weaves them together into a guidebook for social change.

Kuyek provides a valuable list of do's and don'ts for social-justice activists, and her emphasis on building structures for self-reliant communities is important for today's victims of recession.
Calgary Herald

221 pages
Paperback ISBN: 0-921689-86-1 $17.99
Hardcover ISBN: 0-921689-87-X $46.99
L.C. No. 90-83629

MYTH OF THE MARKET
Promises and Illusions
Jeremy Seabrook

The majority of the people place their hope and faith in the mechanism of the market as the bearer of promise for the future, but the spreading of market values leads to social disintegration and the destruction of cultures.

A strong indictment of the market system. All the more timely with the recent moves in global trade.
Peace and Environment News
There are alternatives to the market, but unless we begin to resist the monetization of all human activity, they will be relegated to museums where, fittingly, you'll pay to see them.
Imprint

189 pages
Paperback ISBN: 1-895431-08-5 $18.99
Hardcover ISBN: 1-895431-09-3 $47.99

BLACK ROSE BOOKS

BLACK ROSE BOOKS

has also published the following books of related interest

Montréal: A Citizen's Guide to City Politics, *edited by Jean-Hughes Roy and Brendan Weston*

The Trojan Horse: Alberta and the Future of Canada, *edited by Gordon Laxer and Trevor Harrison*

First Person Plural: A Community Development Approach to Social Change, *by David Smith*

Services and Circuses: Community and the Welfare State, *by Frédéric Lesemann, translated by Lorne Huston and Margaret Heap*

The Search for Community: From Utopia to a Cooperative Society, *by George Melnyk*

Artful Practices: The Political Economy of Everyday Life, *edited by Henri Lustiger-Thaler and Daniel Salée*

Culture and Social Change: Social Movements in Québec and Ontario, *edited by Colin Leys and Marguerite Mendell*

Canada and Radical Social Change, *edited by Dimitrios Roussopoulos*

The Nature of Cooperation, *by John G. Craig*

Who is this "We"? Absence of Community, *by Eleanor Godway and Geraldine Finn*

The City and Radical Social Change, *by Dimitri Roussopoulos*

Green Cities: Ecologically Sound Approaches to Urban Space, *edited by David Gordon*

Local Places: In the Age of the Global City, *edited by Roger Keil, David V.J. Bell and Gerda R. Wekerle*

Political Arrangements: Power and the City, *edited by Henri Lustiger-Thaler*

Bringing the Economy Home From the Market, *by Ross Dobson*

send for a free catalogue of all our titles
BLACK ROSE BOOKS
P.O. Box 1258
Succ. Place du Parc
Montréal, Québec
H3W 2R3 Canada

To order books: (phone) 1-800-565-9523 (fax) 1-800-221-9985
Web site address: http://www.web.net/blackrosebooks

Printed by the workers of
Les Éditions Marquis
Montmagny, Québec
for Black Rose Books Ltd.

COMMUNITY ECONOMIC DEVELOPMENT
In Search of Empowerment and Alternatives
Eric Shragge, ed.

Challenges the notion that the economy should only be privately owned and argues that it should both act in the social interest of the local community and be partially controlled by it.

A critical discussion of both the theory and practice of community economic development.
Journal of Economic Literature

141 pages
Paperback ISBN: 1-895431-86-7 $19.99
Hardcover ISBN: 1-895431-87-5 $48.99
L.C. No. 93-072747
ISSN: 1195-1850

THE POLITICS OF URBAN LIBERATION
Stephen Schecter

A wide-ranging libertarian evaluation dealing with political economy in an urban context, from France to Chile. It also examines the importance of the city in the history of social revolution.

203 pages
Paperback ISBN: 0-919618-78-2 $9.99
Hardcover ISBN: 0-919618-79-0 $38.99

BUREAUCRACY AND COMMUNITY
Linda Davies, Eric Shragge, eds.

This book examines the consequences for both State social workers and community practitioners in face of increasing governmental restraints.

Based on recent empirical work from Québec and the United Kingdom.

... takes a highly critical view of social-services management and the controlling role of government bureaucracies.
Calgary Herald

180 pages, bibliography
Paperback ISBN: 0-921689-56-X $16.99
Hardcover ISBN: 0-921689-57-8 $45.99
L.C. No. 90-81638
ISSN: 1195-1850